AF239435

Björn Schnizler

Resource Allocation in the Grid

Studies on eOrganisation and Market Engineering 6

Universität Karlsruhe (TH)

Herausgeber:

Prof. Dr. Christof Weinhardt
Prof. Dr. Thomas Dreier
Prof. Dr. Rudi Studer

Resource Allocation in the Grid

A Market Engineering Approach

by
Björn Schnizler

universitätsverlag karlsruhe

Dissertation, genehmigt von der Fakultät für Wirtschaftswissenschaften
der Universität Fridericiana zu Karlsruhe, 2007
Referenten: Prof. Dr. Christof Weinhardt, Prof. Dr. Rudi Studer

Impressum

Universitätsverlag Karlsruhe
c/o Universitätsbibliothek
Straße am Forum 2
D-76131 Karlsruhe
www.uvka.de

Universitätsverlag Karlsruhe 2007
Print on Demand

ISSN: 1862-8893
ISBN: 978-3-86644-165-1

Acknowledgements

This work would not have come into being without the support of many colleagues and friends. I am grateful to all those people who supported and inspired me while facing several academic and personal challenges.

In particular, I am grateful to my thesis advisor Professor Dr. Christof Weinhardt. His visionary ideas and his constant support and guidance encouraged me to overcome many hurdles during my PhD studies.

In addition, I thank Professor Dr. Rudi Studer for co-advising me. Thanks to my committee members Professor Dr. Andreas Geyer-Schulz and Professor Dr. Christian Hipp for their support.

The work presented in this book was partially integrated into CATNETS, a project funded by the European Union. I thank Professor Dr. Daniel Veit for managing the project at the University of Karlsruhe and for encouraging me during my work. Thanks to Professor Dr. Torsten Eymann for acquiring and leading the project. Aside from all my project colleagues, I particularly thank Dr. Omer Rana, Liviu Joita, and Pablo Chacin for helping me out with several Grid related challenges.

I am indebted to my colleagues in the research group on Information and Market Engineering at the Institute of Information Systems and Management, University of Karlsruhe. Thank you very much for your support and for being vital and collaborating colleagues. Particular thanks to Dr. Ilka Weber for her mathematical support and Dr. Dirk Neumann for many fruitful discussions and debates. Thanks to Kiet Vo and Dr. Jörg Sandrock for their encouragement and constant support. Several other colleagues deserve thanks for reading my chapters and sharing ideas: Thanks to Carsten Block, Dr. Clemens van Dinther, Dr. Matthias Kunzelmann, and Stefan Luckner.

In addition, I thank Dr. Peter Haase and Holger Rau for their feedback and their constant support. I am grateful to Bess Dawson, Ashley Nicholson, and Nadine Scholz for proofreading parts of the book.

Personally, I am grateful to my mother Inge for enabling my education and for supporting and encouraging me in finishing this work.

Björn Schnizler

Contents

List of Abbreviations

API	Application Programming Interface
CAP	Combinatorial Allocation Problem
CATS	Combinatorial Auction Test Suite
CDA	Continuous Double Auction
CEP	Combinatorial Exchange Problem
CPU	Central Processing Unit
CV	Coefficient of Variation
EGA	Enterprise Grid Alliance
FAFNER	Factoring via Network-Enabled Recursion
FLOPS	Floating point Operations Per Second
FPSB	First-price Sealed-bid
GB	Gigabyte
GGF	Global Grid Forum
GLUE	Grid Laboratory Uniform Environment
GRACE	Grid Architecture for Computational Economy
GRAM	Globus Resource Allocation Manager
GT	Globus Toolkit
GUSTO	Globus Ubiquitous Supercomputing Testbed
GVA	Generalized Vickrey Auction
HTTP	Hypertext Transfer Protocol
I-WAY	Information-Wide-Area-Year
IP	Internet Protocol
jCase	Java Combinatorial Auction Simulation Environment
JMS	Java Messaging Service

JSDL	Job Submission Description Language
MACE	Multi-Attribute Combinatorial Exchange
MAP	MACE Allocation Problem
MIP	Mixed Integer Program
MIPS	Million Instructions per Second
OCEAN	Open Computation Exchange and Arbitration Network
OGF	Open Grid Forum
OGSA	Open Grid Services Architecture
OGSI	Open Grid Services Infrastructure
PDP-1	Programmed Data Processor-1
PPC	Pricing Per Column
QoS	Quality of Service
RSL	Resource Description Language
SLA	Service Level Agreement
SME	Small and Medium-sized Enterprise
SOA	Service Oriented Architecture
SOAP	Simple Object Access Protocol
tsfGrid	Time Sensitive Fair Grid
UDDI	Universal Description, Discovery, and Integration
UML	Unified Modeling Language
URI	Uniform Resource Identifier
VCG	Vickrey-Clarke-Groves
VO	Virtual Organization
W3C	World Wide Web Consortium
WSDL	Web Service Description Language
WSMO	Web Service Modeling Ontology
WSRF	Web Service Resource Framework
XML	Extensible Markup Language

List of Tables

List of Figures

Part I

Foundations

Chapter 1

Introduction

We will probably see the spread of "computer utilities", which, like present electric and
telephone utilities, will service individual homes and offices across the country.
(Kleinrock 1969)

1.1 Motivation

The increasing interconnection between computers has created the vision of Grids: In analogy to the power grid, resources such as processing power, storage space, or software services are accessible in a plug-and-play environment. A user has access to any form of computational resources which are hosted on distributed machines. These resources are not visible to the user – such as a consumer of electric power is unaware of how the demanded electricity is being generated and thereafter transmitted to the power socket.

The implementation of Grids has major ramifications for organizations since they can reduce costs by outsourcing nonessential elements of their IT infrastructure to various forms of computing and application service providers. Such emerging e-utilities – providers offering on-demand access to computing resources – enable organizations to perform computational jobs spontaneously through other resources in the Grid that are not under the control of the user (Foster et al. 2002a).

Most Grid research has been devoted to the development of hard and software infrastructures so that access to resources is dependable, consistent, and pervasive (Foster and Kesselman 2004b). Currently, various open standards define interactions between different computing resources across organizational entities. With the Open Grid Services Architecture (OGSA), which specifies fundamental middleware components for the Grid, the Grid community has laid the foundation for future developments. OGSA defines computer and storage resources as well as networks, programs, and databases as services. Using computational resources as services paves the road for interoperability among heterogeneous computing and application environments (Foster et al. 2002a). OGSA and one of its reference implementations, Globus Toolkit 4, provide the technical infrastructure for accessing computational resources over the Grid. Computers equipped with a Globus installation can access computational resources over the Grid, with transparency for the user. Resource owners can become providers by offering their resources using standardized interfaces and communication protocols.

The technical infrastructure is a necessary requirement to implement Grids in practice. Technical feasibility, however, is not equivalent to actual realization, as also economic issues are important. On the one hand, resource owners will only offer their computational resources if they are adequately compensated. In this context, compensation requires a functioning pricing infrastructure. On the other hand, current resource allocation managers employ batch algorithms which determine allocations based on either naive heuristics such as first-come first-serve or on idiosyncratic cost functions (Buyya et al. 2002). Consequently, these algorithms cannot determine economic efficient resource allocations as they do not guarantee that consumers who have high values for some resources will really receive them.

Market-based approaches are considered to work well in Grid settings (Wolski et al. 2001; Buyya et al. 2005). By assigning values (also called utilities) to their resource requests, users can express their preferences for resources which are subject to usage constraints. If the market mechanism is properly defined, users may be provided with incentives to express their true values for resource requests and offers. This in turn marks the prerequisite for attaining an efficient allocation of resources which maximizes the sum of aggregated valuations.

In recent times, the idea of incorporating market mechanisms into Grid technology has increasingly gained attention. Among others, the proposals include the establishment of Open Grid Markets, where either idle or all available resources can be traded (Shneidman et al. 2005; Lai 2005). Despite this recent interest in market-based approaches, research regarding market mechanisms for Grid resources remains in its infancy. The canon of available market mechanisms only insufficiently copes with the requirements imposed by the Grid.

1.2   Objectives and Contributions

The central objective for this work is the design, implementation, and evaluation of a market mechanism that copes with the requirements upon a resource management system in Grids.

The difficulties in designing and implementing markets for the Grid arise from interdependencies between technical and economical objectives (Weinhardt et al. 2006). When applying markets to the Grid, it is essential to consider these influences that arise from technical fundamentals of Grid systems, potential user requirements, business constraints, and economic objectives. Each of these influencing factors has a profound impact on the outcome and, as a consequence, on the acceptance of the market. The market engineering approach manages these influences by means of a structured, systematic, and theoretically founded procedure of designing, implementing, evaluating, and introducing electronic market platforms (Weinhardt et al. 2003). Using the methodology of market engineering allows a refinement of the central objective into more specific questions.

Research Question 1: Environmental Analysis for the Grid
What are the characteristics of a potential Grid marketplace, and what are the technical and economical requirements upon its underlying mechanism?

Answering this question requires an analysis of the economic environment that comprises the market participants, their preferences as well as the characteristics of Grid resources. The result of this analysis reveals a set of requirements that have to be fulfilled by a Grid market mechanism.

The contribution is a thorough extraction of the requirements concerning the resource allocation problem and the environmental side-constraints for markets in the Grid.

Research Question 2: Design of a Market Mechanism for the Grid
What is the nature of a market mechanism that can be applied to the resource allocation problem in Grids?

The problem of designing a market mechanism is a critical hurdle towards market based resource allocation in Grids. As a solution to this problem, a novel auction mechanism called Multi-Attribute Combinatorial Exchange (MACE) is presented. The auction accounts for bundle bids, quality attributes, time restrictions, and co-allocation constraints of Grid resources. In addition, the bid specification is based on a standardized service level agreement language which makes the auction compliant with common Grid middleware. Finally, a new pricing schema is introduced that is computationally more efficient than other mechanisms proposed for combinatorial exchanges.

The contribution is the derivation of MACE, the first auction mechanism that simultaneously addresses several Grid specific requirements. In addition, the proposed pricing schema is a step towards the design of computationally tractable combinatorial exchanges.

Research Question 3: Implementation into a Software System
How can a Grid market mechanism be implemented into a Grid compliant software system?

This question addresses the problem of implementing combinatorial exchanges into a software system and integrating the system into existing Grid infrastructures. An answer to this question requires the identification of adequate algorithms that can be used to compute an outcome of the auction schema. Subsequently, the implementation requires open interfaces that are compatible with common Grid communication standards.

The contribution is a generic and flexible software system that implements MACE as well as alternative combinatorial mechanisms. The system supports WS-Agreement as a bidding language which allows an integration into service-oriented Grid systems such as OGSA.

Research Question 4: Evaluation of a Grid Market Mechanism
How can a Grid market mechanism be evaluated by means of a simulation?

After the design and implementation of the mechanism, it has to be evaluated with respect to its technical and economical properties. The use of computer simulations is applied to analyze whether or not MACE fulfills the elicited requirements upon a Grid market mechanism. The first challenge of this problem is caused by the lack of empirical data concerning Grid markets. Consequently, one has to adapt and combine existing work proposed in the area of Grid computing and combinatorial auction design. Furthermore, no simulation framework exists that can be used to simulate participants in a Grid market submitting multi-attribute combinatorial bids. Finally, evaluation metrics have to be defined that reflect the technical and economical requirements upon the mechanism.

The contribution of the mechanism evaluation is the design of a simulation model that imitates a Grid marketplace. In addition, a new simulation framework called jCase is developed that can be applied to study various types of combinatorial mechanisms in the context of computer aided market engineering (Weinhardt et al. 2006). Finally, the results of the simulation study are a step towards understanding effects and strengths of combinatorial auction mechanisms and has potential to learn more about combinatorial auctions.

1.3   Outline

The work at hand is structured into three main parts as depicted in Figure 1.1. Part I introduces the most important foundations of Grids and markets. Subsequently, Part II is concerned with the design and implementation of a Grid market mechanism. Finally, Part III covers the numerical evaluation of the technical and economical properties of the mechanism.

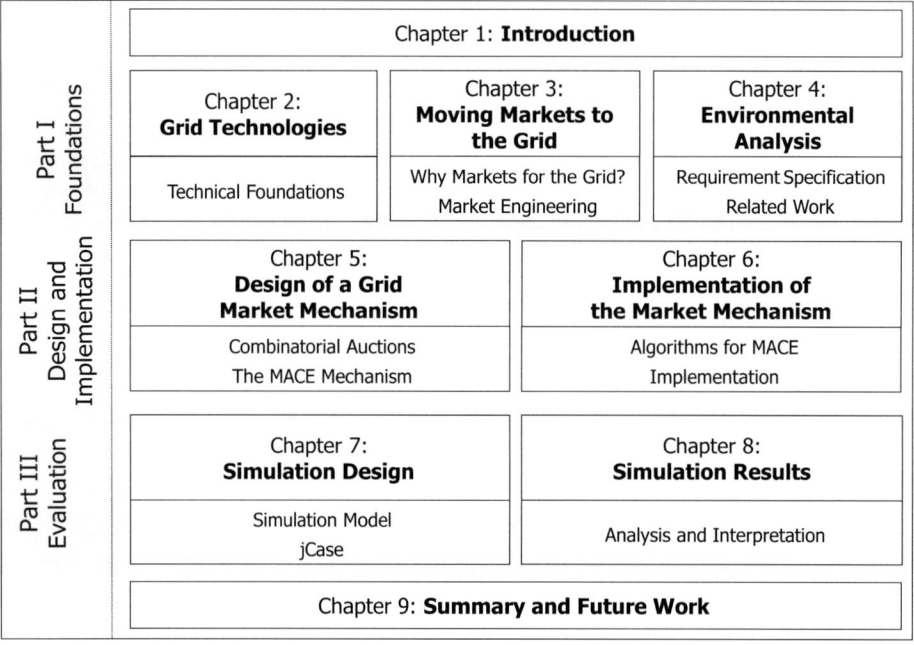

Figure 1.1: Structure of this work

Part I – Foundations: Chapter 2 introduces the basic concepts and terminologies of Grid computing and Grid resource management. Next, Chapter 3 motivates why markets should be applied to coordinate resource allocations in Grids. Furthermore, the chapter provides a common understanding of markets and market engineering. Chapter 4 analyzes the economic environment of a Grid marketplace, elicits a set of requirements upon an apt mechanism, and reviews related work. The result of the first part is a common understanding of Grid technologies and markets. In addition, the first research question is answered by an extraction of the environmental side-constraints and the requirements upon Grid market mechanisms.

Part II – Design and Implementation: The second part of the work is concerned with the design and implementation of a Grid market mechanism. First, Chapter 5 outlines the basic concepts of combinatorial auction design and introduces MACE as an auction for the Grid. After that, Chapter 6 presents a set of algorithms that are required to implement the conceptual model into a software system. This part answers the second and third research question by designing and implementing a market mechanism that accounts for Grid specific requirements.

Part III – Evaluation: The evaluation of the proposed mechanism is described in the third part of this work. Chapter 7 provides a set of evaluation metrics that measure the adherence of the mechanism to economical and technical properties. In addition, a simulation model is introduced that imitates a Grid marketplace and that can be used to measure the defined metrics. A simulation framework called jCase is described that is applied to perform the simulation study. Chapter 8 describes and analyzes the results of the simulation with regard to the elicited list of requirements. This part answers the last research question by providing a set of metrics, a Grid market model, and a simulation framework to evaluate Grid market mechanisms.

Chapter 9 concludes with a summary, an overview of open questions, and an outlook on future research.

Chapter 2

Grid Technologies

Sceptics may wonder why private companies would ever want to share computing resources co-operatively, as particle physicists are doing. The security risks may seem insurmountable, and the economic benefits questionable. Yet sceptics beware. Twelve years ago [...] a young CERN engineer named Tim Berners-Lee gave out T-shirts advertising a new and rather obscure scientific-networking tool of dubious economic value: it was called the world wide web.

(The Economist 2004b)

Over the past few years, the emergence and popularity of Grids have been driven by an increased development of technologies that support geographically distributed computing. Several different types of middleware, programming libraries, and toolkits have been proposed that allow single applications to utilize multiple computing resources. On the one hand, this is achieved by the design of flexible architectures, which incorporate technical issues like resource heterogeneity, as well as social issues like organizational policy restrictions. On the other hand, resource management systems have been developed to discover, allocate, monitor, and negotiate the required resources. For a wide application of Grids, both the underlying architecture, as well as the resource management system represent crucial building blocks. Therefore, the aim of this chapter is to outline the basic concepts and related terminologies of current state of the art Grid architectures and resource management systems.

The chapter is structured as follows: Section 2.1 outlines the evolution of Grid technologies from proprietary, scientific computing infrastructures towards holistic systems for coordinated resource sharing based on standardized and open protocols. Section 2.2 describes the Open Grid Services Architecture (OGSA) as the current standard architecture for the Grid. Section 2.3 introduces the most important concepts of resource management systems. Finally, Section 2.4 summarizes and concludes the chapter.

2.1 Evolution of Grid Technologies

Grid technologies emerged in the mid-1990s to provide a distributed computing infrastructure for advanced science and engineering (Foster and Kesselmann 2004). In the meantime, the term *Grid* and its related technology stack have undergone a change: Grids evolved from a proprietary infrastructure for distributed high-performance computing towards a flexible

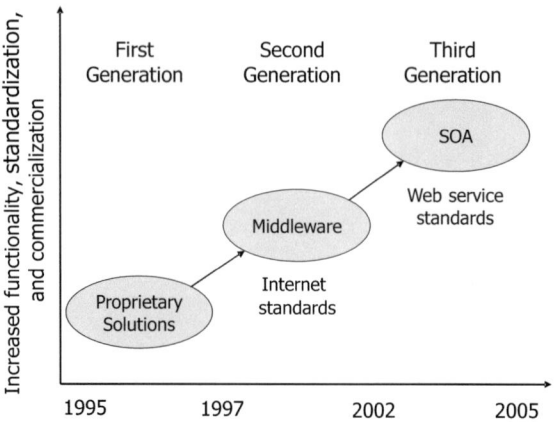

Figure 2.1: Evolution of Grid Technologies following Foster and Kesselmann (2004, p. 9)

approach for coordinated resource sharing, by means of standardized and open protocols (Foster 2002). Moreover, the target of Grid technologies has moved from pure scientific applications towards a multitude of different areas, including business domains. Representative examples for Grid business applications comprise, among others, risk analysis for portfolio management and crash test simulations for automobiles.

De Roure et al. (2003) sketch three different stages in the evolution of Grid technologies, which are depicted in Figure 2.1 following Foster and Kesselmann (2004): first generation Grids deploy proprietary systems in order to connect high performance supercomputers between scientific institutions. Second generation Grids focus on middleware technology, to overcome the heterogeneity and scalability challenges of distributed systems. Most of these systems are built upon Internet protocols to foster standardized communication processes. Third generation Grids amplify the standardization process of Grid technologies and enlarge their target application domains. They are designed according to the principles of service oriented architectures (SOAs) and make use of the Web service technology stack. These technologies facilitate a flexible and dynamic deployment of Grids. In the following sections, this evolution of Grid technologies and its corresponding technology stack are briefly outlined.

2.1.1   First Generation Grids

Early Grid developments originated from the efforts of linking supercomputing sites within the U.S. Gigabit testbed (De Roure et al. 2003). The objective of these efforts was the provision of computational resources to enable the execution of high performance applications. These developments are called metacomputing systems, i.e., networks of heterogeneous, computational resources linked by software (Catlett and Smarr 1992). Several architectures and implementations have been proposed to enable metacomputing. The two representative projects of the first generation are FAFNER (Factoring via Network-Enabled Recursion) and I-WAY (Information-Wide-Area-Year):

FAFNER: FAFNER is aimed at factorizing very large numbers.[1] A parallel algorithm has been developed to break down the factorization problem into smaller subproblems. These subproblems are solved independently on several distributed machines in parallel. FAFNER was one of the first web-based metacomputing projects and paved the way for a wave of successor projects such as SETI@Home (Sullivan et al. 1997).

I-WAY: I-WAY is the effort of linking high performance computers and visualization environments via a network (DeFanti et al. 1996). I-WAY is designed to execute individual high performance applications, such as simulation or video rendering jobs. As one of the innovations, I-WAY applies a resource broker to discover and allocate jobs automatically and to maintain status information of different machines. Most components of the I-WAY system are integrated into its successor system Globus Toolkit 1 (GT 1) (Foster and Kesselman 1997).

Both proposed systems are designed to fulfill individual requirements: factorizing large numbers and executing specialized high performance applications which require powerful resources. However, a large-scale deployment of these systems is hampered by their lack of flexibility and scalability (De Roure et al. 2003). For instance, FAFNER requires human interaction to distribute the subproblems and to collect results. I-WAY focuses on specialized supercomputing sites and is thus hard to deploy on standard machines. Moreover, both systems only provide limited functionality concerning security, scalability, and robustness (Foster and Kesselman 2004a).

Despite the aforementioned weaknesses of first generation systems, FAFNER and I-WAY were both highly innovative and successful. The experiences gained with the development and deployment of these systems yielded towards second generation Grids.

2.1.2   Second Generation Grids

Second generation Grids expand on earlier approaches by providing systems that can be deployed in large-scale settings. For this purpose, several components are developed covering common problems that arise in distributed computing systems. For instance, such components comprise functions for authentication, resource discovery, and resource access (Foster and Kesselman 2004a). Infrastructures building upon such components were called Computational Grids, a term coined in analogy to the electrical power grid (Stevens et al. 1997). At that time, Foster and Kesselman (1998, p. 17) characterized a *Computational Grid* as a *"hardware and software infrastructure that provides dependable, consistent, pervasive, and inexpensive access to high-end computational capabilities"*. In contrast to current definitions of Grids that emphasize the controlled sharing of any computational resource (cf. Definition 2.2), this early characterization focused on high-end computational resources.

The design and implementation of reusable and flexible software components that are mostly encapsulated in form of middleware realizes the aforementioned access to computational resources. This hides the heterogeneity of resources running on different machines. The two most prominent Grid middleware implementations of the second generation are GT 1 (Foster and Kesselman 1997) and Legion (Grimshaw et al. 1997). Both systems are used in several different scenarios, e.g., a distributed interactive simulation and a tele-immersion[2]

---

[1] See http://cs-www.bu.edu/cgi-bin/FAFNER/factor.pl for details (accessed 09.01.2006).
[2] Tele-immersion combines video conferencing and virtual reality to enable users in different locations the collaboration in a shared, virtual, or simulated environment (Kauff et al. 2000).

system deployed in GUSTO[3] (Brunett et al. 1998) or for clustering geographic environmental data (Mahinthakumar et al. 1999).

Social and policy issues concerning resource sharing arose with an increasing interest in Grid computing and the practical feasibility of existing middleware implementations. The emphasis of Grids moved from computing driven infrastructures for scientists towards the controlled sharing of any network enabled entity, such as processing power, storage space, and application services for business and scientific areas of interest. In such settings, resource providers and consumers control the sharing of resources: they define what is shared, who is allowed to use the shared resources, and the conditions under which sharing occurs (Foster and Kesselmann 2004). Former Grid definitions and implementations did not meet the arisen requirements of distributed resource sharing. For this reason Foster et al. (2001) refined the definition and objective of Grids to support *"coordinated resource sharing and problem solving in dynamic, multi-institutional virtual organizations"* (Foster et al. 2001, p. 200). In this context, a set of individuals defined by such sharing rules is denoted as a virtual organization (VO). In literature, the term *virtual organization* is widely discussed and its meaning oftentimes defined differently (Davidow and Malone 1992). Common to most definitions is that a VO is defined as a federated collection of distributed individuals that collaborate concerning a common interest by means of agreements (Boudreau et al. 1998). Grids focus on virtualizing computing infrastructures and software applications, and thus, Grids provide the technological foundations for individuals to collaborate independently of geographic matters. Furthermore, Grids foster the compliance with contracted agreements for any form of computational jobs in a standardized fashion.

Foster et al. (2001) propose an architecture supporting such a controlled sharing within VOs: Its objective is the conceptual definition of fundamental components and protocols required for a variety of Grid application scenarios (Foster and Kesselman 2004a). The architecture – as depicted in Figure 2.2 – is organized by means of layers, i.e., modular components that build upon each other. Layering provides insulation so that changes in different parts of the system can occur independently (Clark and Pasquale 1996). The architecture comprises the following five layers (Foster et al. 2001):

Fabric Layer: The fabric layer includes protocols and interfaces that provide sharing facilities of logical resources[4], such as computational resources, storage systems, networks, and sensors. These logical resources, however, use internal protocols that are not concerned with the architecture. For instance, the fabric provided by a logical storage resource cannot be represented by a raw hard disk but has to provide a corresponding file system.

Connectivity Layer: The connectivity layer defines basic Grid specific network protocols. This includes communication protocols to exchange messages with resources provided by the fabric layer. Furthermore, authentication protocols ensure a controlled resource sharing. Existing standardized Internet protocols such as routing or transport protocols facilitate the functions offered by this layer.

---

[3]The Globus Ubiquitous Supercomputing Testbed (GUSTO) is a large-scale testbed that spans over 20 sites and includes over 3000 nodes for a total compute power of over 2 TFLOPS (Brunett et al. 1998).

[4]A physical resource is an entity that exists physically, e.g., a CPU of a server (Song and Li 2005). In contrast, a logical resource represents a set of distributed physical resources that a VO posses according to their underlying policies, rules, and availability (Xing et al. 2005).

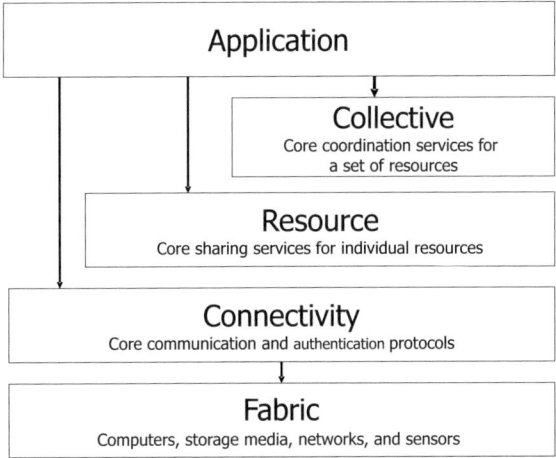

Figure 2.2: Layered Grid architecture (Foster et al. 2001, p. 207)

Resource Layer: The resource layer consists of protocols for a secure negotiation, sharing, initiation, monitoring, control, accounting, and payment of resources. Protocols of this layer are only responsible for local resources: hence, they ignore issues concerning collections of distributed resources within a network.

Collective Layer: The collective layer defines protocols and services for global resource management. It provides functions and interaction protocols required for collections of distributed resources. While the resource layer is concerned with the interaction of single and local resources, the collective layer is associated with global interactions across several distributed resources. For instance, the collective layer provides a directory for discovering resources and a resource broker for allocating and monitoring them.

Application Layer: The application layer comprises of a variety of Grid enabled user applications. These applications make use of the protocols provided at each layer, i.e., protocols for authentication, resource access, and resource discovery.

The layered Grid architecture is implemented in the Globus Toolkit 2 (GT 2), the successor of I-WAY and GT 1. By providing modular software components for common problems, such as authentication, resource discovery, and resource access, GT 2 facilitates the construction of various different Grid applications (Foster and Kesselmann 2004).

In summary, second generation Grids evolved from propriety solutions (I-WAY) over partially flexible implementations (GT 1) towards protocol driven middleware systems (GT 2). These implementations enable the building of large-scale applications for different domains.

However, in order to build new and flexible Grid applications covering business domains, one must reuse existing components, assemble them in a flexible manner, and extend and replace them easily. Unfortunately, this flexibility is hardly given by GT 2 and comparable efforts, such as Condor, a workload management system for compute-intensive jobs (Frey et al. 2001), or Legion, a framework for aggregating several computers into one single virtual machine (Grimshaw et al. 1997; Natrajan et al. 2001). Most parts of second generation implementations are neither formally standardized nor publicly reviewed (Foster and Kessel-mann 2004). Furthermore, most interfaces of these systems are incompatible with other ex-isting Grid implementations. The lack of standardization, reusability, and interoperability of second generation Grids, on the one hand, and the emergence of Web service technologies, on the other hand, drove the evolution of Grids towards the third generation.

2.1.3   Third Generation Grids

Second generation Grids enable the sharing of computational resources, in order to achieve large-scale computation. With an increasing number of new Grid applications, however, additional requirements became apparent from business and scientific areas of application. In order to deploy new Grid applications, one must reuse existing software and information components and assemble them in a flexible manner. Second generation systems such as GT 2 do not achieve this flexibility. Furthermore, it is often required that resources guarantee certain quality characteristics, such as an average response time, a lower limit for free storage space, or a minimum security provision. When a resource offers such a guarantee to an application, it also offers quality of service (QoS) (Foster and Kesselman 2004a). Although proprietary QoS solutions are implemented in second generation Grids (Roy and Sander 2004), they lack standardization and generalization.

Third generation Grids address these requirements by applying the principles of SOAs to the Grid. A SOA is defined as a set of loosely-coupled services in a network which have well-defined interfaces and which can communicate with each other (Kaye 2003). Such a design principle allows a flexible composition of distributed services in a network and a standardized message exchange between the entities involved. This standardized process enables the exchange of resource information, such as its capability descriptions and its offered QoS levels.

Building Grid architectures based on a SOA implicates that computer and storage re-sources, as well as networks, programs, and databases are virtualized as services, i.e., network-enabled entities that provide some capability. Thereby, the underlying technical complexity of different computational resources and applications is hidden by standard ser-vice interfaces (Taylor 2004). In Grids, it is required that interaction with resources is re-alized by standardized interfaces. Such an interaction comprises administrative processes, such as deploying, configuring, monitoring, metering, tuning, and troubleshooting the re-source (Global Grid Forum 2005b). If a resource allows such a standardized interaction, it is considered to be *manageable*. Derived from service orientation and standardized resource interaction, a general definition of a Grid resource is formulated as follows:

Definition 2.1: Grid Resource
A Grid resource is a computational entity that provides manageable interfaces (Global Grid Forum 2005c, p. 4).

For better readability and in terms of maintaining common terminologies, the term *re-source* is used to denote any Grid resource, that is – in most cases – a *manageable* Web service[5]. The term *service* is only used when a concrete service representation of a logical entity is discussed. For instance, the term *service* is used to denote a storage service.

The virtualization of resources enables interoperability among heterogeneous computing and application environments (Foster et al. 2002a). While second generation Grids focus

---

[5]It is not mandatory that a Grid resources is based on a Web service.

on protocols required for interoperability among distributed resources, third generation architectures specify the nature of resource interfaces that respond to these protocol messages.
Third generation systems stress behavior and functionality of Grid components and complement former protocol-oriented concepts (Foster et al. 2002b).

As a result of these developments reflecting a holistic view on distributed resource sharing, the term Grid is defined as follows (Foster 2002, p. 2–3):

Definition 2.2: Grid
*A Grid is a system that uses open, standardized, and general-purpose protocols to federate
distributed computational resources and to deliver nontrivial qualities of services.*

Systems of the third generation focus on open and generalized protocols in order to enable information exchange between heterogeneous and distributed entities. In addition, the
specification of open protocols fosters the automation and self-organization of Grid systems.
This is necessary as humans can no longer deal with the scale and heterogeneity, but delegate
to software to do so (De Roure et al. 2003). For instance, resource discovery cannot remain
a manual task in a large-scale environment and thus must to be automated. This can only
be achieved if essential information, such as resource capabilities and user requirements, is
described and exchanged by the use of standardized communication protocols.

The de facto architecture of the third generation is OGSA. Its design principles and its
implications on Grids are discussed in the following section.

2.2 Open Grid Services Architecture – State of the Art

Grids are concerned with the creation, management, and application of distributed resources.
Within a Grid, resources can vary in their functionality, quality, and lifespan. For instance,
storage services can have different sizes and seek times. Common to all shared resources is,
however, the delivery of the service on a contracted level of QoS which comprises service-
level management, security semantics, and failover functionality (Joseph and Fellenstein
2004). The provision of a desired QoS level spanning heterogeneous services deployed on
different machines requires the specification of a well-defined and standardized architecture.
OGSA as proposed by Foster et al. (2002b) addresses these requirements. The architecture is
supported by the Open Grid Forum (OGF)[6] in order to expedite the standardization process
of Grid technologies.

Building on existing Grid technologies, such as GT 2, OGSA aligns Grid concepts with
SOAs and Web services. This alignment is originated from the similarities of Grids and Web
services: both technologies have the objective of distributed resource sharing (Abbas 2004).
In case of a Web service this includes the sharing of business and process logics to external
partners. Grid sharing concerns physical and logical resources such as computation, storage,
and application services. In both cases the access to resources is distributed and independent
of the resources' physical location.

OGSA builds on the principles of SOAs and Web services. These principles and concepts
are outlined in Section 2.2.1. Subsequently, Section 2.2.2 introduces the OGSA platform
architecture and Section 2.2.3 gives an overview over Globus Toolkit 4 (GT 4) as one of its
reference implementations.

---

[6]OGF is an organization that leads the global standardization effort for Grids. OGF resulted from the merger
of the Global Grid Forum (GGF) and the Enterprise Grid Alliance (EGA). See http://www.ogf.org/ for
details (accessed: 12.10.2006).

2.2.1   Service Oriented Architectures and Web Services

Service-Oriented Architecture (SOA):   A SOA is a specific type of distributed system in which all entities are services that perform some well-defined operations (Joseph et al. 2004). These services have to provide network-addressable interfaces and communicate via standard protocols and standard data formats. The communication process between entities involved is based on a well-defined message exchange, independent of the service's underlying platform and vendor-specific implementation details.

SOAs enable the deployment of applications composed by loosely-coupled services rather than appearing as monolithic systems (Kaye 2003). As such, their application facilitates the reuse of existing application components. SOAs address fundamental challenges of open systems, that are to operate efficiently and to achieve autonomy in heterogeneous environments (Huhns and Singh 2005). As such, a Grid architecture based on the principles of a SOA is deemed promising to fulfill the requirements upon third generation Grid systems.

In a SOA, application providers can publish their services in a global registry. Subsequently, these services are discovered dynamically and utilized by service requesters at run-time. For instance, a service provider can publish a storage service in such a registry. A simulation application that requires disk space to store some data can discover this storage service and invoke it by standardized interfaces. Subsequently, it can store data without being aware of how this data is stored, e.g., by the use of a distributed file system.

Web Services: SOAs are typically realized by means of Web services. A Web service is a software system that supports interoperable machine-to-machine interaction over a network (W3C 2003). This is realized by transferring XML documents between applications and the use of standard Internet protocols. Web services are embedded into the Web service technology stack which comprises a set of relevant specifications for communication, service description, and service discovery.[7] In the context of SOAs, the following three standards are the most salient ones (Curbera et al. 2002):

- the *Simple Object Access Protocol* (SOAP) for enabling communication between Web services,

- the *Web Service Description Language* (WSDL) for describing the interface of a Web service, and

- the *Universal Description, Discovery, and Integration* (UDDI) mechanism as a repository for publishing and discovering Web services.

SOAP is an XML-based protocol to exchange information in distributed systems. It provides an enveloping mechanism that defines the content of a message. The standard determines which messages are processed by defining a set of encoding rules for expressing data types and a convention for representing remote procedure calls and responses (W3C 2000). SOAP messages are exchanged using a wide set of transport protocols, such as HTTP, FTP, or Java Messaging Service (JMS) (Foster et al. 2002b).

SOAP enables communication between services. However, the standard does not define which messages have to be exchanged in order to communicate with a service successfully.

---

[7]The specifications and standards are defined by the Web Services Activity group of the World Wide Web Consortium (W3C). See http://www.w3.org/2002/ws/ for details (accessed: 14.10.2004).

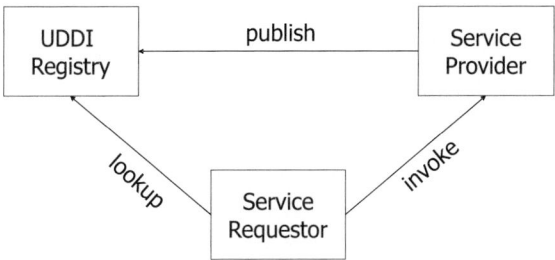

Figure 2.3: Interplay of SOAP, WSDL, and UDDI

Thus, standard conventions for describing the name of a Web service and its input and out-put parameter are defined. This information is made explicit by WSDL. WSDL is an XML encoded specification that is used to describe a service interface independent of its imple-mentation. WSDL documents contain information about the functionality of services, their location (e.g., their IP-addresses), and the protocol required for contacting them (e.g., using HTTP). WSDL documents are separated in an *abstract* and *concrete* part. The abstract part describes the service interface, i.e., the supported methods and parameters. The concrete part defines protocol bindings and other information. Suppose, for instance, a WSDL document that describes a storage service. The abstract part specifies the operations supported by the service (e.g., an operation to retrieve files), the required input message (e.g., the filename), and output message (e.g., the file content encoded as a string).[8] The concrete part specifies the message encoding and the protocol bindings for all operations, e.g., the use of SOAP and HTTP.

SOAP and WSDL are used for the invocation and description of Web services. For a far-reaching deployment of Web services in a SOA, service requesters need further knowledge about the existence of services and their providers. UDDI provides a framework to discover services and to publish their descriptions. The core element of UDDI is a repository, more specifically, an XML document that contains information about service capabilities and its supplier. A UDDI repository is queried using a predefined API in combination with a query language.[9] The UDDI registry itself is also a Web service which is invoked by the use of WSDL and SOAP.

Figure 2.3 depicts the interplay of SOAP, WSDL, and UDDI (Wojciechowski and Wein-hardt 2002). A service provider is publishing a particular Web service in the UDDI registry using SOAP and WSDL. After that, a service requestor queries the registry for this particular service. Finally, the requestor invokes the service at the providers hosting environment using SOAP and WSDL.

Web Service Resource Framework (WSRF): Web services in combination with WSDL, SOAP, and UDDI are fundamental specifications for targeting SOAs. The specifications

---

[8]The concrete names of the operators are ambiguous. Service requesters have to know the meaning of each parameter. The ontology community provides amendment description languages such as OWL-S (http://www.daml.org/services/owl-s/1.1/) and WSMO (http://www.wsmo.org/) to model explicit meanings of these parameters.

[9]Currently, only few and rather simple query languages exists for UDDI. As such, the process of querying a UDDI is seen as cumbersome (Alonso et al. 2004).

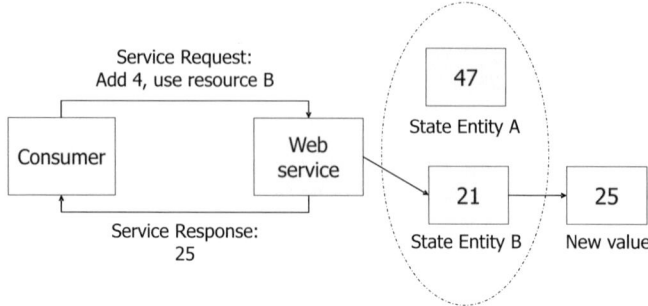

Figure 2.4: WSRF approach to statefulness following Sotomayor and Childers (2006, p. 32–33)

determine how service providers and consumers interact over a network. However, no further status concerning this interaction is stored as Web services are *stateless*. Messages exchanged between a service provider and a consumer rest exclusively upon the information contained in the input messages.

A Grid system, however, must maintain the status of its managed resources. Considering a computation service, such a status includes information about current workload, processor status, and reservations made by consumers. Grid resources require a stateful management, as their behavior is dependent of their underlying status (Joseph et al. 2004). Grid resources necessarily require standardized interfaces that provide access to the status of the service.

In order to enable a standardized management of stateful services, OGSA is based on the Web Service Resource Framework (WSRF).[10] WSRF models the stateful management of Web services by introducing a separate entity which is referred to as *state entity*[11]. A state entity is used to store status information for the interaction with a particular Web service. Each state entity has a unique identifier that is concatenated with its service. This identifier is known to the service consumer and is used for the entire interaction session with the service. Thus, the Web service has access to the corresponding resource and can use it to retrieve and store relevant status information.

Example 2.1: WSRF
Figure 2.4 exemplifies the interaction of a service consumer, a Web service, and its state entity. A consumer invokes a service which is capable of adding up numbers. The corresponding state entity for the session is *B*. The consumer has already submitted several numbers to the service so that the current sum in *state entity B* is 21. Thus, a service request with the parameter *add 4* to the current status in *state entity B* results in a response of 25.

The pairing of a Web service and a state entity is called *WS-Resource*. The communication with a WS-Resource, i.e., communicating to the Web service which state entity is to

---

[10]Former specifications of OGSA based on the Open Grid Services Infrastructure (OGSI). OGSI is a comparable effort for dynamic and stateful management of Web services. However, OGSI is not integrated into the family of Web service standards and is seen as too complex (Joseph et al. 2004). Thus, it was replaced by WSRF. For a detailed comparison of WSRF and OGSI, the reader is referred to Czajkowski et al. (2004).

[11]In literature, this state entity is usually called *resource*. However, it is refrained from this common terminology in favour of a clear separation of a state entity and a Grid resource.

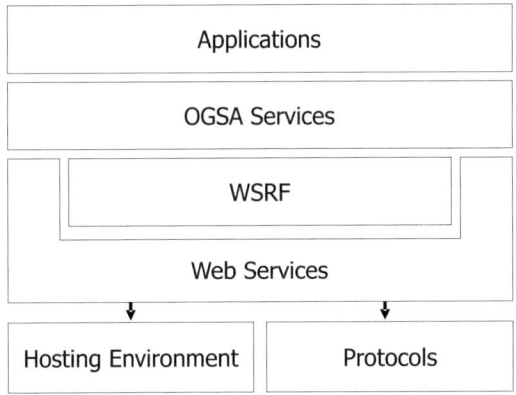

Figure 2.5: OGSA platform architecture (Joseph et al. 2004, p. 628)

be used, is realized by means of *WS-Addressing*. The WS-Addressing specification defines a construct called *endpoint reference* that contains, among others, a URI pointing to the Web service and a pointer to the state entity identifier. On the basis of this addressing schema, a WS-Resource is defined as follows:

Definition 2.3: WS-Resource
A WS-Resource is a composition of a Web service and a state entity that is [...] addressed and accessed according to the implied resource pattern, a conventional use of WS-Addressing endpoint references (Czajkowski et al. 2004, p. 5).[12]

A WS-Resource represents both, a Web service and its state entity. The service represents a logical or physical entity and has a number of interfaces to reserve, access, and monitor the resource. The state entity is responsible for managing the status of an interaction with a Web service.

For global management of such interfaces, WSRF provides a collection of specifications which support access and creation of WS-Resources, as well as lifetime and fault management (Czajkowski et al. 2004). WS-Resources and WSRF provide manageable interfaces which are required for Grid resources (cf. Definition 2.1). As such, a WS-Resource is an example for a Grid resource.

2.2.2 OGSA Platform Architecture

OGSA is the conflation of SOAs and Grid computing efforts. Figure 2.5 outlines the OGSA platform architecture, according to Foster et al. (2002b) and Joseph et al. (2004). The architecture consists of four layers: a *hosting environment and protocol* layer, a *Web services and WSRF* layer, an *OGSA services* layer, and an *application* layer.

Hosting Environment and Protocols: A hosting environment is responsible for instantiating and executing services. It includes physical and logical resources, operating systems, and a service container, such as J2EE or .NET. Furthermore, fundamental

---

[12]In the original definition, the term *resource* is used instead of *state entity*.

communication protocols are provided, such as routing and transport protocols, for exchanging messages between OGSA instances.

Web Services and WSRF: The Web services and WSRF layer virtualizes physical and logical entities as WS-Resources. The layer hides the heterogeneity and complexity of the underlying hosting environment to higher-level layers by providing standardized and manageable interfaces.

OGSA Services: OGSA services are core services required to maintain Grid applications. These services cover general management functions for Grids. Among others, the set of OGSA services comprises of resource management functionalities which are used to discover, monitor, bill, and account services.

Applications: The application layer represents a set of services developed for the Grid.

The OGSA platform architecture is a uniform SOA for the Grid. It integrates Web service standards into emerging Grid technologies. The architecture virtualizes all components of a Grid environment and enables the provisioning of logical and physical resources, regardless of their implementation and hosting platform. OGSA fosters interoperability and reusability of services. Thus, the architectural concepts of OGSA qualify to accomplish the requirements upon third generation Grids. Its reference implementation Globus Toolkit 4 (GT 4) is discussed in the following.

2.2.3   Globus Toolkit 4 as a Reference Implementation

GT 4[13] is an open source toolkit which can be used to build Grid applications. The toolkit is organized as a set of loosely-coupled components which provide common functionality for the deployment and execution of Grid applications. These components comprise of security issues, services for data and execution management, information services, and a common runtime library. GT 4 is an implementation of the OGSA requirements and is currently the de facto standard toolkit for most Grid applications (Sotomayor and Childers 2006).[14]

The architectural outline of GT 4 is depicted in Figure 2.6. GT 4 is divided into three sets of components: *infrastructure services*, *containers*, and *clients*.

Infrastructure services: These services implement interfaces for the management of computational, storage, and application services. For instance, they include execution management services (such as GRAM), monitoring and discovery services (such as Index), and services for data access and movement (such as GridFTP). Most of these services are implemented as Java Web services using Apache Axis[15] and communicate via Web service compliant protocols. However, some of them are implemented by the use of alternative transport and security protocols. For instance, GridFTP is implemented in C.

---

[13]Former specifications of OGSA based on OGSI are implemented in the Globus Toolkit 3 (GT 3).

[14]Several alternative implementations of OGSA based recommendations are currently under development. For instance, Brooke et al. (2004) and Humphrey (2003) each develop an OGSA compliant Grid service middleware.

[15]Apache Axis is a Java based implementation of SOAP. See http://ws.apache.org/axis/ for details (accessed 21.10.2005).

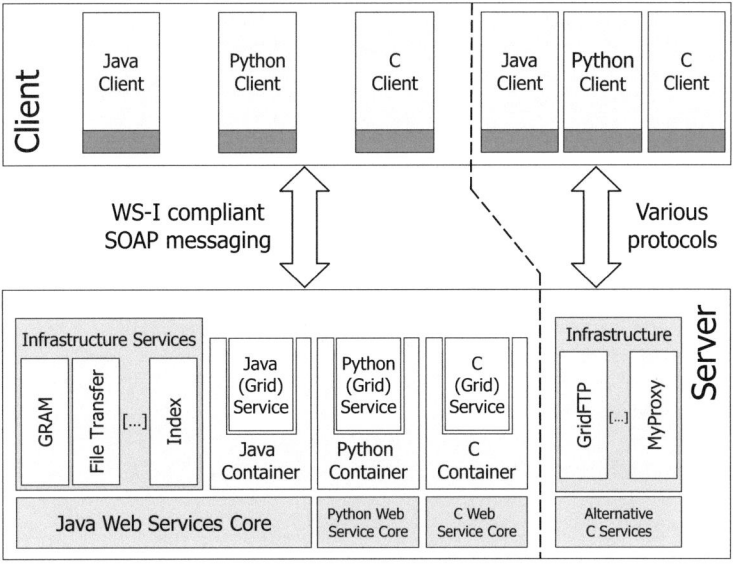

Figure 2.6: GT 4 architecture (Foster 2005, p. 2)

Containers: GT 4 provides three different containers for user-developed services. These services are implemented either in Java, Python, or C. A container provides commonly required functionalities for developing and deploying Grid services. Among others, these functions concern security, discovery, and status management mechanisms. A container extends the underlying hosting platform by adding a set of Web service specifications such as WSRF and WS-Security. Grid applications, just as a storage service or a SAP R/3 service, are managed within this container.

Clients: A client can use a set of predefined libraries which are typically required for the invocation of a distributed service. Subsequently, the client can access any user-developed service from a service provider using either Web service messaging or alternative communication protocols.

GT 4 is a fundamental technological enabler for deploying Grids in scientific and business domains. The toolkit enables the building of different applications for sharing any kind of services.

2.3 Resource Management in Grids

OGSA and its reference implementation GT 4 enable the formation of loosely-coupled high-performance computational environments. As pointed above, fundamental to such systems is the ability to discover various types of computational and application resources, to arrange for their use, to utilize them, and to monitor their state (Czajkowski et al. 2004). This process is usually referred to as resource management. Among others, resource management is responsible for typical management operations of distributed systems, such as resource reservation and allocation, security management, monitoring functionalities, billing and accounting, fault management, and resource aggregation (Global Grid Forum 2005c). Following Czajkowski et al. (2004, p. 259), resource management in the Grid defined as follows:

Definition 2.4: Resource management
Resource management in the Grid refers to the operations applied to control the behavior of Grid resources that are made available to other entities.

A key issue of resource management in Grids is the ability to decide which resources are allocated to which consumer and scheduled at what time. In Grids, this process is called resource allocation.[16] It comprises functionalities to describe the capabilities of resources, to discover candidate resources fulfilling the required capabilities, and to schedule the allocation of them.

Definition 2.5: Resource allocation
Resource allocation in the Grid comprises all functionality that is required to determine which Grid resources are allocated from which providers to which consumers.

With regard to local resources in traditional computing systems, such as desktop or cluster machines, resource management and allocation is a well-studied problem (Foster and Kesselmann 2004). Several local management systems are implemented for different application scenarios as batch schedulers, workflow engines, and operating systems (Czajkowski et al. 2004). These systems have full control over each of their underlying resources and have complete knowledge of their state and utilization. Resource allocation decisions are usually based on system specific objective functions, such as the maximization of total resource utilization. Local resource managers work fairly well in closed and controlled environments. In a distributed system, such as the Grid, however, these managers fail as they do not have full control over a set of distributed resources. Resources in the Grid are heterogeneous and have a multitude of different characteristics with varying configurations (Czajkowski et al. 2004). For instance, the local resource manager implemented in a Linux operating system cannot allocate a processing unit on a Solaris system. Among others, both systems implement different job management engines that cannot communicate directly with each other. As such, the Linux system neither has information concerning the status of the resources controlled by the Solaris system, nor the Linux system is capable of determining an allocation of resources on it. Furthermore, Grid resources are subject to various organizational and administrative policies (Foster et al. 2002b). For instance, such policy restrictions of an organization can prohibit the allocation of a resource from outside the European Union. In summary, local resource managers can neither manage the status and the allocation of distributed resource, nor respect policy restrictions of the participants.

The objective of resource management systems in Grids is to overcome these barriers and to provide basic management functionalities in order to discover, allocate, schedule, and monitor a wide range of different distributed resources (Czajkowski et al. 2004). Groundwork for achieving this goal lies in the development of efficient and flexible resource allocation systems. On that note, Subsection 2.3.1 describes a set of common technical requirements of a resource allocation system for the Grid. Subsequently, Subsection 2.3.2 introduces a generic resource allocation process and a selection of corresponding technologies which are required to fulfill the elicited requirements.

---

[16]In literature, this process is sometimes also called resource scheduling (e.g., in Schopf (2004)).

2.3.1   Requirements upon a Resource Allocation Manager

In literature, several requirements upon resource allocation managers for Grids are discussed. These requirements are mostly based on experiences with Grid test beds (Russell et al. 2004) and cluster and parallel computing infrastructures (Czajkowski et al. 1998). Besides application and domain specific requirements, the following generic requirements upon resource allocation managers are specified: (Czajkowski et al. 2004; Russell et al. 2004; Schwiegelshohn and Yahyapour 2004)

Requirement 2.1: Computational Tractability
The apt resource allocation manager has to determine an allocation within a meaningful time frame. In the context of trading Grid resources, a meaningful time frame is consistent with the maximum time limit that an allocation process may last. The review of related literature suggests that an allocation process that is shorter than 5 minutes for 500 job requests and offers is adequate (Shan et al. 2003; Shan et al. 2004).[17]

Requirement 2.2: Automated Resource Allocation
In order to facilitate the automation of Grid systems as introduced by third generation systems, a resource allocation mechanism has to select appropriate resources automatically.

Requirement 2.3: Double sided Mechanism
A resource allocation mechanism apt for the Grid has to enable multiple resource owners to publish their resources and multiple resource requesters to discover them.

Requirement 2.4: Support for Heterogeneous Resources
In the Grid, different heterogeneous types of resources have to be managed by the resource allocation system. For instance, the manager has to provide functionalities which can be used to allocate storage services as well as computation services.

Requirement 2.5: Support for Different Resource Characteristics
Resources in the Grid are typically not completely standardized. Similar resources can differ in their quality characteristics. For instance, storage services can differ by their capacity and access time. Resource consumers require different quality characteristics of the same type of resource. A complex rendering application, for instance, requires more capacity of a storage service than a conversion tool for single music files. As such, a resource allocation manager must support the specification and adherence of minimum capability requirements.[18]

Requirement 2.6: Bundling of Resources
Resource consumers usually demand a combination of different resources as a bundle in order to perform a task (Subramoniam et al. 2002; Cheliotis et al. 2005). Grid resources are complementarities, meaning that participants have super-additive valuations for the resources, since the sum of the utilities for single resources is less than the value for the whole bundle. Suppose a consumer requires a storage service and a computation service in order to perform a rendering job. If any of the two services, e.g., the storage service, is not allocated to him, the remaining bundle has no value for him. In order to avoid this exposure risk (i.e., receiving only a subset of the bundle), the resource allocation manager must support the simultaneous allocation of multiple resources in form of bundles.

---

[17]It is to note that this value is estimated and should only serve as a clue for the maximum runtime of an allocation manager.

[18]This assumes, that resource providers can estimate their available resource capacities, e.g., by the use of performance prediction models such as proposed by Wolski (1998) or Schopf and Yang (2004). Furthermore, it is assumed that resource consumers can specify their capability requirements (Smith 2004), e.g., that an application requires a storage service with 300 GB of capacity.

Requirement 2.7: Co-Allocation of Resources
Capacity-demanding applications usually require the simultaneous allocation of several homogenous resources from different providers. For example, a large-scale simulation can require several computation services to get completed in time. Research literature often refers to the simultaneous allocation of multiple homogenous resources as co-allocation. In this context, two cases must be considered: First, it is desirable to limit the maximum number of resource co-allocations, i.e., the maximum number of resource divisions. Second, it may be logical to couple multiple resources of a bundle in order to guarantee that these resources are allocated from the same provider and – more importantly – will be executed on the same machine.

Requirement 2.8: Guaranteed Resource Usage Time
Resource consumers usually require resources for a certain time span, e.g., a storage service is required for 3 hours. A resource manager must support the specification of resource usage time and must manage these confirmations in the allocation process.

Requirement 2.9: Advanced Reservation of Resource
Resource consumers may want to express their future resource requirements, e.g., the consumer may require a set of resources in 5 hours. In some cases, resource consumers may want to express boundaries in form of start and end time slots. For instance, the consumer may be indifferent whether the resource is allocated at 10 a.m. or at 11 a.m., as long as the whole job is finished at a certain time, say 3 p.m. Likewise, resource providers may also express their idle resources in the future, e.g., a computer center may want to offer its resources at night. Such scheduling of resources in the future is referred to as advanced reservation.[19]

Requirement 2.10: Substitutability of Resources
In the Grid, resource consumers may be indifferent between several resource configurations. For instance, a consumer is indifferent whether a storage service with 300 GB is allocated to him for 4 hours or a different storage service with only 200 GB is allocated to him for 7 hours. However, the consumer may want to be ensured that only one service is allocated at most. In this case, the resources are substitutes, i.e., a consumer has sub-additive valuations for them. To express the substitutability of resources, the resource allocation manager must allow consumers to express XOR[20] dependencies between several resource configurations. For resource providers, such an operator may not be necessary as Grid resources are non-storable commodities, e.g., a computation service currently available cannot be stored for a later time.

Requirement 2.11: Network Quality
The performance of applications in the Grid can be subject to numerous network constraints (Russell et al. 2004). Thus, a resource allocation manager has to take the given network quality into account when allocating resources. For instance, it is inefficient to allocate a storage service hosted on a node with a slow network connection to a data intensive application.

On the basis of these requirements, a general resource allocation process is introduced in the following. The process builds the basis for any resource management system that attempts to fulfill the above elicited requirements.

---

[19]Advanced reservation of resources and the ability to submit time boundaries may require that the underlying Grid middleware supports checkpointing in order to perform jobs discontinuously. For this, a checkpoint file of the job is generated to allow for a later continuation (Schwiegelshohn and Yahyapour 2004). Furthermore, application migration techniques are required to port an application from one resource to another one.

[20]A XOR B ($A \oplus B$) means either $\emptyset$, A, or B, but not AB.

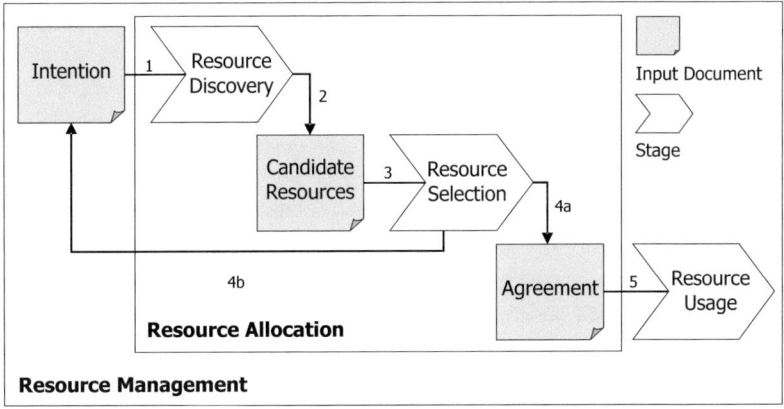

Figure 2.7: Resource allocation process following Schopf (2004, p. 18)

2.3.2   Resource Allocation Process

In the Grid, a resource allocation manager has to provide functionality to specify, discover, allocate, and schedule distributed resources. Following Schopf (2004) a general resource allocation process is depicted in Figure 2.7. Furthermore, the figure pinpoints the intersections of the resource allocation process and general resource management functionalities.

The objective of the given process is to reach a QoS level agreement between a resource provider and a consumer. Such an agreement specifies which resources are allocated from which provider to which consumer, with respect to a specified QoS level. On that note, an intention to establish such an agreement is submitted to the resource allocation manager. This intention is the input for the discovery mechanism (1) to find candidate resources which fulfill the user's requirements (2). Based on the resulting candidate list, an appropriate resource has to be selected and an agreement has to be negotiated (3). If such an agreement is established (4a), the resource can be used (5), i.e., the service can be executed. Otherwise (4b), the user may submit an alternative intention.

These three stages of the resource management process and their corresponding technology stacks are discussed in the following.

2.3.2.1   Stage 1 – Resource Discovery

In order to utilize a resource, a consumer has to be aware of the resource's existence, its characteristics, and its usage conditions. Likewise, a resource provider must have the opportunity to publish relevant characteristics and details about its provided resources. This information is managed and provided by a resource registry. Applications or users can query this registry to discover relevant services.

A prerequisite for publishing and discovering resources, as well as describing resource capabilities and organizational policies are standardized specification languages. Such languages are used to express intentions for providing and obtaining resources which fulfill required characteristics and usage conditions. In Grids, these intentions, in terms of service level agreements (SLAs), are usually formalized by means of the WS-Agreement specification (Andrieux et al. 2005). WS-Agreement provides a language and a protocol for ad-

vertising capabilities of Web services and creating agreements based on offers, as well as
for monitoring agreement compliance at runtime. Initially, an agreement initiator (e.g., a
resource consumer) receives an agreement template from a provider. Subsequently, the initiator fills out all relevant parameter and submits the filled template to the provider (Ludwig
et al. 2004). If the provider accepts the parameter specifications, an agreement is established.
Likewise, it is also possible that a resource consumer can specify the resource requirements
and policy restrictions in an agreement template and submit it to a resource provider. In both
cases, the objective of the discovery mechanism is to find candidate counterparts.

An essential part of an agreement between a resource provider and consumer is the type
of resource being provided and the underlying policy restrictions under which the provision occurs.[21] For describing the type of resources, several generic languages exist, such
as WSDL, OWL-S, and WSMO. Furthermore, for computational resources, specialized resource description languages can be applied in order to express resource attribute metrics,
such as bandwidth, latency, and space. The Resource Description Language (RSL) (Czajkowski et al. 1998) and ClassAds (Raman et al. 2004) are the two most common languages
applied in several Grid implementations. Furthermore, the OGF impels the standardization of the Job Submission Description Language (JSDL) for specifying requirements of
computational jobs (Global Grid Forum 2005a). In addition, the Grid Laboratory Uniform
Environment (GLUE) defines a model for describing Grid resources such as computing and
storage elements (Andreozzi et al. 2005). In order to describe policy restrictions, several policy languages from Web service developments can be applied to Grids, e.g., the WS-Policy
specification (Bajaj et al. 2006).[22] Most common service descriptions and policy languages
can be integrated into WS-Agreement.

Example 2.2: WS-Agreement
Figure 2.8 depicts a part of an exemplarily WS-Agreement intention. By means of this
intention, a user is requesting a computational service in order to execute an application.
The service capabilities are described using JSDL and denote that the service must either
have 32 or 8 processors (XOR constraint). The latest possible end time of the computational
job is February, 2nd, 2006.

After the specification of the requirements and conditions, the intention document is
submitted to a resource discovery mechanism which can be queried for a set of candidate
resources. Such discovery mechanisms are either implemented in a centralized, hierarchical,
or in a decentralized manner. For instance, Condor applies a centralized information pool
for collecting resource requests and offers (Thain et al. 2005). The MDS2 system as part of
the Globus Toolkit 2 is organized as a hierarchical architecture including several distributed
resource information servers (Czajkowski et al. 2001). In addition, Curbera et al. (2002), Al-
Ali et al. (2003), and Aloisio et al. (2005) propose UDDI registries in a central or hierarchical
manner as Grid discovery mechanisms. Decentralized resource discovery mechanisms, such
as proposed by Kashani et al. (2004) and Iamnitchi and Foster (2001), are usually based on
Peer-to-Peer technologies.

---

[21]Further parts of an agreement such as security, monitoring, accounting, and addressing issues play also a
crucial role in Grid settings. They are, however, out of scope for the work at hand.

[22]For a comparison of different policy description languages, the reader is referred to Anderson (2005).

```
<wsag:AgreementOffer> [...] <wsag:Terms> <wsag:All>
  <wsag:ServiceDescriptionTerm wsag:Name="executable"
      wsag:ServiceName="Compute">
  </wsag:ServiceDescriptionTerm>
  <wsag:ExactlyOne>
   <wsag:All>
    <wsag:ServiceDescriptionTerm wsag:Name="numberOfCPUs"
        wsag:ServiceName="Compute">
     <job:numberOfCPUs>32</job:numberOfCPUs>
    </wsag:ServiceDescriptionTerm>
   </wsag:All>
   <wsag:All>
    <wsag:ServiceDescriptionTerm wsag:Name="numberOfCPUs"
        wsag:ServiceName="Compute">
     <job:numberOfCPUs>8</job:numberOfCPUs>
    </wsag:ServiceDescriptionTerm>
   </wsag:All>
  </wsag:ExactlyOne>
  <wsag:GuaranteeTerm wsag:Name="MaxEndTime">
   <wsag:ServiceScope>
    <wsag:ServiceName>ComputeJob1</wsag:ServiceName>
   </wsag:ServiceScope>
   <wsag:ServiceLevelObjective>endTime IS_BEFORE 2006-02-02
   </wsag:ServiceLevelObjective>
  </wsag:GuaranteeTerm>
</wsag:All> </wsag:Terms> [...] </wsag:AgreementOffer>
```

Figure 2.8: Part of a WS-Agreement intention

2.3.2.2 Stage 2 – Resource Selection

Given a list of possible resources which meet minimum requirements, a set of resources has to be selected to perform a job. This selection stage is sometimes combined with a second information step in order to gather further dynamic information about the preferred resource, e.g., its network connectivity (Schopf 2004). Several different strategies of how to select an appropriate resource are discussed in literature. These strategies usually depend on user and application requirements. They can be classified as manual and automatic selection strategies:

Manual Selection: A manual selection strategy is often applied when a user wants to have full control over the resource selection. This strategy is advantageous if the variety of offered services is low (e.g., in an in-house Grid as applied in Meliksetian et al. (2004)) or the required services are rare and highly specialized. For instance, suppose a biochemist wants to use a specialized database service that provides results of a specific biochemical experiment. Such a resource is a rare and a non standardized commodity. Furthermore, its capabilities are hard to describe using standardized description languages. In such cases, the biochemist may select an appropriate resource manually in order to ensure that the minimum capability requirements are met.

Automated Selection: In most Grid scenarios, however, an automatic selection of candidate resources is advantageous compared to a manual selection strategy. This is especially the case if the candidate resources are commodities such as computation or storage services, that can be described using standardized specification languages. Most of the proposed automatic selection strategies for the Grid are based on matchmaking algorithms. In such systems, the values of the capabilities of resource providers are compared with those required by consumers (Veit 2003). One of the most famous matchmaking systems in the Grid is the Condor matchmaking framework (Raman et al. 1998) and its extension Gang-Matching (Raman et al. 2003). Furthermore, ontology based matchmakers, such as proposed by Tangmunarunkit et al. (2003), are applied for a semantic matchmaking of resource offers and requests. In case multiple resources match the required capabilities, matchmaking algorithms usually select a resource according to a system specific strategy, e.g., using a first-come first-serve mechanism.[23] In most automatic resource selection strategies, the resource discovery and selection stage are intertwined and realized in one single component. As such, a clear distinction between resource discovery and selection does not exist.

Besides manual and automatic selection algorithms, several hybrid strategies exist in literature and practice. Such algorithms usually restrict the set of candidate services to a smaller subset of potential resources. Subsequently, the user decides which resource should be obtained (Meliksetian et al. 2004).

Having selected a specific resource, the counterparts can reach an agreement upon resource usage. If such an agreement is established, the resource can be used by the consumer.

2.3.2.3   Stage 3 – Resource Usage

After an agreement is established between a resource provider and consumer, a job can be performed using the allocated resources. Before a job is started, the resource provider has to reserve local resources in order to fulfill the agreed QoS level. This is typically realized using a Grid middleware in combination with a local resource manager. Having reserved the resources, the job is executed. In some cases, it is necessary to transfer data to the resource provider in order to perform the job. For instance, suppose a computational service provider that offers a cluster to a consumer. In this case, it may be required to transfer a specific application to that node, e.g., using GridFTP (Allcock et al. 2002). When the job is executed, the user can monitor the status of the job and of the resource. After the job is finished, the user is notified and if necessary retrieves files from the resource.

2.4   Summary

This chapter introduced the basic concepts of Grid architectures and resource management systems. Section 2.1 outlined the historical evolution of Grid technologies which shifted from proprietary high-performance computing infrastructures towards holistic systems for coordinated resource sharing based on standardized and open protocols. The evolution further showed an increased functionality, standardization, and commercialization of Grid technologies. As a result, current Grid architectures rely on principles of SOAs in order to achieve flexibility in heterogeneous environments.

Section 2.2 introduced OGSA as the current state of the art Grid architecture. For this, basic principles of SOAs, Web services, and WSRF are first discussed. Furthermore, it is outlined how these specifications complement and refine existing Grid technologies. Based

---

[23]For a comprehensive study on automatic resource selectors in the Grid, the reader is referred to Krauter et al. (2002).

on these specifications, the OGSA platform architecture, as well as its reference implementation GT 4, are briefly outlined. These technologies enable the formation of loosely-coupled, high-performance computational environments.

Essential for a wide application of Grid technologies is the ability to discover, arrange, utilize, and monitor resources. These functionalities are comprised by resource management systems which are discussed in Section 2.3. At first, general requirements of a resource allocation system for the Grid are elicited. Subsequently, a resource allocation process is introduced which builds the base for fulfilling the specified requirements.

In the following Chapter 3 it is argued why current technical resource management systems fail to achieve an economically efficient outcome. Furthermore, it is discussed why the use of market mechanisms for allocating Grid resources is deemed promising.

Chapter 3

Moving Markets to the Grid

In the long term, the real test of our success will be not merely how well we understand the
general principles which govern economic interactions, but how well we can bring this
knowledge to bear on practical questions of microeconomic engineering.
(Roth 1991, p. 113)

Most of the research carried out in the area of Grids has been devoted to the hardware and
software infrastructure to provide access to any form of distributed resources. Technical infrastructure is a necessary requirement to implement Grids in practice. Technical feasibility,
however, is not equivalent to actual realization, as also institutional arrangements are becoming increasingly important. In essence, current middleware provides insufficient incentive to
participate in the Grid. This lack of incentive stems from the fact that most Grid middleware resource management systems employ batch algorithms which determine the allocation based on either naive heuristics or on idiosyncratic cost functions (Buyya et al. 2002).
From an economic point of view, however, these algorithms are suboptimal as they strive to
maximize a system-wide performance objective, such as throughput or mean response time,
rather than determining an economically efficient allocation of resources by maximizing the
total value over all participants. Thus, these batch algorithms cannot guarantee that buyers
with a high valuation for some resources will really receive them.

Recently, researchers have increasingly suggested employing markets for the resource
allocation problem in Grids (Wolski et al. 2001; Buyya et al. 2001). If the market rules are
properly designed, users may be provided incentives to express their true values for service
requests and offers. This, in turn, marks the prerequisite for attaining an efficient allocation
of Grid resources.

The objective of this chapter is threefold: First, the chapter motivates the use of markets
for allocating resources in the Grid. Second, it introduces the foundations and functionality
of markets with a focus on concepts that are related to Grid markets. Third, the chapter
outlines a systematic approach to design, implement, and evaluate markets. The structure
of this chapter is as follows: Section 3.1 provides an answer to the question why markets
should be applied to allocate and schedule resources in the Grid. Subsequently, Section 3.2
outlines the general structure of a market and introduces a theory to analyze the impact of
different market rules. As the design of a market for the Grid is rather difficult, Section 3.3
outlines the market engineering approach, a systematic procedure for engineering markets.
Finally, Section 3.4 concludes with a summary.

		Incentive mechanism	
		Static	**Dynamic**
Focus	**Cooperation**	Community sharing	Priority sharing
	Competition	Fixed pricing	Markets

Table 3.1: Classification of resource allocation models

3.1 Why Markets for the Grid?

In literature and practice, various mechanisms have been proposed to allocate resources in distributed computing systems. In order to determine an allocation of resources, each mechanism attempts to implement a particular social choice function, that is, they implement a rule to determine which resources are allocated to which requesting participant (Shneidman et al. 2005). Such a social choice function may maximize the overall system utilization or the total revenue of a particular Grid operator.[1] From an economic point of view, a social choice function that determines an efficient allocation typically meets the goal that the mechanism designer wants to achieve (Neumann 2004). An efficient resource allocation maximizes the total utility of all participants.

Independent from their particular peculiarities, one can classify resource allocation mechanisms by their *focus* and their *incentive mechanism*: The focus of a resource allocation mechanism can be either *cooperation* or *competition*. Cooperative models assume that rational individuals will *"cooperate in pursuing their common interests if the conditions permit them to do so"* (Harsanyi and Selten 1998, p. 356). An example for a cooperative model is the sharing of computing power to perform a corporate physical experiment among scientists. In contrast, competition assumes that there is a *"contest between rivals"* (Merriam-Webster 2006). As an example for a competitive behavior of agents suppose two rival companies that compete for the access to one single supercomputer. Aside from their focus, resource allocation mechanisms differ from their underlying incentive mechanism. This mechanism impels the willingness of agents to participate in the system. Such mechanisms can be either *static* or *dynamic*. Static models constitute fixed entry fees or fixed accounting schemes such as a fixed price to access a computer node. Dynamic mechanisms adapt their participation conditions according to the change of available resource quantities. A common example for a dynamic mechanism is a market mechanism whose price system dynamically reflects information about supply and demand for a resource.

Table 3.1 illustrates the classification of resource allocation models for the Grid and constitutes a practical mechanism for each criterion. These mechanisms and their applicability to Grids are briefly reviewed in the following.

3.1.1 Community Sharing

Currently, most resource allocation mechanisms that are applied in practice base on community sharing models known from Peer-to-Peer networks such as Gnutella[2] or BitTorrent[3]. The principle of such models is that agents can participate in the network if they offer a part of their idle resources as a fixed entry fee. Usually this entry fee is only a small and static

---

[1]Likewise to financial markets, there may be several different Grid operators in the future.
[2]See http://www.gnutella.org/ for details.
[3]See http://www.bittorrent.com/ for details

fraction of the consumable resources. The entry fee could prescribe that one computer has to be shared to get access to a cluster of machines. In this situation, the term *agent* is used to denote any participating user such as an individual, an agency, a government department, or a company.

The basis for sharing models is cooperation rather than competition. From a social-psychological point of view, the willingness to share resources or information as public goods is explained by altruistic or reciprocal behavior (Antoniadis et al. 2004). In practice, however, such behavior rarely exists: Adar and Huberman (2000) report that nearly 70% of the Gnutella agents share no files.[4] Furthermore, nearly 50% of all responses are returned by the top 1% of sharing nodes. This is explained by the fact that agents act rationally by reducing their shared resources to a minimum and only consume offered resources (Becker and Clement 2004). Current community sharing models do not provide sufficient incentives to share more than a minimum resource endowment. One can transfer these experiences to the Grid and come to the assumption that the willingness to share computer resources as public goods is small. Most computational resources, such as clusters, are cost-intensive and require outlays for their permanent administration. As such, it is not reasonable to believe that agents share more Grid resources than required.

If agents request more resources than shared, demand exceeds supply. In such cases, a resource allocator must decide which agents are supplied with the given resource endowment. This decision reflects its implemented social choice function. Traditionally, within community sharing models, resource managers base either on naive heuristics, such as first-come first-serve, or on idiosyncratic cost functions, such as the maximization of system utilization (Buyya et al. 2005). However, these functions do not guarantee that users who value the resources most will also receive them. For instance, suppose a company runs two concurrent applications that require computational resources. One application, a stock portfolio optimizer, is very critical for the company; another application, for instance an annual report generator, is not that important at that instance. A first-come first-serve strategy does not guarantee that the portfolio optimizer is preferred by the allocation decision, as priorities are not taken into account. As a result, the described resource managers cannot guarantee the achievement of economically efficient outcomes.

The use of community sharing models for the Grid has two main shortcomings: First, resource owners only offer a small fraction of their available resources to the Grid. Second, allocation decisions can be inefficient due to first-come first-serve strategies. Unfortunately, the first shortcoming makes the second one more severe, as only a minimum of resources are contributed to the Grid and demand for resources may be very large[5]. Consequently, there will be a situation of an extremely large excess demand for resources (Schnizler et al. 2005).

3.1.2 Priority Sharing

Priority sharing models extend community based mechanisms by including dynamically adaptable agent weight functions into the allocation decision. As such, the importance of different jobs competing for resources can be rated. This may lead to efficient allocations.

---

[4]In the Gnutella network, users can participate even without sharing files.

[5]For instance, in PlanetLab – a test bed for scientific networking and distributed computing – demand is usually higher than supply a few weeks before the submission deadlines of popular conferences (Fu et al. 2003).

Proportional Share is a frequently discussed example of a priority based model applied in distributed systems (Waldspurger and Weihl 1994; AuYoung et al. 2004):

Proportional share accounts for job priorities by assigning a weight function w_i to each agent $i \in \mathcal{I}$. On the basis of these weight functions, the mechanism allocates each agent i a $w_i / \sum_{i \in \mathcal{I}} w_i$ share of all resources. For instance, if the portfolio optimizer $i = 1$ of the aforementioned example has a priority value of $w_1 = 2$ and the report generator $i = 2$ has a priority value of $w_2 = 1$, the optimizer gets two-thirds and the report generator gets one-third of the resources. Assume the weights simultaneously reflect the true value of each application, the resulting allocation is efficient. Now, suppose the report generator becomes more important, as annual financial statements have to be generated. Furthermore, the stock portfolio optimizer becomes a non-critical application for the company. In such a case, proportional share will still be efficient if the stock portfolio optimizer reduces the weight w_1 and the report generator increases the weight w_2. Thus, the report generator will get a higher value and will be allocated to more resources. However, there is no incentive for the portfolio optimizer to reduce the weight w_1. A faster optimization of the portfolio due to more resources still creates a small benefit for the application maintainer, although the benefit for the whole company would be higher if the weight of the optimizer was reduced. The application maintainer of the portfolio optimizer behaves in a non-cooperative manner that leads to inefficient outcomes. This socioeconomic phenomenon – actions of an individual that cause the society as a whole to suffer – is known as *the tragedy of the commons* (Hardin 1968). With regard to a free market economy, this phenomenon mainly applies to resources which are not suitable for private ownership. Suppose, for example, the pollution problem in an economy. If an agent puts his waste into a river, his individual share of the costs for the whole economy is less than the costs of purifying the waste before releasing it. This fact is true for every agent in the economy. Hardin (1968, p. 1245) summarizes that *"we are locked into a system of fouling our own nest, so long as we behave only as independent, rational, free-enterprisers."*.

One solution for the tragedy of the commons is to install an administrator as a central entity who controls the system and dynamically adapts the weight values for the resources. For the Grid, however, such a manual task is seen as to too expensive and error prone (Lai 2005). Moreover, a central monitoring of application requirements is almost impossible to realize if organizational barriers are crossed.

Another way to preclude a tragedy of the commons situation in Grids is to price the access to resources (Cheliotis et al. 2005). This shifts the focus from cooperative based models towards competitive mechanisms.

3.1.3   Fixed Pricing

In practice, fixed pricing schemes are applied to control and to price access of resources. Popular examples for such schemes are flat rates for pricing network bandwidth and fixed prices for the use of computer resources.[6]

In the example mentioned above, a fixed pricing scheme clearly reduces the demand of the portfolio optimization application due to budget restrictions. Moreover, such pricing schemes can lead to efficient outcomes if values for resources are static. Fixed pricing

---

[6]For instance, Sun Microsystems sells unused CPU cycles for $1 per CPU hour and storage at $1 per gigabyte per month. See http://www.network.com/ for details (accessed 11.12.2006).

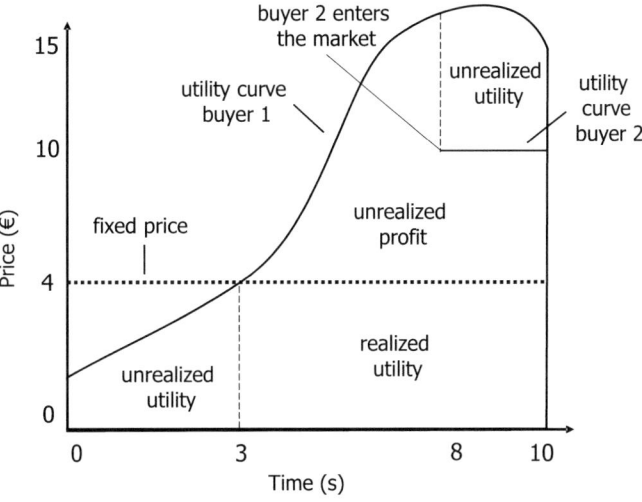

Figure 3.1: Utility curves of two buyers competing for a fixed price resource following Lai (2005, p.2)

schemes are, however, inefficient if these values change dynamically. This obstacle is depicted in Figure 3.1 following Lai (2005, p. 2): The graph shows the utility curves of two buyers for the same resource which is offered by a seller for a fixed price of $p = 4$ €. Until time step $t = 3$, buyer 1's utility is below the fixed price and, as a consequence, buyer 1 is unwilling to pay the fixed price for the resource. In these time steps, the outcome of the mechanism is inefficient, as the (small) utility of buyer 1 is not realized. After time step $t = 3$, buyer 1 is willing to pay more than the fixed price for the resource. Consequently, buyer 1 can use the resource and can realize some utility. Although an efficient allocation is achieved, the seller does not realize all potential profit, i.e., the seller is not realizing the difference between the utility curve of buyer 1 and the fixed price. In time step $t = 8$, buyer 2 enters the market and also wants to purchase the resource. In this case, the seller cannot distinguish among the utility curves of both buyers, as this information is private. As such, the seller cannot guarantee to allocate the resource efficiently. For instance, if the seller allocates the resource to buyer 2, the outcome is inefficient as buyer 1 has a higher utility for it.

In general, the more dynamic the values, the higher the efficiency loss caused by the fixed pricing scheme (Lai 2005). Grid resources have a dynamic value which depends on a combination of workload requirements and scarcity (Cheliotis et al. 2005). For instance, the computational workload of an automotive producer is high during a crash-test simulation and low during summer, when the employees are on holidays. Likewise, the idle resources are scarce during the simulation and plentiful during the holidays. Such a variation of workload and availability of idle resources influences the values for the resources. In order to allocate resources efficiently, a pricing scheme has to take such dynamics into account. Thus, the application of a fixed pricing mechanism for the Grid is limited.

3.1.4   Markets

In contrast to sharing models and fixed price mechanisms, markets can be an effective institution for allocating resources efficiently that have a dynamic value. This is achieved by the
interplay of supply and demand and due to the information feedback inherent to the price
system (Hurwicz 1972). By assigning a value to their resource requests, agents can reveal
their relative urgency or costs, which in turn is subject to resource usage constraints.

   If the market mechanism is designed properly, agents may be provided with incentives
to express their true values for resource requests and offers. As such, markets can be an
adequate mechanism to determine efficient resource allocation decisions and, thus, make the
Grid attractive for agents. In addition, markets inherently offer a business model for resource
owners as they are payed for their resource provision (Schnizler et al. 2006a).

3.2   Foundations of Markets

An application of markets to the Grid requires an understanding of what a market is and
how it determines allocations and prices. This knowledge builds the basis for the subsequent
engineering of a Grid market. This section aims to provide a consistent understanding of
markets: Section 3.2.1 introduces the terminology of markets that is used throughout this
work. It introduces a formal microeconomic framework that provides a common view on
the structure and the concepts of markets. Although the framework offers ways to describe
a set of different markets and their implemented rules, it does not give any hint on the consequences of the underlying rules. Section 3.2.2 introduces *mechanism design*, a theory that
questions the consequences of different types of rules (Bichler 2001). Finally, Section 3.2.3
outlines how these theoretical concepts are practically implemented.

3.2.1   Microeconomic System Framework

The microeconomic system framework proposed by Smith (1982) sketches a common view
on the structure of any economic system.[7] It provides very few well-accepted concepts and
denotes their interactions (Smith 2003). The framework serves as a starting point to define a
consistent terminology and a common understanding of markets.[8]

   The framework, as depicted in Figure 3.2, is comprised of five basic concepts and denotes
their dependencies: The economic environment embraces all factors that affect supply and
demand and that are exogenously given. This includes, among others, the agents and their
preferences, as well as the traded resources and their characteristics. Agents communicate
their preferences to other agents on the basis of a market language[9] that is defined by the
institution. The potential message space is usually restricted by the institution and limits the
choice behavior of the agents. Aside from the market language, the institution defines a set
of rules to establish an outcome, i.e., it defines ways to determine allocations and prices. The
system performance denotes the quality of the outcome with respect to the environment. In
the following paragraphs, these concepts are discussed in more detail.

---

[7]In this context, the term *system* is understood as a collection of entities that act and interact towards the
achievement of some logical end (Law and Kelton 2000).

[8]Holtmann and Neumann (2003) provide an extended version of this framework that accounts for business
structures and technical infrastructures.

[9]Without loss of generality, the market language is understood as a way to encode and decode information
of agents.

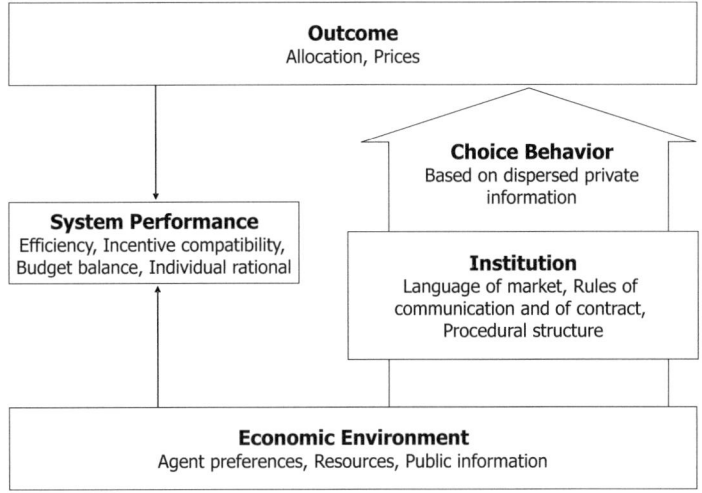

Figure 3.2: Microeconomic system framework (Smith 1989; Neumann 2004)

3.2.1.1 Economic Environment

The economic environment summarizes all factors that influence the performance of the system but are outside of the mechanism designer's control. This includes information about the agents, their initial information and their preferences for different outcomes, the resource characteristics, and legal restrictions. With regard to a market for the Grid, technical limitations of middleware systems are also part of the economic environment.

Definition 3.1: Economic Environment
The economic environment $e = (e_1, \ldots, e_I)$ describes the set of circumstances that have an impact on the performance of the system but are exogenously given, where e_i defines the individual environment characteristics of agent i and I is the number of agents.

For a Grid market, the focus of the economic environment lies on the agents and their preferences, as well as the resources and their characteristics.

Agents: The environment comprises a set of agents $\mathcal{I}$, where $i \in \mathcal{I}$ denotes an agent that participates in the resource allocation process. Agents have different preferences concerning the outcome $o \in \mathcal{O}$ that is determined by an institution. For instance, an agent i might prefer the outcome o_1 over the outcome o_2 ($o_1 \succeq o_2$), whereas agent j might prefer o_2 over o_1 ($o_1 \preceq o_2$). Such a diversity of preferences is formalized by the introduction of the *type* of an agent, more specifically, $\theta_i \in \Theta_i$ denotes the type of agent i from the set of all potential types Θ_i. The type determines the preferences of an agent over different outcomes and is assumed to be private information. Based upon this type, preferences are expressed by a utility function $u_i(o, \theta_i)$. For instance, if an agent i prefers $o_1 \succeq o_2$, the utility function fulfills the inequality $u_i(o_1, \theta_i) \geq u_i(o_2, \theta_i)$.

Agents express their values for an outcome o by their valuation function: Let θ_i be the type of agent i and let $\mathcal{P}_i$ denote a set of public information that is available to the agent. In this case, the set of public information $\mathcal{P}_i$ comprises real-valued variables that influence the valuation of an agent. For instance, this could be the current market price for a hard disk. The value of an agent i for an outcome o thus depends on the type θ_i and the public information $\mathcal{P}_i$. As a consequence, it is denoted as $v_i(o, \theta_i, \mathcal{P}_i)$ with $v_i : \mathcal{O} \times \Theta_i \times \mathcal{P}_i \rightarrow \mathbb{R}$ (Milgrom and Weber 1982). Besides his valuation, the risk attitude of an agent further influences the behavior. The most common model applied in literature is that of risk neutral agents: Agents are indifferent between an amount of money that is certain and an equal expected value of an allocation (Milgrom 2004). If the agent is risk averse, he would prefer the sure amount of money. In case of risk seeking models, the agent would prefer the allocation decision. As a special case, consider risk neutral agents that do not have any public information. This case is referred to as independent private value model, whereby the valuation of an agent i is simplified denoted as $v_i(o, \theta_i)$.

Resources: The second parameter set of the environment describes the resources. These are the commodities that are to be allocated by the institution. Resources may have different peculiarities that have an impact on both the valuations of agents and the rules of the institution. The most salient characteristics of Grid resources are briefly outlined in the following:[10]

Let $\mathcal{G}$ be the set of resources that are comprised by the environment, where $g_k \in \mathcal{G}$ denotes a particular resource that can be either physical or logical. Resources can be consumed in discrete amounts or continuously. A resource is said to be discrete when only integer units of the resource can be allocated. An allocation of discrete items is formalized as follows: Let $x_i(g_k) = q$ denote a variable that denotes the number of units $q \in \mathbb{N}$ of resource g_k that are allocated to agent i. If real-valued allocations of a resource are possible, it is said to be continuous. This is denoted by $y_i(g_k) = l$, where $l \in \mathbb{R}^+$. As a special case, suppose there is at most one unit of each resource g_k to be allocated ($q \wedge l \leq 1$). Thus, $x_i(g_k)$ becomes a binary variable with $x_i(g_k) \in \{0, 1\}$ and $y_i(g_k)$ gets restricted to $y_i(g_k) \in [0, 1]$.

If an agent considers two resources as identical, the resources are characterized as homogeneous. When there are differences between them, they are called heterogeneous. If resources are heterogeneous, there may be interdependencies between them. As a result, the utility of an agent changes if it consumes them simultaneously. If the resources are complements, the utility of receiving multiple resources is greater than the sum of the utilities for each item. As a consequence, the agent has a super-additive utility function as $u_i(g_k) + u_i(g_j) < u_i(g_k \cup g_j)$. At this, the term $u_i(g_k)$ denotes the utility of agent i with type θ_i if an outcome o is computed that allocates resource g_k to agent i. Resources are substitutes if the utility of receiving a set of resources is less than the values attached to the single items (Varian 1992). In such a case, an agent has a sub-additive utility function as $u_i(g_k) + u_i(g_j) > u_i(g_k \cup g_j)$. If there are no dependencies between the resources, the agent has an additive utility function that is characterized as $u_i(g_k) + u_i(g_j) = u_i(g_k \cup g_j)$.

If the valuation for a resource only depends on its price, the resource has a single attribute. If physical or material conditions also affect the preferences of an agent, the resource has to be described by multiple attributes. For instance, not only the price for a storage service may influence the agent's valuation but also its available space. Such additional attributes can be formalized by a set of attributes $\mathcal{A}_{g_k}$ that are associated with the resource g_k, where $a_i^k \in \mathcal{A}_{g_k}$ denotes a particular attribute i of the resource g_k.

---

[10]Neumann (2004) analyzes further characteristics of resources. Such a detailed view is, however, out of scope for the work at hand.

This formal description helps to characterize and to analyze the resources that are to be allocated by the institution. Furthermore, the description is indispensable for the design of the message space and the choice rules of the institution.

3.2.1.2 Institution

In a resource allocation problem, an institution defines the set of rules (i) that specifies the message exchange between agents and (ii) that determines which messages lead to allocations and prices (Smith 2003). These rules can be either formal such as in organized stock exchanges or informal due to traditional or implicit norms.

The institution provides a language $M = (M_1, \ldots, M_I)$ that consists of messages $m = (m_1, \ldots, m_I)$, where $m_i \in M_i$ is the set of messages that can be submitted by an agent i and I denotes the number of agents. For example, such a message might be a bid in an English auction. Furthermore, the institution defines a set of allocation rules $\mathcal{K} = (k_1(m), \ldots, k_I(m))$, where $k_i(m)$ denotes an allocation to agent i on the basis of all messages m. The payment rule $\mathcal{P} = (p_1(m), \ldots, p_I(m))$ denotes the payments (or transfers) that have to be made by each agent depending on the submitted messages m. Suppose an agent i bids 10 € in a first-price sealed-bid auction and is allocated the resource g_k. The corresponding payment rule would imply that the agent has to pay $p_i(m) = 10$ € for the resource. Finally, the institution defines a set of adjustment rules $\mathcal{R} = (r_1(t_0, t, T), \ldots, r_I(t_0, t, T))$ that specify under which conditions messages can be submitted or modified during the exchange process. Thereby, a particular adjustment rule $r_i(t_0, t, T)$ consists of a starting rule, a transition rule, and a closing rule. The starting rule $r_i(t_0, \cdot, \cdot)$ determines the start of the message exchange. For instance, this specifies the opening time in an English auction. The transition rule $r_i(\cdot, t, \cdot)$ governs the sequencing and exchange of messages. This rule can specify when an agent is allowed to resubmit a bid in an English auction. The closing rule $r_i(\cdot, \cdot, T)$ specifies when the message exchange process is stopped. Based upon these rules, an economic institution is defined as follows:

Definition 3.2: Institution
An institution is defined as $H = (H_1, \ldots, H_I)$, where

$$H_i = (M_i, k_i(m), p_i(m), r_i(t_0, t, T))$$

defines agent $i's$ rights in communication and in exchange (Smith 1982, p. 925).

The definition of an institution helps to define the term *market*. Traditionally, a market is defined as a virtual or physical meeting point of supply and demand which are balanced by means of a price mechanism. Referring to the aforementioned concepts, the environment determines supply and demand. Furthermore, the price mechanism that is specified by the institution brings them into balance (Neumann 2004):

Definition 3.3: Market
A market is a combination of the economic environment and the price system that is specified by the institution.

A special case of this definition is an electronic market which uses an information system for communication and determining an outcome.

3.2.1.3 Agent Behavior

The behavior of agents connects their individual motivation with the institution in order to yield an outcome (Smith 2003). Agents have different preferences, knowledge, and priorities when they want to acquire a resource. They use messages to communicate their motivations and interests to other agents. The message space is, however, limited by the institution. Thus, agents are restricted when expressing their preferences. Agent behavior characterizes these restrictions as a mapping from individual circumstances and institutional restrictions into messages.

Agent behavior can be described by means of a static description (outcome behavior) or by means of a dynamic description (response behavior). A static description of agent behavior is applied when the communication process takes place in a single step (one-shot). Agents communicate their messages once. After that, an allocation is determined with respect to the rules defined by the institution. As an example, such a description is applied in a first-price sealed-bid auction. Agents submit their bids to the auctioneer who subsequently determines an allocation and a price. Formally denoted, a static description of messages is realized by a function $\beta(e_i|H)$ with $m_i = \beta(e_i|H)$, where e_i represents the local environment of agent i and H denotes the institution. A dynamic description of agent behavior is used when the communication process is iterative. Agents can submit several messages, where the message content bases on historical information. An example for a dynamic description of agent behavior is an English auction where agents can submit multiple bids to the auctioneer based upon the highest bid of the previous round. In mathematical terms, a dynamic description of agent behavior is given by $m_i(t) = f_i(m(t-1)|e_i, H)$, where t is the time when an agent submits a message, $m(t-1)$ denotes the messages received along the market process, e_i denotes the local environment of agent i, and H represents the institution.

One way to describe and analyze the behavior of agents is the use of game theory. Game theory is used to study systems of agents that make strategic decisions. The choices and behavior of agents are described by means of *strategies*. A strategy represents a complete and contingent plan that defines the actions an agent will select in every distinguishable state of a game (Parkes 2001). In formal terms, a strategy s_i of agent i is defined as $s_i(\theta_i) \in \Omega_i$, where θ_i denotes the type of an agent i and Ω_i represents all possible strategies of the agent. Modelling agent behavior by means of game theory is advantageous, as existing concepts and solutions from this theory can be applied to the study of markets.

Game theory strives to find equilibriums in games. States where no agent gains an advantage by changing his own strategy unilaterally are constituting such an equilibrium. In a market setting, the concept of equilibrium is interpreted as a state where no agent can improve his utility by submitting another message to the institution. For instance, equilibrium in an English auction is constituted if no agent bids higher than the current highest price.

Another important concept of game theory regards dominant strategy, the maximization of the expected utility of an agent for all possible strategies of other agents (Parkes 2001). Formally expressed, let $u_i^E(\cdot)$ denote the expected utility of an agent i, $s_i(\theta_i)$ be the own strategy, and $s_{-i}(\theta_{-i})$ denote the strategy of every other agent. If $s_i(\theta_i)$ is a dominant strategy, the following inequality holds:

$$u_i^E(s_i(\theta_i), s_{-i}(\theta_{-i}), \theta_i) \geq u_i^E(s_i'(\theta_i), s_{-i}(\theta_{-i}), \theta_i),$$
$$\forall s_i'(\theta_i) \neq s_i(\theta_i), s_i(\theta_i) \wedge s_i'(\theta_i) \in \Omega_i, s_{-i}(\theta_{-i}) \in \Omega_{-i}$$

The expected utility of an agent i that plays strategy $s_i(\theta_i)$ is always greater or equal than the expected utility of every other strategy $s'_i(\theta_i)$, independent of the strategies $s_{-i}(\theta_{-i})$ selected by other agents. The concept of a dominant strategy is a desirable property of agent behavior as their message exchange with the institution is not affected by other agents. Equilibrium in dominant strategies denotes the situation in which every agent has the same utility maximizing strategy for all strategies of other agents (Parkes 2001). In such case, all agents in the system do best in playing their dominant strategy.

The concept of strategies allows the introduction of a *mechanism* that is used to combine the economic environment that comprises of a set of agents $i \in \mathcal{I}$, their behavior, and the institution. The message space that influences the agent's behavior is represented as a set of strategies Ω_i that are available to each agent i. Furthermore, the institution is denoted as an outcome function $\delta_{\mathcal{M}}(\cdot)$ that consists of a choice rule $k(\cdot)$ and a payment rule $p(\cdot)$. Based upon these definitions, a mechanism is defined as follows (Parkes 2001, p. 30):

Definition 3.4: Mechanism
A mechanism $\mathcal{M} = (\Omega_1, \ldots, \Omega_I, \delta_{\mathcal{M}})$ defines the set of strategies Ω_i that are available to each agent i and defines an outcome rule $\delta_{\mathcal{M}} : \Omega_1 \times, \ldots, \times \Omega_I \to \mathcal{O}$ that determines the allocation and payments.

The mechanism determines the strategy space of the agents (e.g., bid at least higher than the current highest bid) and a function to compute an outcome (e.g., the bidder with the highest bid receives the resource and has to pay the second highest bid).

3.2.1.4 System Performance

Mechanisms are installed to attain a desired outcome. On the basis of the outcome (allocation and prices) and the economic environment (preferences of agents), a set of system performance metrics can be measured. This performance strongly depends on the behavior of the agents. To control this behavior, the objective of designing a mechanism is to install the right incentives for agents to behave in a certain way (Neumann 2004). With the knowledge of the agents' behavior, the mechanism designer can specify a set of institutional rules that attempt to achieve the desired outcome.

The desired outcome of a mechanism is defined by a *social choice function* $f : \Theta_1 \times \ldots \times \Theta_I \to \mathcal{O}$. This function selects the optimal outcome $f(\theta) \in \mathcal{O}$ on the basis of the agents' types $\theta = (\theta_1 \times \ldots \times \theta_I)$ (Parkes 2001). As the *type* of an agent is private information, the agent is not willing to reveal it to other agents. The objective of a mechanism is to implement a set of adequate rules so that agents reveal some of their private information to the mechanism. If an agent reveals sufficient information, the mechanism will attain the same outcome $f(\theta)$. Reiter (1977) illustrates this problem as depicted in Figure 3.3: The social function $f(\theta)$ determines the optimal outcome on the basis of the agents' types θ. However, such an abstract function is unrealistic as agents may not reveal their private information. They rather submit partial, and not necessarily truthful, information to maximize their own utility. It is denoted as the *mechanism design problem* to provide a strategy space $s(\theta)$ in a way that the outcome of the social function can also be attained by the mechanism such as $f(\theta) = \delta(s(\theta))$. This is usually achieved by providing incentives in attempt to have agents revealing sufficient private information that is required to achieve a desired goal.

Having defined the construct of a mechanism, a set of objectives upon its outcome is formulated. In essence, the idea is to define a social choice function that meets the specified

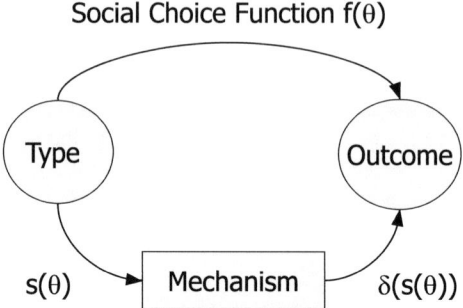

Figure 3.3: Connection between a social choice function and a mechanism (Reiter 1977)

requirements and, subsequently, to implement a mechanism that attains the same outcome. The following discussion outlines the most significant desiderata for a Grid market (Schnizler et al. 2006b). For a comprehensive discussion on alternative objectives, the reader is referred to Neumann (2004).

Desiderata 3.1: Allocative efficiency

A mechanism is allocative efficient if the total value over all agents is maximized. If $o \in \mathcal{O}$ is an efficient allocation, no alternative outcome $o' \in \mathcal{O}$ would attain a higher utility for the agents:

$$\sum_{i \in \mathcal{I}} u_i(o, \theta_i) \geq \sum_{i \in \mathcal{I}} u_i(o', \theta_i), \qquad \forall o' \in \mathcal{O} \tag{3.1}$$

In most cases, a mechanism can only attain allocative efficiency if the market agents report their valuation truthfully. This requires incentive compatibility in equilibrium.

Desiderata 3.2: Incentive compatibility

A mechanism is incentive compatible if every agent's expected utility maximizing strategy in equilibrium with respect to every other agent is to report his true preferences (Parkes 2001). Agents may not have an incentive to untruthfully report their preferences in order to increase their individual utility. A mechanism is *strategy-proof* when truthful revelation of the preferences constitutes a dominant-strategy equilibrium.

Desiderata 3.3: Budget-balance

The property of budget-balance is concerned with the question whether the mechanism requires payments from outside the system or not. A mechanism is budget-balanced if all payments made to the mechanism are redistributed among the agents. Let $p_i(\theta)$ be the payment made by agent i, a mechanism is budget-balanced if

$$\sum_{i \in \mathcal{I}} p_i(\theta) = 0. \tag{3.2}$$

Payments are positive for buyers and negative for sellers. Funds are neither removed from the system, nor is the system subsidized from outside. A weaker property is the concept of *weak budget-balance*: Net payments are made from the agents to the mechanism, but no net payment from the mechanism to the agents. In mathematical terms, a mechanism is weak budget-balanced if

$$\sum_{i \in \mathcal{I}} p_i(\theta) \geq 0. \tag{3.3}$$

Desiderata 3.4: Individual rationality
The constraint of individual rationality requires the utility after participating in the mechanism to be greater or equal than before. Let $u_i(o, \theta_i)$ be the utility of agent i for participating in the mechanism and let $\bar{u}_i(o, \theta_i)$ be the utility for non-participation. A mechanism is individually rational if

$$u_i(o, \theta_i) \geq \bar{u}_i(o, \theta_i), \quad \forall i \in \mathcal{I}. \tag{3.4}$$

A weaker property is that of interim individual rationality. A mechanism is interim individually rational if the expected utility $u_i^E(o, \theta_i)$ for participating in the mechanism is greater or equal than the expected utility $\bar{u}_i^E(o, \theta_i)$ from non-participating:

$$u_i^E(o, \theta_i) \geq \bar{u}_i^E(o, \theta_i), \quad \forall i \in \mathcal{I}. \tag{3.5}$$

Desiderata 3.5: Computational tractability
Computational tractability considers the complexity of computing the outcome of a mechanism based on the agent's strategies (Kalagnanam and Parkes 2004). With an increasing size of the message space, the allocation problem can become very demanding. Computational constraints may delimit the design of choice and transfer rules.

In general, an allocative efficient outcome is the objective a mechanism designer wants to achieve (Neumann 2004). The remaining desiderata are side-constraints which are essential in fulfilling this objective. However, the goal of achieving allocative efficiency usually conflicts with revenue maximization (Myerson 1981; Jehiel and Moldovanu 2003): In a revenue maximization problem – also called *optimal auction design* – an outcome function is specified which maximizes the revenue of the agents. The argumentation towards revenue maximization stems from auction theory and means that a seller in an auction is not interested in efficiency, rather in profit maximization. On the other hand, Parkes (2001, p. 60) argues that if a mechanism *"does not compute efficient allocations then agents will go else where."*[11] Although there are settings in which the efficient allocation also maximizes the expected revenue (Krishna and Perry 2000), it is often not possible to attain both objectives simultaneously. For the work at hand, the desired objective is to attain an efficient allocation.

3.2.2 Mechanism Design

Mechanism design considers the design of institutions and how the design affects the outcomes of interactions (Jackson 2002). The focus of mechanism design lies on the design of institutions that attain a set of objectives, assuming that agents interacting through institutions are self-interested and have private information about their preferences (Parkes 2001). Mechanism design provides a set of theories that give insight into which type of social function can or cannot be implemented by a mechanism.

In the following, the basic concepts of mechanism design are outlined: Section 3.2.2.1 introduces the revelation principle as a central tool used to analyze possible and impossible results of mechanism design. Section 3.2.2.2 outlines the Vickrey-Clarke-Groves mechanism as an efficient, strategy-proof, and individually rational mechanism for agents with specific utility functions. Finally, Section 3.2.2.3 briefly introduces two important impossibility theorems that show what cannot be achieved by a mechanism.

---

[11]This assumes that the market operator is not a monopolist.

3.2.2.1   Revelation Principle

One can distinguish between direct and indirect mechanisms: In a direct mechanism, agents submit their messages once and, subsequently, an outcome is computed. In an indirect mechanism, agents can submit several messages and receive information feedback from the mechanism. In a direct mechanism, the behavior of agents is modeled by the use of a static description, whereas an indirect mechanism is designed utilizing a dynamic description (cf. Section 3.2.1.3).

Assume that agents of type θ_i report their private information (possibly untruthful) as $\hat{\theta}_i$. Then, a direct mechanism computes the outcome $\delta(\hat{\theta})$, where $\hat{\theta} = (\hat{\theta}_1, \ldots, \hat{\theta}_N)$ denotes the reported types of the agents. In an indirect mechanism, the mechanism computes a provisional outcome $\delta(\hat{\theta}(\delta(t-1)), t)$ in each round t, where $\hat{\theta}(\delta(t-1), t)$ represents the reported types of the agents in time t. This reported type depends on the feedback information $\delta(t-1)$ received by the mechanism. The rules of the mechanisms imply the amount of information that is revealed to the agents. In an English auction, for instance, the revealed information is the current highest bid for a resource.

The revelation principle implies that it is sufficient to restrict to direct incentive compatible mechanisms.[12] The principle states that any mechanism $\mathcal{M}$ (direct or indirect) which implements a social choice function $f(\cdot)$ in dominant strategies is also implementable by a strategy-proof direct mechanism (Parkes 2001). The intuition behind the principle is as follows: Suppose a mechanism $\mathcal{M}$ that leads to an outcome $\delta(s^*(\theta)) = f(\theta)$, where $s^*(\theta)$ denotes the strategy profiles of the agents in equilibrium. Now, the behavior of these agents, i.e., their strategies, is simulated by another mechanism $\mathcal{M}'$. This mechanism computes the optimal strategies of the agents based on their reported preferences. It is a dominant strategy that every agent reports the preferences truthfully to $\mathcal{M}'$, as the *simulator* $\mathcal{M}'$ computes the optimal strategies on the basis of the report type. As a consequence, the direct incentive compatible mechanism $\mathcal{M}'$ implements the same social choice function $f(\cdot)$ as $\mathcal{M}$.

The implication of the revelation principle is as follows: If a social choice function can be implemented by any mechanism, it is sufficient to restrict to direct mechanisms (Jackson 2002). An indirect mechanism, for example, can become quite complex as no assumptions on the set of strategies are made. An analysis of such mechanisms can become impossible, as agents play complex strategies by reacting to historical information $\bar{\delta}(t-1)$ in each round. The revelation principle states that it is sufficient to concentrate on a simpler class of mechanisms, namely the class of direct mechanisms (Krishna 2002). The computations made by agents during their strategy formulation in an indirect mechanism can thus be shifted to the direct mechanism: An indirect mechanism can only attain a particular property if a direct mechanism can be constructed with the same property (Kalagnanam and Parkes 2004).

The revelation principles simplifies the design and analysis of mechanisms. For instance, the transition rules $r_i(t_0, t, T)$ that model dynamic behavior of agents can be neglected for analyzing the properties that a mechanism attains. Hence, it is useful for the designer to restrict to direct mechanisms as a simple class of mechanisms (McAfee and McMillan 1987).[13]

---

[12]The principle was originally developed by Gibbard (1973) and later extended by Green and Laffont (1977), and Myerson (1979, 1981) .

[13]The principle assumes that a direct mechanism that is computational tractable always exists. However, this assumption may fail in settings that require complex mechanisms. A detailed discussion of the computational practicability of the revelation principle is given in Conitzer and Sandholm (2003).

3.2.2.2   Vickrey-Clarke-Groves Mechanism

An important direct mechanism is the Vickrey-Clarke-Groves (VCG) mechanism as proposed by Vickrey (1961), Clarke (1971), and Groves (1973).

In the following discussion, the independent private value model and agents with quasi-linear utility functions are assumed (cf. Section 3.2.1.1). Thus, utility can be transferred across all agents by means of side-payments (Parkes 2001). Quasi-linear utility functions have the form

$$u_i(o, \theta_i) = v_i(o, \theta_i) - p_i, \tag{3.6}$$

where $v_i(o, \theta_i)$ is the valuation of an agent i and p_i the payment. This type of function allows a separation of the choices $k_i(\cdot)$ and the corresponding payments $p_i(\cdot)$.

Groves Mechanisms: A VCG mechanism is a special case of a Groves mechanism (Groves 1973). In a Groves mechanism, agents communicate their preferences $\hat{\theta}_i = s_i(\theta_i)$ directly to the mechanism, where $\hat{\theta}_i$ denotes the reported type of agent i, which is not necessarily truthfully reported. Subsequently, the mechanism computes an allocation by solving the choice function

$$k^*(\hat{\theta}) = \arg\max_{k \in \mathcal{K}} \sum_{i \in \mathcal{I}} v_i(k, \hat{\theta}_i). \tag{3.7}$$

The function $k^*(\hat{\theta})$ maximizes the total reported valuations over all agents. On the basis of the computed allocation, the payment rule $p_i(\hat{\theta})$ determines the payments of each agent, where $p_i(\hat{\theta})$ is defined as

$$p_i(\hat{\theta}) = \pi_i(\hat{\theta}_{-i}) - \sum_{j \neq i} v_j(k^*(\hat{\theta}), \hat{\theta}_j).$$

The first term $\pi_i(\hat{\theta}_{-i})$ denotes the *transfer rule*, an arbitrary function $\pi_i : \Theta_{-i} \to \mathbb{R}$ that depends on all but agent i reported types (Parkes 2001). This freedom of defining $\pi_i(\hat{\theta}_{-i})$ leads to a set of different mechanisms that all belong to the Groves family.

Groves mechanisms are important for the design of mechanisms, as they have some desirable economic properties discussed below.

Theorem 3.1:   Efficiency of Groves Mechanisms
For agents with quasi-linear utility functions, Groves mechanisms are allocative-efficient and strategy-proof (Green and Laffont 1977).

Proof. As long as agents report their types truthfully, the implemented choice rule (Equation 3.7) of a Groves mechanism computes an efficient allocation (cf. Equation 3.1). As such, it is sufficient to show that the mechanism is strategy-proof: Following the argumentation of Parkes (2001), the utility of agent i that reported the type $\hat{\theta}_i$ is defined as

$$u_i(\hat{\theta}_i) = v_i(k^*(\hat{\theta}), \theta_i) - p_i(\hat{\theta}) = v_i(k^*(\hat{\theta}), \theta_i) - \pi_i(\hat{\theta}_{-i}) + \sum_{j \neq i} v_j(k^*(\hat{\theta}), \hat{\theta}_j)$$

In order to determine the best strategy selection of agent i, the term $\pi_i(\hat{\theta}_{-i})$ can be ignored, as it is independent from i. The utility of agent i is thus maximized by

$$\max_{\hat{\theta}_i \in \Theta_i} [v_i(k^*(\hat{\theta}), \theta_i) + \sum_{j \neq i} v_j(k^*(\hat{\theta}), \hat{\theta}_j)].$$

Thus, the reported type $\hat{\theta}_i$ of agent i only affects the allocation function $k^*(\hat{\theta})$. From agent i's perspective, the function $k^*(\hat{\theta})$ is only maximized if the agent reports the true type $\hat{\theta}_i = \theta_i$. As a result, the mechanism solves

$$k^*(\theta_i, \hat{\theta}_{-i}) = \arg \max_{k \in \mathcal{K}} [v_i(k, \theta_i) + \sum_{j \neq i} v_j(k, \hat{\theta}_j)].$$

As a consequence, it is a dominant strategy for agent i to report its type truthfully. $\square$

Moreover, it is proven that Groves mechanisms are the only mechanisms that are allocative efficient and strategy-proof:

Theorem 3.2: Uniqueness of Groves Mechanisms
Groves mechanisms are the only mechanisms that are allocative efficient and strategy-proof for agents with quasi-linear utility functions (Green and Laffont 1977, p. 432).

A proof for this theorem can be found in Green and Laffont (1977, p. 432–33).

In regard to the revelation principle, this theorem also states that any iterative mechanism that is allocative efficient and strategy-proof implements a Groves mechanism.

Aside from these strong economic characteristics, the property of individual rationality strongly depends on the choice of $\pi_i(\hat{\theta}_{-i})$. For instance, defining $\pi_i(\hat{\theta}_{-i}) = 0$ results in a mechanism that is not individually rational for agent i. In this case, he has to transfer a positive value to other agents if he is not part of the allocation.

VCG Mechanism: One individually rational mechanism of the Groves family is the VCG mechanism.[14] The mechanism defines the transfer rule $\pi_i(\hat{\theta}_{-i})$ as

$$\pi_i(\hat{\theta}_{-i}) = \sum_{j \neq i} v_j(k^*_{-i}(\hat{\theta}_{-i}), \hat{\theta}_j),$$

with

$$k^*_{-i}(\hat{\theta}_{-i}) = \arg \max_{k \in \mathcal{K}} \sum_{j \neq i} v_j(k, \hat{\theta}_j).$$

The function $k^*_{-i}(\hat{\theta}_{-i})$ denotes the outcome with all agents except agent i. As a consequence, $\pi_i(\hat{\theta}_{-i})$ determines the value of the outcome that would have been computed in absence of agent i. In other words, the transfer function $\pi_i(\hat{\theta}_{-i})$ reflects the impact of the participation of agent i. When an agent i is not part of the allocation, the transfer is zero.

Theorem 3.3: Individual Rationality of VCG Mechanism
The VCG mechanism is individually rational for agents with quasi-linear utility functions.

Proof. Given the utility of agent i with $u_i(o^*, \theta_i) = v_i(k^*(\hat{\theta}), \hat{\theta}_i) - p_i(\hat{\theta})$ and the VCG payment function $p_i(\hat{\theta}) = \sum_{j \neq i} v_j(k^*_{-i}(\hat{\theta}_{-i}), \hat{\theta}_j) - \sum_{j \neq i} v_j(k^*(\hat{\theta}), \hat{\theta}_j)$. On the basis of this, the utility of an agent i is computed as

$$u_i(o^*, \theta_i) = v_i(k^*(\hat{\theta}), \hat{\theta}_i) - \left[\sum_{j \neq i} v_j(k^*_{-i}(\hat{\theta}_{-i}), \hat{\theta}_j) - \sum_{j \neq i} v_j(k^*(\hat{\theta}), \hat{\theta}_j) \right] \qquad (3.8)$$

$$u_i(o^*, \theta_i) = \sum_{i \in \mathcal{I}} v_j(k^*_{-i}(\hat{\theta}_{-i}), \hat{\theta}_j) - \sum_{j \neq i} v_j(k^*_{-i}(\hat{\theta}_{-i}), \hat{\theta}_j) \qquad (3.9)$$

---

[14]The VCG mechanism is sometimes also referred as Pivotal or Clarke mechanism.

The term $\sum_{i \in \mathcal{I}} v_j(k^*_{-i}(\hat{\theta}_{-i}), \hat{\theta}_j)$ values the allocation with agent i and $\sum_{j \neq i} v_j(k^*_{-i}(\hat{\theta}_{-i}), \hat{\theta}_j)$ values the attained allocation without agent i. Thus, $u_i(o^*, \theta_i) \geq 0$ as the best solution with i, cannot be worse than the solution without agent i. $\qquad\square$

Furthermore, the VCG mechanism is an instance of a Groves mechanism and, as a consequence, it is allocative efficient and strategy-proof.[15]

3.2.2.3 Impossibility Theorems

The family of Groves mechanisms and in particular the VCG mechanism demonstrate what *can* be achieved by a mechanism. In the following section, two important impossibility theorems are discussed that show what *cannot* be achieved by a mechanism. The general idea behind these theorems is to show the impossibility of a direct mechanism and, subsequently, to generalize the results to all mechanisms by means of the revelation principle.

Hurwicz (1972) was one of the first to demonstrate the trade off between efficiency and incentive compatibility: Hurwicz (1972) and Green and Laffont (1977) show, that it is impossible to design a mechanism that is allocative efficient, budget-balanced, and strategy-proof in an exchange with agents that have quasi-linear utility functions. Here, the term *exchange* refers to an economic environment with multiple buyers and sellers that act simultaneously.

Theorem 3.4: Hurwicz-Green-Laffont
There exists no mechanism that is allocative efficient, budget-balanced, and strategy-proof in an exchange with agents that have quasi-linear utility functions (Parkes 2001, p. 52).

The theorem is based on a set of theorems that are derived by Hurwicz (1972) and Green and Laffont (1977)

Myerson and Satterthwaite (1983) extend the Hurwicz-Green-Laffont theorem to Bayesian implementation problems in which individual rationality is also required. The dominant strategy property for truth-telling is formulated by means of Bayesian-Nash incentive compatibility. A mechanism is Bayesian-Nash incentive compatible when any agent's expected utility maximizing strategy in equilibrium with every other agent is to report preferences truthfully (Parkes 2001).

Theorem 3.5: Myerson-Satterthwaite
There exists no mechanism that is allocative efficient, budget-balanced, individually rational, and Bayesian-Nash incentive compatible (Myerson and Satterthwaite 1983).

The theorem holds even for interim individual rationality, where every agent participates in the mechanism if the expected utility from participating is not negative (Jackson 2002).

Both theorems emphasize, that it is impossible to design an exchange that is allocative efficient, budget-balance, and individually rational. As such, the goal of the mechanism designer is to find mechanisms where at least two of these properties are in effect (Parkes 2001).

---

[15]In some cases, the VCG mechanism is also budget-balanced: In settings with one seller and multiple buyers, the VCG mechanism determines a budget-balanced outcome.

3.2.3 Practical Mechanism Design

Negotiations and auctions are specific mechanisms that have gained practical importance within mechanism design. Literature and practice emphasize several successful applications of negotiations and auctions for different domains that have different requirements and objectives.

The differences between negotiations and auctions have diminished with the emergence of Internet technologies. Whereas traditional negotiations (also denoted as *bargaining* situations) have been conducted face-to-face, the use of information systems allows for more activities undertaken in negotiations (Bichler et al. 2003). Current negotiation support systems implement sophisticated tools that help agents to discover and match relevant counterparts and that support them during the negotiation process. As such, a clear distinction between negotiations and auctions can no longer be made. The most fundamental difference is pointed out by Kersten et al. (2000, p. 6) stating that *"auctions deal with known and well-defined objects while negotiations may be about defining these objects and collaborating in order to obtain a common definition."* One possible deduction from this statement could be that negotiations may be superior to auctions if the underlying resource is complex and not defined precisely. Examples for such resources are houses or business contracts. Counteractively, the use of auctions may be advantageous if the traded resources are mostly standardized, such as DVD players or stocks.

3.2.3.1 Negotiations

The analysis of negotiations is focused by many different research disciplines, such as economic and social science, computer science, as well as information systems. As a consequence, the definition and meaning of negotiations is widely and sometimes diversely discussed. A definition that attempts to encompass most of the different research directions is given by Bichler et al. (2003, p. 316): They define a negotiation *"as an iterative communication and decision making process between two or more agents [...] who (1) cannot achieve their objectives through unilateral actions, (2) exchange information comprising offers, counter-offers and arguments, (3) deal with interdependent tasks, and (4) search for a consensus which is a compromise decision"*. The process of communicating offers and counter-offers is often called a *"negotiation dance"* (Raiffa 1982): In a negotiation, agents may not accept the initial offers from their counter parties. An agreement can only be reached if agents adapt their offers slightly towards mutual improvements. One objective of negotiation theory is to analyze whether or not such agreements can be found in a particular negotiation setting. Furthermore, negotiation theory provides techniques that support agents in their strategy selection in order to achieve such improvements.

The communication and decision making process that is applied to reach an agreement can be implemented in different ways: Some negotiations ignore them (unstructured negotiation), some implement them in a flexible manner (semi-structured negotiation), and some specify the underlying message space as well as the choice and transfer rules in detail (structured negotiation). The type of negotiation applied to a particular setting strongly depends on the economic environment, i.e., on the requirements of the agents and on the characteristics of the negotiated resource.

Negotiations are oftentimes supported by the use of information systems: These systems may support the whole negotiation process (negotiation support system) (Kersten 2004), an individual negotiator in its decision making process (Kersten and Noronha 1999; Thiessen and Soberg 2003), the negotiators by means of a communication channel (Schoop et al. 2004), or may automate the process completely by means of software agents (Jennings et al. 2001).

The key advantage of negotiations is their ability to adapt the objectives between the participating agents during the process (Kersten et al. 2000). However, a drawback of most negotiation processes is their high communication effort that is required to reach an agreement. For instance, in multilateral negotiations, the communication effort rises the more negotiators are contacted. In settings, where multiple sellers offer a single buyer the same resource, the communication effort can become the bottleneck of the system. The buyer may be unable to negotiate with all potential sellers simultaneously, leading to economically inefficient outcomes.

3.2.3.2 Auctions

Auctions are popular mechanisms for conducting market transactions. They have been successfully applied in private, industrial, and governmental domains. With the emergence of Internet technologies, the application area of auctions even increased: Auction sites such as eBay, Yahoo!, and Amazon list millions of items for sale and attract a multitude of users.

In general, agents (either buyers or sellers) submit their preferences to the auctioneer by means of bids. Bids are formulated according to a pre-defined bidding language that denotes the message space of the auction institution. Subsequently, the auctioneer determines the winners of the auction (clearing, winner determination) and computes the corresponding prices (price determination). On the basis of this process, an auction is defined as follows:

Definition 3.5: Auction
An auction is a market institution with an explicit set of rules determining resource allocation and prices on the basis of bids from the market participants (McAfee and McMillan 1987, p. 701).

The most common types of auctions are single sided and double sided auctions. In the following paragraphs, these two types and some of their instances are discussed. For further descriptions of the capabilities and properties of different auction mechanisms, the reader is referred to Wurman et al. (2001) and Krishna (2002).

Single Sided Auctions: Single sided auctions are mechanisms, where only buyers or sellers can submit bids ($1 : n$ or $m : 1$ relations). In the following, the most prominent single sided auctions are outlined:

- **Vickrey Auction:** The Vickrey auction is an instance of a VCG mechanism. The auction is organized as a sealed bid auction where bidders submit one single bid to the auctioneer. Finally, the bidder who submitted the highest bid is awarded with the resource at the price of the second highest bid. It can be shown that truthful bidding is a dominant strategy in a Vickrey auction (Green and Laffont 1977).

- **First-Price Sealed-Bid:** In the first-price sealed-bid (FPSB) auction, bidders submit one single bid to the auctioneer without knowing the other's bids (sealed bid). The bidder with the highest bid wins the auction and pays the amount of the winning bid. In general, there is no dominant strategy for agents in the FPSB auction.

- **Dutch Auction:** In the Dutch auction, the auctioneer calls out a price and lowers this price incrementally as long as no bidder is willing to accept it. Once a bidder accepts the announced price, he wins the auction and has to pay his bid. As a strategy in the Dutch Auction, the bidder has to define a price that he is willing to accept (Milgrom 1989). This price is below the valuation in order to draw positive utility from the auction.

- **English Auction:** In the English auction, the auctioneer announces a price and increases that price incrementally as long as there are at least two bidders interested. When the second last bidder refuses to stay in the bidding process, the last bidder receives the item. Obviously, the price the winner has to pay (approximately) equals the second highest bid. The dominant strategy of the English auction under private value settings is thus to bid as high as the private valuation.

- **Combinatorial Auction:** Combinatorial auctions are multi-item auctions, where an agent can submit bids on multiple heterogeneous resources as a bundle. As such, the agent can express super-additive utility functions by means of expressing the valuation for a bundle of resources. A bundle consists of logical AND concatenated bids on a set of resources. Such bids ensure that an agent is allocated to either all resources of the bundle or to none of it. A practical example for a combinatorial auction is to bid for a bundle that comprises of a hotel room, a flight, and a rental car. If the agent would only receive the rental car without the hotel and the flight, the allocation would be useless. By means of bidding on these items in the form of a bundle, the agent can ensure that he gets all or none of the resources. Furthermore, combinatorial auctions allow expressing sub-additive valuations. This is realized by allowing multiple XOR concatenated bids on a set of bundles, where the XOR operator ensures that at most one bundle is allocated to an agent. Extending the aforementioned example, this allows the agent to bid on both, a holiday bundle in Greece as well as on a holiday bundle in Cuba. The XOR operator ensures, that at most one package is allocated. Combinatorial auctions are implemented as direct auctions (e.g., the Generalized Vickrey Auction (GVA) (Varian 1995)) or as iterative auctions (e.g., iBundle (Parkes 2001)).

Single sided auctions are – from an economic point of view – well understood and applied successfully in different domains. They attain (approximate) efficient outcomes if the distribution of the agents in the economic environment represents the $1 : n$ or $m : 1$ relations. For instance, this is the case when an art dealer sells a painting or an enterprise wants to commission a project by means of an auction. If the relations of the agents are violated, single sided auctions may lead to inefficient outcomes. The relation is violated if there are multiple buyers and multiple sellers trading the same type of resource. In such a case, the application of a double side auction is superior.

Double Sided Auctions: Double sided auctions or short exchanges are those auctions where competitive bidding takes place on both sides ($m : n$ relation). In comparison to traditional single sided auctions, exchanges have received much less attention by modern economic theory. One reason for this is given by McAfee and McMillan (1987): They argue that the strategic behavior of multiple buyers and sellers that compete against each other is difficult to model game-theoretically. Another hurdle in the design of exchanges is the impossibility theorem by Myerson and Satterthwaite (1983) (cf. Section 3.2.2.3): The authors show that there cannot be any exchange which is efficient, budget-balanced, and individually rational at the same time. As such, at least one of the desired economic properties must be leveraged. An example for this is given by Parkes et al. (2001): The efficiency of an exchange can be approximated, while cleaving on the budget-balance and individually rational properties.

A key consideration of exchanges is the timing of the clearing process which determines the auction winners and thereby the allocation of the resources. Exchanges can be either cleared continuously (continuous double auction) or periodically (periodic double auction, call market): A continuous double auction (CDA) is an exchange where buyers and sellers simultaneously and asynchronously announce their bids. Whenever a new bid enters the market, the auctioneer tries to clear the market immediately. Thus, the CDA is especially advantageous in terms of immediacy. A call market is an exchange with periodic clearing, e.g., the auctioneer clears the market every fives minutes. All bids that arrive during this period are collected in an order-book and cleared periodically.

Following literature and practice, single item exchanges and combinatorial exchanges represent the most prominent instances of double sided auctions:

- **Single Item Exchange:** A single item exchange denotes a double auction, where a single type of resource is traded. The k-double auction is thereby the simplest form of a single item exchange (Friedman 1991): Buyers and sellers submit their bids to the auctioneer. On the basis of the individual bids, the auctioneer subsequently forms supply and demand curves and determines the prices where supply and demand are balanced. Using a given parameter $k \in [0, 1]$, a market clearing price $p = (1-k)a+kb$ is chosen from the interval $[a, b]$ that bounds the range of all possible clearing prices. Buyers which submit bids that are higher than this market-clearing price will trade with those sellers, who submitted lower bids than the clearing price (Satterthwaite and Williams 2002).

  Traditionally, single item exchanges are applied to trade standardized resource such as stocks (Friedman 1991) or electricity (Nicolaisen et al. 2001). Recently, there has been a huge interest in applying exchanges to alternative application areas: One example for this are forecasting markets, where agents trade their exceptions on future events by means of an exchange (Luckner et al. 2005).

- **Combinatorial Exchange:** A combinatorial exchange is the conflation of a combinatorial auction and a single-item exchange. In essence, a combinatorial exchange allows multiple buyers and sellers to trade a set of heterogeneous resources simultaneously. It allows agents to express complex utility functions such as additive, sub-additive, or super-additive functions. For instance, an agent can express the value for the transaction *sell stock A and buy stock B and C* by means of a bundle bid.

  The theoretical study of combinatorial exchanges has invited much less attention than single item exchanges (Parkes et al. 2001; Jain and Varaiya 2004; Parkes et al. 2005). One reason for this lies in the complexity of such exchanges: Solving the winner determination problem in such an exchange can become intractable in many settings. However, if such problems can be solved, combinatorial exchanges have several application domains, such as trading stocks (Fan et al. 1999; Grunenberg et al. 2004) or for allocating airport takeoff and landing rights (Ball et al. 2006).

In summary, there exists several different areas for an application of auctions. Moreover, recent advances in auction theory and information technology paved the way towards the development of new mechanisms that allow agents to express complex preference structures.

The design and implementation of such complex mechanisms has become an emerging and interdisciplinary research field combining economics, game theory, optimization, and computer science (Cramton et al. 2006).

3.3   Market Engineering

The difficulty in designing and implementing markets for the Grid is the interdependence of technical and economical objectives (Weinhardt et al. 2006). From an economic viewpoint, a market for the Grid must encompass common economic performance desiderata such as allocative efficiency (cf. Section 3.2.1.4). Relying on existing market mechanisms known from other contexts may, however, result in poor efficiency (Lai 2005). The mechanism designer also has to account for the technical conditions of the target domain. These conditions comprise the underlying environment in terms of Grid middleware and the requirements of potential Grid users and applications. The market should act as a resource allocation manager, hence, fulfilling general requirements upon such a manager. This allows the introduction of the precondition that a market apt for the Grid has to be realized as an electronic market. Otherwise, the market cannot fulfill an automated resource allocation as required by a Grid resource management system (cf. Requirement 2.2).

Different requirements from technical and economical viewpoints may lead to different and oftentimes conflicting objectives. Lai (2005, p.4) points out that *"a pure mechanism designer is likely to design an economic mechanism with high economic efficiency, but with little concern for traditional metrics of computational efficiency, reliability, security, complexity, and ease-of-use. Pure system designers have generally done the inverse."* As such, neither a pure mechanism design driven nor a pure system design driven approach may lead to a useful overall design and implementation of an adequate Grid market.

When applying markets to the Grid, it is essential to comprise different influences that arise from technical fundamentals of Grid systems, potential user requirements, business constraints[16], and economic objectives. Each of these influences has a profound impact on the outcome and, as a consequence, on the acceptance of the market (Weinhardt et al. 2003). The market engineering approach manages these influences by means of a structured, systematic, and theoretically founded procedure of designing, implementing, evaluating, and introducing electronic market platforms (Weinhardt et al. 2003; Neumann 2004; Holtmann 2004). As such, the application of the market engineering approach is suitable for moving markets to the Grid.

The market engineering approach is structured by means of a process as depicted in Figure 3.4: In the first stage, the requirements of the new market mechanism are deduced. Subsequently, the new market mechanism is designed and implemented in the second stage. After the implementation, the mechanism is tested on its technical and economical properties. Finally, the market platform is introduced. At any stage of the market engineering process, there is a decision whether to proceed with the next step or more advantageous to repeat the prior one. The market engineering process does not only structure the design process as it also provides the designer with a whole array of methods that may support separate sub-tasks. In the following, these stages and a selection of supporting methods are outlined briefly on the basis of Neumann (2004).

---

[16]Market engineering also comprises the structured design of business models for market operators (Weinhardt et al. 2003). For the work at hand, however, the design of such business models for Grid market operators is out of scope.

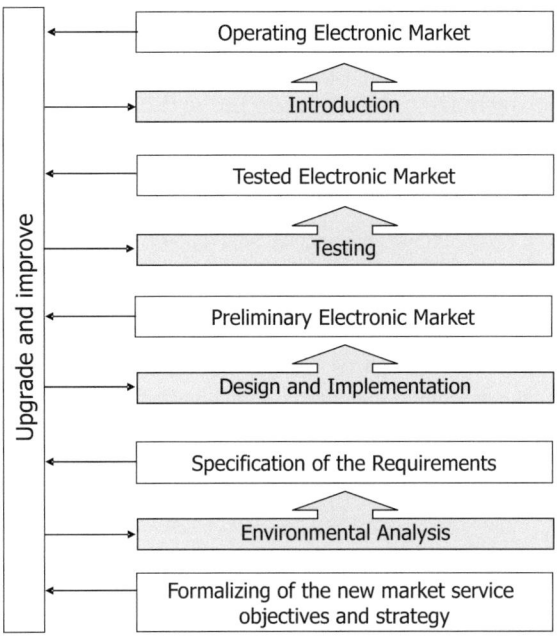

Figure 3.4: Stages of the market engineering process (Neumann 2004, p. 155)

3.3.1   Stage 1 – Environmental Analysis

The objective of the environmental analysis is to formalize the strategies and objectives of the new electronic market. The stage comprises two phases: the environment definition and the requirement analysis.

The goal of the environment definition is to characterize the economic environment for which the market mechanism is to be engineered. This phase comprises the collection and analysis of potential trading objects, market segments, and agents that may interact on a particular segment. The environment definition usually starts with the analysis of potential trading objects. On the basis of this analysis, potential market segments for trading these resources are identified and evaluated comparatively. Having selected a target market, information about potential agents is deduced.

The target market reveals the economic environment for which the market is intended. In order to gain potential agents acting on it, the market mechanism must fulfill the needs and requirements of these agents. The requirement analysis consists of a thorough extraction of these needs concerning the resource allocation problem and the environmental side-constraints. Cramton (2003, p. 8) motivates the requirement analysis as follows: *"Good market design begins with a thorough understanding of the market participants, their incentives, and the economic problem that the market is trying to solve."*

On the basis of the requirement analysis, the market engineer decides whether to engineer a new mechanism from scratch or to reuse and adapt an existing one for the target problem. This decision is usually supported by a literature review.

3.3.2   Stage 2 – Design and Implementation

The second stage of the process comprises the design of the market mechanism and its implementation into an information system. Analogous to the engineering design process from mechanical engineering (Pahl and Beitz 1984), the design stage is decomposed into four major phases known as the conceptual design, embodiment design, detail design, and implementation.

In the conceptual design stage, the market mechanism is deduced as an allocation and payment function. At this stage, the engineer is supported by different tools and methodologies such as mechanism design and linear programming[17]. These purely conceptual functions are refined in the embodiment design phase into a practical market scheme which is subsequently transformed into a formal process model. In the detail design phase, all remaining design issues are tackled and subsequently implemented. This phase is supported by traditional software engineering concepts and tools, such as UML (Arlow and Neustadt 2005), design patterns (Gamma et al. 1995), or the Rational Unified Process (Kroll and MacIsaac 2006). The output of this phase is a fully implemented prototype of an electronic market.

Market engineering provides different tools that assist the engineer in designing and implementing market mechanisms. For instance, the market engineer can rely on the generic market system meet2trade[18] that supports different auction mechanisms and negotiation schemes (Weinhardt et al. 2006).

3.3.3   Stage 3 – Testing

Having implemented the market mechanism, it is tested upon its technical and economical properties. The testing stage comprises functionality tests to ensure the correctness of the software implementation and economic tests to measure the outcome performance of the market.

Functionality tests are made to ensure that the information system works as it is designed. In other words, these tests ensure that the information system correctly reflects the institutional rules. This phase is also supported by traditional software engineering techniques (Whittaker 2000). Depending on the complexity of the underlying information system, this phase also comprises of technical performance tests such as runtime analysis.

The objective of the economical tests is to ascertain whether or not the electronic market attains the desired economic outcome. This phase is supported by analytical and experimental evaluation methods. Experimental methods are comprised of laboratory experiments (Weber 2006; Gimpel 2007), numerical simulations (Kunzelmann 2006), or agent-based simulations (van Dinther 2006).

After functional and economical tests are performed, additional pilot runs are made. These runs provide information about the agent's acceptance of the market and, if necessary, allow the engineer to adjust the underlying institutional rules.

---

[17]For instance, most auction schemes can be represented as a linear program (Bikhchandani et al. 2001).
[18]For more more details refer to http://www.meet2trade.de/.

3.3.4 Stage 4 – Introduction

In the last stage of the process, the electronic market is introduced. The design and refinement of the institutional rules ends with this stage. The introduction of the electronic market initiates its operation cycle (Neumann 2004).

3.4 Summary

In the context of engineering Grid markets, this chapter outlined three prerequisites for the engineering of a Grid market: (i) a clarification to whether or not markets should be applied in Grids, (ii) a brief overview of the theoretical background of markets, and (iii) an introduction into a structured approach for engineering them.

Section 3.1 answered the question why markets should be applied in Grids: Different resource allocation models for distributed systems are analyzed in regard to their ability to allocate resources in the Grid efficiently. As a result of the discussion, markets are emphasized as a resource allocation mechanism for the Grid, as they can be an effective institution to efficiently allocate resources that have a dynamic value.

Subsequently, Section 3.2 introduced a common understanding of the foundations and functionalities of markets: Firstly, Section 3.2.1 outlined a formal microeconomic framework that provides a common view on the structure and the concepts of markets. Secondly, Section 3.2.2 introduced mechanism design, a theory that supports the design and analysis of market mechanisms. Finally, Section 3.2.3 showed how these theoretical concepts are practically implemented as negotiations and auctions.

As the design of a market for the Grid is a rather complex and interdependent task, Section 3.3 outlined the market engineering approach. This view provides a structured, systematic, and theoretically founded procedure of designing, evaluating, and introducing electronic market platforms.

The concepts that are presented in this chapter serve as a basis for the further engineering of a Grid market. Following the lines of market engineering, the subsequent chapters are structured as follows: Chapter 4 analyzes the environment of a potential Grid market. On the basis of the resulting requirement list, Chapter 5 outlines the design of a new Grid market and Chapter 6 shows how this is implemented in an information system. Finally, the implemented mechanism is evaluated in Chapter 7 and Chapter 8.

Chapter 4

Environmental Analysis

Some day, firms will indeed stop maintaining huge, complex and expensive computer systems that often sit idle and cannot communicate with the computers of suppliers and customers. Instead, they will outsource their computing to specialists and pay for it as they use it, just as they now pay for their electricity, gas and water.

(The Economist 2004a)

The previous chapter motivated the application of markets for coordinating the allocation of resources in the Grid. For the design of such a market, the discussion further suggested the use of a market engineering approach to encompass the interdependencies of technical and economical requirements.

Corresponding with the market engineering process, the aim of this chapter is to process an environmental analysis of a Grid market. At this point, the environmental analysis comprises two different phases: the environment definition and the requirement analysis. The objective of the environment definition is to collect information about transaction objects (e.g., what resources are traded), participants (e.g., who are the potential participants), as well as their preferences, endowments, and constraints. This information helps to determine a set of potential market segments for which mechanisms could be engineered. These segments are evaluated against each other and, as a result, a target market segment is selected. Subsequently, the needs and requirements of the participants for the target market are extracted in the requirement analysis. As a last step of the analysis, there is a survey probing into whether an existing market mechanism fulfills the specified requirements or a new mechanism must be engineered.

The outline of this chapter is as follows: Section 4.1 starts the analysis with an environment definition. The result of this phase is a clear trading object definition, a target market selection, and an analysis of potential participants. Section 4.2 specifies the requirements upon a suitable mechanism for the target market. Section 4.3 reviews state of the art market mechanisms that are applied to the Grid. The review analyzes these mechanisms with regard to their adherence of the elicited requirements. Finally, Section 4.4 summarizes and concludes the chapter.

4.1   Environment Definition

Engineering an adequate market mechanism requires a full understanding of the trading object and its characteristics. The specification of the trading object has a profound impact on the choice of the target market and, as a consequence, on the number of potential agents and their needs. Several economics oriented papers suggest market mechanisms used for an abstract good which is called "Grid". Those papers are well founded from the market design perspective, but they miss a clear definition of the trading object. When referring to markets in the Grid, it is essential to understand the technical fundamentals to understand what can really be traded and how.

In the following, potential trading objects in a Grid are identified and characterized. Based on this, potential market segments are highlighted and evaluated and, subsequently, a target market segment is selected. Finally, the number of potential agents and their needs in the target market are elicited.

4.1.1   Trading Object Definition

Trading objects in a Grid market constitute rights to use certain computational resources on different machines (Shneidman et al. 2005). Such resources are heterogeneous in regard to their capabilities and their potential fields of application. Some of them may attract various agents while others are irrelevant for most users. Accordingly, the number of potential market participants depends on the type of resource being traded. As the number of market participants has a profound impact on the design of a market mechanism, different types of resources are analyzed with respect to their expected degree of supply and demand.

Figure 4.1 depicts a three layered view on potential resources in the Grid: *Standardized elementary services*, *standardized application services*, and *non-standardized application services* construct each layer respectively.[1] Furthermore, the bottom line represents physical resources through which the service is performed. These resources can be either primitive resources (e.g., a CPU or a sensor) or a set of resources in the form of a cluster. Physical resources are, however, not potential trading objects in the Grid, as they become virtualized by the middleware.

Standardized Elementary Services: The first layer comprises services that virtualize physical resources. This includes, for instance, a computational service that virtualizes a cluster or a desktop machine. These resources are denoted as standardized elementary services. Although type and behavior of these services are mostly standardized, the services have multiple attributes in which the characteristics may vary. For instance, storage services may differ according to their capacity (in Gigabyte (GB)), access time (in milliseconds (ms)), and data throughput (in bits per second (bits/s)). These varying characteristics of the same type of resource, as well as the resource itself can be described by means of standardized description languages such as RSL or GLUE. As these services virtualize physical resources, they constitute elementary entities for a Grid that are required by various different users and applications.

Standardized Application Services: Application services with a broad scope of application are represented by the second layer. The input and output semantics of these

---

[1]Resources can also be classified by a more granular distinction. However, for the work at hand, the proposed three-layered view suffices.

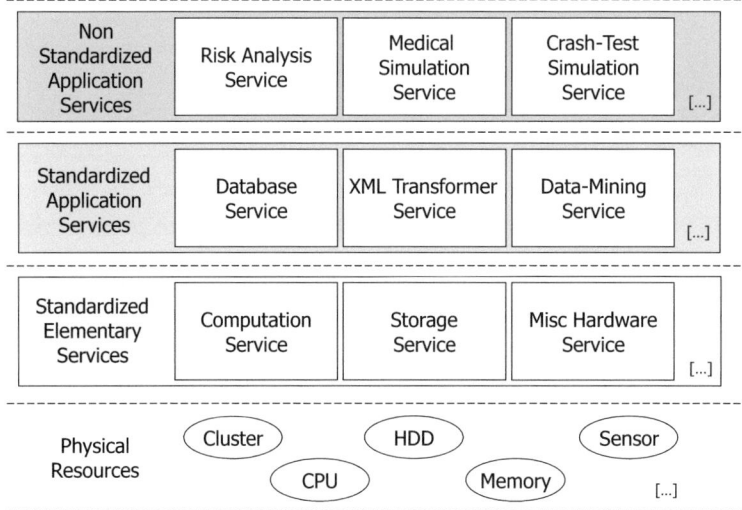

Figure 4.1: Layered view on different resource types in the Grid

so-called standardized application services are well-accepted and interpretable by a major part of Grid users.[2] Exemplary services of this layer are database services and XML transformation services. Services in this layer are required for several different higher-level applications and, as a consequence, are utilized by a multitude of different users. They may further utilize services of the layer below. For instance, a database service makes use of a storage service. Similar to elementary services, the provided quality of service levels for the same type of service may vary. For instance, a set of XML transformation services may vary from their offered response time (in ms); however, it is assumed that these characteristics can also be described in a standardized form.

Non-Standardized Application Services: Services represented by the third layer are non-standardized application services. Such services are only used for specific application areas such as a simulation service that is is required for medical research. Hence, these services are oftentimes only utilized by a small number of Grid participants. Usually, their characteristics and capabilities cannot be described by means of standardized, well-accepted, and interpretable description languages.

Non-standardized services as described above are highly specialized. In consequence, only few market agents will be interested in trading them. In contrast, services from the first and second layer are mostly standardized and attract many agents in a market. Thus, these two layers can be summarized by one layer for standardized services.

4.1.2 Market Segmentation

Markets as coordination mechanisms for using Grid resources can be established for standardized and for non-standardized services. However, the requirements upon each under-

---

[2]In some cases, this can also be realized by the use of ontology-based description languages such as OWL-S.

	Market for trading	
	Standardized Services	Non-Standardized Services
Number of providers and requesters	high	low
Commodity type	standardized	unstandardized, scarce
Different types of resources	low	high
Degree of automated usability	high	low

Table 4.1: Characterization of standardized and non-standardized services

lying market mechanism differ due to the various characteristics of the transaction objects. Table 4.1 illustrates these differences: For standardized services, on the one hand, the number of potential providers and consumers is assumed to be high. The target resources are standardized transaction objects and, in some cases, even standard commodities. The number of different types of standardized services is limited, as only few services exist that are generic and fundamental enough to utilize in various different fields of application. Due to their high degree of standardization, the provision and utilization of these services can both be automated. Non-standardized services of the same type are, on the other hand, scarce. For instance, only few providers can offer highly specialized medical simulation services of the same type with the same functionality. As a result, the number of potential providers and consumers for such services is assumed to be low. In contrast to standardized services, various different types of non-standardized services exist; however, due to their specificity and their lack of standardized descriptiveness, they can hardly be discovered and invoked automatically.

The different characteristics of standardized and non-standardized services result in diametrical requirements upon a market for trading them. With respect to these differences, experiences gained from traditional procurement scenarios such as reported in Bajari et al. (2004) can be transferred: Standardized services in the Grid can be compared to manufactured goods in procurement, such as rubbers and DVD players. For such commodities, literature emphasizes the benefits of auctions as adequate transaction mechanisms (Krishna 2002; Milgrom 2004). Auctions, however, may not be appropriate for trading non-standardized services. These services, just as airplanes or buildings in procurement scenarios, are characterized by their complexity and their individual natures. A consumer of a non-standardized service may require several interaction steps with a supplier in order to clarify configurations and properties of the traded service. As such, communication and coordination interactions between the service counterparts are important requirements for trading non-standardized services. Such interaction capabilities are, however, not given by traditional auctions. For instance, in a sealed-bid auction, bids are the only messages exchanged by the market participants. In such cases, the use of bilateral negotiations may be superior to auctions, as negotiations facilitate communication and coordination among agents.[3]

A holistic market mechanism that meets the requirements of both types of services may not exist. As a result, the different characteristics of potential markets for trading standardized and non-standardized services require individual and contrarily market mechanisms. As such, a target market segment will be selected in the following.

---

[3]Comprehensive studies comparing auctions and negotiations in different applications scenarios can be found in Thomas and Wilson (2002) and Bajari et al. (2004).

4.1.3   Market Targeting

The work at hand targets a market for trading standardized services. This is rationalized by the fact that such a market attracts many different agents and pertains to different application areas. For instance, such a market can be used to coordinate the computational resources of a single company by means of an in-house Grid such as proposed by Meliksetian et al. (2004). In addition, the market can be applied to facilitate the vision of an Open-Grid market which is the most holistic scenario for applying markets to the Grid. An Open-Grid market allows all interested parties to access the platform and trade their resources (Neumann 2006).

On the basis of the general Definition 2.1 of a Grid resource and the properties of standardized elementary services and standardized application services, the trading object in the target Grid market is defined as follows:

Definition 4.1:   Trading Object in the Grid
A trading object in the envisioned Grid market is a Grid resource that belongs to the group of standardized elementary or standardized application services. The characteristics of a particular resource can be described by a set of quality attributes $\mathcal{A}_{g_k}$ where $a_i^k \in \mathcal{A}_{g_k}$ denotes a particular attribute of the resource g_k.

Based upon this definition, potential market participants and their needs are identified and characterized in the following.

4.1.4   Potential Participants

The characteristics of the major players in the targeted Grid market are manifold: On the one hand, telecommunication companies (e.g., British Telecom) have a great need for a Grid market aimed at in-sourcing the entire IT hardware of their clients as new business model (Schnizler et al. 2006a). Resource owners like SUN or IBM also investigate the development of the Grid in order to offer their hardware and software infrastructure to potential customers. On the other hand, customers in a Grid are resource consumers who require computational resources. This includes, for instance, scientists at universities who require storage services for their experiments or SMEs who need a data mining service to analyze their marketing data.

Although the participants of the envisioned Grid market stem from different domains, their common requirements for a Grid market mechanism include its seamless integration into the given Grid middleware. In order to enable such an integration into existing middleware, the market has to replace the resource allocation manager and, as such, account for the general requirements upon a resource allocation manager (cf. Section 2.3.1). In addition, the market should enable an automation of the whole transaction process. It is assumed that market participants are not willing to submit bids for resources and monitor the state of the market manually (Neumann et al. 2006; Schnizler et al. 2006).[4]

Besides the needs of the potential participants, the average number of buyers and sellers in such a market plays another crucial role. The number of participants, however, strongly depends on the focus of the underlying application area. For instance, in an in-house Grid market, the number of potential participants is assumed to be low. Conversely, scenarios that envision an Open-Grid market assume a high number of potential participants. At the moment, neither an in-house market, nor an Open-Grid market in practice exist. As such,

---

[4]For this work, further requirements of potential participants such as security standards are out of scope.

the options to perform an empirical analysis to determine the number of agents are limited. However, several test beds and experimental evaluation studies which serve as clues exist. Distinctive projects and infrastructure in this area are, among others, the Grid 2003 Project (Foster et al. 2004), the NorduGrid project (Eerola et al. 2003), and PlanetLab (Bavier et al. 2004).

In the following, PlanetLab[5] serves as a destination test bed for an empirical analysis of the user characteristics. Essentially, PlanetLab is a test bed for networking and distributed computing among several scientific institutes worldwide. The network is currently the largest infrastructure for sharing distributed resources. Although the network is mainly restricted to scientific purposes, PlanetLab is considered suitable as a forerunner of an Open-Grid platform.

The user information of PlanetLab was obtained using the data provided by the All-Pairs-Pings project. Every 15 minutes, all registered nodes are contacted to check their availability status.[6] The available data from November 2005 until March 2006 was collected and analyzed. As a result of the study, PlanetLab has, on average, $\mu = 170.89$ active machines which can be used to perform computational jobs (with a standard deviation of $\sigma = 21.33$). The coefficient of variation (CV) for the values $CV = \sigma/\mu = 0.12$ shows that the variability in reference to the size of the mean is low. Thus, the determined average constitutes to be a stable value. Transferring the PlanetLab characteristics to a market scenario schema implies 170 sellers on average. Assuming an equal number of buyers and sellers, the average number of agents in the PlanetLab scenario is 340. As such, the number of agents measured in PlanetLab denotes a lower boundary of potential participants in a market platform targeted in the work at hand.

Based on this environment definition, the requirements upon a Grid market mechanism are elicited in the following.

4.2   Requirement Analysis

In order to become practicable, a market mechanism for the Grid must match the requirements upon a resource allocation manager as described in Section 2.3.1. Furthermore, the outcome of the mechanism should have desirable economic properties as outlined in Section 3.2.1.4. Thus, the requirement specification for a Grid market mechanism is a conflation of desirable mechanism design properties and general requirements upon a resource allocation manager. The result of this conflation is summarized in Table 4.2. The focus of each requirement is assigned to either mechanism design properties or resource management requirements.[7]

The general objective that a mechanism designer desires to achieve is allocative efficiency (R1) (cf. Section 3.2.1.4). Other requirements (R2-R15) are side-constraints to fulfill this objective. As an example for the requirements suppose R9 that addresses complementarities of resources. A market mechanism which is not able to handle bids on bundles cannot ensure to achieve efficient allocations. This is supported by the fact that higher values on bundles of resources are not considered by the allocation (Bykowsky et al. 2000).

---

[5]See http://www.planet-lab.org/ for details.

[6]See http://ping.ececs.uc.edu/ping/ for details (accessed: 05.04.2006).

[7]A special case is requirement 5 (R5), as it can be assigned to both groups. On the one hand, it is a required property of computational mechanism design. On the other hand, a resource allocation manager has to determine an outcome computationally efficient.

Requirement	Description	Driven by	
		Mechanism Design	Resource Manager
R1	Efficient Allocation	•	
R2	Incentive Compatible	•	
R3	Individually Rational	•	
R4	Budget-Balance	•	
R5	Computational Tractable	•	•
R6	Automated Resource Allocation		•
R7	Double sided Mechanism		•
R8	Support for Heterogeneous Resources		•
R9	Support for Different Resource Characteristics		•
R10	Bundling of Resources		•
R11	Co-Allocation of Resources		•
R12	Guaranteed Resource Usage Time		•
R13	Advanced Reservation of Resources		•
R14	Substitutability of Resources		•
R15	Network Quality		•

Table 4.2: Requirements upon a Grid market mechanism

In the following, existing market implementations for the Grid are reviewed in regard to their adherence to the specified requirements.

4.3 Meeting the Requirements

The use of market mechanisms for allocating computer resources is not an entirely new phenomenon. In literature, several auction mechanisms and negotiation protocols have been proposed for different kinds of distributed systems. Markets for coordinating computational resources were originally applied to traditional distributed systems. As these propositions influenced current research on moving markets to the Grid, Section 4.3.1 discusses fundamental work on market-based load balancing systems and parallel computing[8] infrastructures. Subsequently, Section 4.3.2 reviews the current state of the art market based coordination mechanisms in Grids.

4.3.1 Market Mechanisms for Load Balancing and Parallel Computing

In the following paragraphs, the most fundamental work regarding the application of markets for allocating resources in traditional distributed systems is reviewed. The discussion briefly outlines the target environment for the proposed market, the underlying market mechanisms, and the trading objects.

4.3.1.1 PDP Auctions at Harvard University

Sutherland (1968) is one of the first who proposed the use of auction mechanisms for allocating computer resources. He applies a modified English auction for the allocation of a

---

[8]Unfortunately, a clear differentiation of the proposed systems is oftentimes impossible. Some systems are classified as parallel computing market systems, but may also be applicable in meta-computing environments.

PDP-1[9] at Harvard University. Users can submit bids manually on a blackboard to purchase computing hours. Through offers made during the bidding process, they can reveal their urgency for using the computer. The user with the highest bid is granted exclusive access to the machine. In experimental studies, Sutherland (1968) shows that the use of auctions increases the total utilization of the PDP-1 significantly. The proposed approach points the way towards market-based allocation of computer resources.

4.3.1.2   Ferguson's Load Balancing Approach

Ferguson et al. (1988) introduce market mechanisms for coordinating resources in a load balancing scenario. In opposition to technical schedulers, that rely on cooperation and consensus, the authors assume competitive and independent agents that compete for computational resources. In their approach, they use single sided auctions for allocating CPU cycles and communication resources. Each processor on a computing node implements an auction algorithm to determine which job is granted the node's CPU cycles for a slice of time. Nodes publish information concerning their auction outcomes and clearing prices at a bulletin board in order to inform jobs that require resources. Based on of this information, a job can select a particular auction node to bid for the required resources.

In experimental studies by means of a simulation, the authors use a FPSB auction and a Dutch auction. They compare the use of auctions with a technical scheduler and measure technical metrics such as the latency of jobs. As a main result, they show, in regard to the measured metrics, that the economic approaches perform as well as the technical scheduler. In addition, the authors show that the technical scalability of auctions is superior to traditional schedulers. This is a result of the decentralized information processing by means of distributed entities. However, the authors do not measure economic metrics such as efficiency.

4.3.1.3   The Spawn System

Waldspurger et al. (1992) propose a distributed system that uses market mechanisms for allocating computational resources called Spawn. The system allows load sharing and resource management for competing computational jobs. Spawn supports tree-based applications, i.e., applications that can be split into subtasks which can be executed concurrently. In such applications, partial results are computed on different levels of the tree and are subsequently sent to a leaf on a higher level of the tree. On each leaf, a manager combines and aggregates the results received from its children. Subsequently, this manager reports the aggregated results to its higher leaf on the tree. Such a form of computation – different tasks competing for computational resources on different levels of the tree – can be efficiently implemented in a decentralized fashion.

In Spawn, the managers of each leaf serve as funding sponsors for their children. This funding is used to purchase CPU resources for subtasks associated with each leaf. These resources are purchased by participating in Vickrey auctions which are instantiated by each node that offers idle CPU slices. The auction instances and their corresponding price information are only advertised to the neighbors of each node. As no central blackboard exists, the applied propagation mechanism is comparable to existing Peer-to-Peer advertisement algorithms. Out of all available auctions, a requesting leaf randomly joins one particular auction.

---

[9]The PDP-1 (Programmed Data Processor-1) is a computer system manufactured in 1960.

In case an agreement is reached after the auction process, a resource manager controls the communication with and the monitoring of the supplied resources.

Via a simulation and also with a prototypical implementation of the system, the authors show that the use of Vickrey auctions leads to economically efficient outcomes. In addition, the use of a one-shot auction results in lesser communication costs compared to an iterative auction. Furthermore, the authors show that the distributed nature of the system has advantages in terms of scalability compared to centralized systems. However, the decentralization has drawbacks concerning the information propagation. As the information is only propagated to neighbors, new information is disseminated with delays. This raises the risk of unstable price fluctuations due to imperfect knowledge (Huberman and Hogg 1995). As a result, this may lead to economical inefficient outcomes. Moreover, the results obtained by Spawn are limited due to the assumption of concurrent applications that do not communicate (Chun 2001).

4.3.1.4 Popcorn

Popcorn, as proposed by Nisan et al. (1998), is a Web-based computing system for scheduling Java-based parallel applications. Tasks can bid on CPU times of distributed workstations. This CPU time is measured in Java operations and, as such, the system can account for system heterogeneity.

The Popcorn system implements three different kinds of auction mechanisms: Vickrey auctions, first-price double auctions, and a k-price double auctions (Regev and Nisan 2000). Both double auction schemes are implemented as call markets. For the announcement of new auction instances, their states, and current market prices, Popcorn installs a central repository by means of a Web platform.[10] Thus, information dispersion similar to that experienced in the Spawn system is bypassed. As a disadvantage of this central information aggregation, the Web platform becomes a communication bottleneck in large-scale settings.

The system is evaluated by means of a field experiment and simulations. As a result of their experiments, the authors show that all applied mechanisms attain approximately efficient outcomes. The highest efficiency is attained by the k-price double auction which makes this type of auction suitable for an application in a distributed computation setting.

4.3.1.5 Resource Coordination with ADAMCO

Lohmann (1999) proposes a market-based allocation of CPU cycles by means of a multi agent system. In his setting, agents can set up different types of auctions in order to coordinate their resource requirements in a decentralized manner. The author investigates four different types of single sided auctions: for coordinating single jobs, he applies the English auction, the Dutch auction, and the Vickrey auction; for coordinating multiple jobs, he applies the GVA as a single sided combinatorial auction.

The proposed mechanisms are implemented in the multi agent system ADAMCO (Lohmann et al. 1997). For evaluating the mechanisms, MACRODYN serves as a target application. MACRODYN is a software package for the numerical simulation of dynamic systems (Böhm and Schenk-Hoppé 1998). The application is used to generate different problem settings that have varying demand of CPU cycles.

---

[10]Gagliano et al. (1995) propose a similar information repository to overcome the problem of distributed information propagation.

System	Market Mechanism	Trading Object	Target Environment
PDP Auctions (Sutherland 1968)	English Auction	Computer Machine	Computer Pool
Ferguson's Load Balancing (Ferguson et al. 1988)	FPSB Auction Dutch Auction	CPU cycles, Network	Load Balancing
Spawn (Waldspurger et al. 1992)	Vickrey Auction	CPU cycles	Parallel Computing
Popcorn (Nisan et al. 1998)	Vickrey Auction First Price Exchange k-Price Exchange	CPU cycles	Parallel Computing
ADAMCO (Lohmann 1999)	Vickrey Auction English Auction GVA	CPU cycles	Load Balancing

Table 4.3: Summary of market mechanisms for traditional distributed systems

The applied auction schemes are compared to a technical resource manager that bases on a genetic algorithm. For evaluating the mechanisms, Lohmann (1999) measures technical metrics such as the processing time of a job. The evaluation shows, that auctions perform better than traditional schedulers in dynamic and heterogeneous environments. However, in static and homogenous settings, the applied genetic algorithm results in faster processing times of the jobs. As such, the author proposes the simultaneous deployment of technical and economic-based coordination mechanisms for distributed systems. A suitable mechanism – either with a technical or economical objective – should be selected according to the current workload setting.

4.3.1.6 Reflection

Table 4.3 summarizes the outlined work on market-based resource allocation in traditional distributed computing environments. The trading objects in most of these systems comprise of idle CPU cycles that are made available to resource requesters. All proposed systems implement basic auction types for allocating the resources. In compliance with the theoretical results obtained from common auction theory, most proposed mechanisms achieve economically efficient results.

As an important result, the deployment and evaluation of the proposed systems show that proper designed market mechanisms and traditional schedulers achieve similar technical performance, such as response latency (Ferguson et al. 1988). Furthermore, Spawn and Popcorn demonstrate the trade-off between information aggregation and scalability. On the one hand, the decentralization of Spawn has performance advantages in large-scale settings (Waldspurger et al. 1992). However, the simulation experiments reveal the economical inefficiency of the applied decentralized information propagation techniques. On the other hand, Popcorn aggregates all market relevant information and propagates them by means of a central Web portal (Nisan et al. 1998). This results in economically efficient outcomes. Unfortunately, the Web portal becomes a communication bottleneck in large-scale settings.

The proposed mechanisms clearly influence further research on market-based resource allocation in Grids. A direct application of the proposed systems to the Grid is inhibited, as these mechanisms do not address Grid specific requirements. For instance, the mechanisms neglect the simultaneous trading of heterogeneous resources with multiple different quality characteristics. Despite their inapplicability for the Grid, however, the experiences gained by the development of these systems build the basis for the design and the implementation of markets for Grids.

4.3.2   Market Mechanisms for Grids

With the emergence of Grid technologies, the interest in applying market mechanisms to the resource allocation problem has risen significantly. Aside from several proposals that adapt and extend classical market mechanisms from traditional distributed systems, several novel and complex auction mechanisms and negotiation protocols were proposed for allocating resources in the Grid.

In the following, the most fundamental propositions of market mechanisms for Grids are reviewed according to their applicability for trading standardized services.[11]

4.3.2.1   Nimrod/G and the Computational Economy

Buyya et al. (2000) were among the first researchers to motivate the transfer of market-based systems from distributed systems to Grids. They propose the resource broker Nimrod/G, which is capable of integrating different kinds of economic models. This enables an economic based scheduling and allocating of the available resources. Nimrod/G provides a layer that allows a user to submit budget constraints and technical resource requirements for any kind of computational job. Subsequently, this layer bids on the required resources and tries to reserve them. Nimrod/G can communicate with different types of trading mechanisms such as bargaining mechanisms, posted price models, and auctions (Buyya 2002). In order to purchase the required resources, the platform selects a particular trading mechanism on the basis of the current price information and user policy restrictions.

Nimrod/G is embedded into the Grid Architecture for Computational Economy (GRACE) framework (Buyya et al. 2001). GRACE allows a generic integration of economic-based resource brokers such as Nimrod/G, programming environments, and core Grid middleware such as GT 4. GRACE provides a Grid market directory that can be used to propagate instantiated market mechanisms such as auctions. A broker that wants to purchase resources can use this repository to investigate for relevant market instances.

Several different market mechanisms are implemented within GRACE and Nimrod/G; unfortunately, the implemented mechanisms cover rather basic mechanisms such as English auctions and bilateral bargaining models. Although Grid specific requirements are supported by the broker, the underlying mechanisms widely neglect these parameters. For instance, an English auction supports neither multiple resource attributes, nor time restrictions for advanced reservation. As such, the mechanisms that are currently applied in Nimrod/G and GRACE do not fulfill the requirements elicited in Section 4.2. The architectural concepts provided by GRACE are, however, deemed promising for facilitating a market-based resource management in Grids.

4.3.2.2   G-Commerce

Wolski et al. (2001) propose G-Commerce, a computational economy for coordinating resource allocations in Grids. The authors introduce commodity markets and repeated Vickrey

---

[11] A comprehensive survey of further economic based models for the Grid can be found in Buyya et al. (2002) and Sim (2006).

auctions for trading CPU cycles and storage space. For these trading objects, they assume that buyers and sellers each have equal supply and demand functions which can both be communicated.

In the commodity market, prices are publicly agreed upon for each type of commodity and are announced by a Walrasian auctioneer. Subsequently, buyers and sellers decide whether they want to buy or sell this resource for the announced price. The resulting allocation constitutes a *competitive equilibrium* (also called *Walrasian equilibrium*) if buyers and sellers maximize their utilities and if the aggregated supply of each commodity equals its demand (Mas-Colell et al. 1995). In case the announced prices do not constitute such an equilibrium, they are adjusted by lowering or heighten them. For this, Wolski et al. (2001) apply the *Global Newton* process proposed by Smale (1976), which determines equilibrium prices. In general, the Newton method requires complete information concerning the supply and demand functions of buyers and sellers. In this context, Saari and Simon (1978, p. 1099) argue that *"this is a staggering amount of information"*. Wolski et al. (2001) reduce the required amount of information by introducing an approximation called *First Bank of G*. This approximation uses a large-degree polynomial in order to approximate the required excess demand functions instead of polling this information frequently.

Although the market mechanism computes equilibrium prices for the traded resources, the assumption that the supply and demand functions of all buyers and sellers each are equal still remains. With respect to different policy and service requirements of Grid applications, this assumption may be violated in practice. Furthermore, a sufficient condition under which a stable equilibrium can be achieved in competitive markets is *gross substitutability*. This property holds if the net demand for other goods does not decrease if the price for one particular good rises (Mas-Colell et al. 1995). Gross substitutability is violated if there are complementarities in preferences or technologies (Wellman 1993). In the context of a Grid market, complementary valuations may exist. As such, the gross substitutability may be violated, which results in inefficient outcomes. In addition, Bikhchandani and Ostroy (2000) show that for a bundle of resources which are complementarities (e.g., CPU cycles and storage space), uniform prices, such as computed by Spawn, may not exist in competitive equilibrium. As such, a direct application of the proposed model to the envisioned target market is not possible.

As an important result of their simulations, Wolski et al. (2001) show that a multiplayer market in form of the commodity market achieves better economic outcomes than the application of repeated classical single sided auctions. As such, their work is a forerunner for applying double sided markets to the Grid.

4.3.2.3   The Open Computation Exchange and Arbitration Network

The Open Computation Exchange and Arbitration Network (OCEAN) provides an open and portable software infrastructure for automated commercial buying and selling of computing resources over the Internet (Padala et al. 2003). The trading objects in OCEAN comprise of CPU time, memory usage, and network bandwidth. With respect to the layered view on potential trading objects such as outlined in Section 4.1.1, OCEAN focuses on physical resources.

In OCEAN, each workstation represents an OCEAN node that can act as a buyer or a seller of resources.[12] In case nodes want to purchase some resources, they describe their

---

[12]The architecture also allows a node to act as a buyer and as a seller simultaneously.

requirements of the resources by means of a resource description language. The language provided by the OCEAN framework can be used to describe any type of resource characteristics, including computational resource descriptions and time attributes. The proposed proprietary language is comparable to current communication languages applied in Grids, such as WS-Agreement and GLUE. After the requirements are described using the resource description language, the node starts to discover potential sellers on the network. This is realized by a Peer-to-Peer based search protocol and a matchmaking algorithm. As a result of the peer discovery process, the requesting OCEAN node receives a list of potential seller nodes. Based upon this list, it starts bilateral bargaining negotiations with a set of selected sellers. This negotiation process is realized by exchanging several XML-based intention documents. If a buyer and a seller agree upon a specified quality of service level, the buyer can use the resources of the seller.

Besides the negotiation facilities, OCEAN provides additional components that are required for operating Grid markets. For instance, the framework offers a reputation system that allows nodes to rate each other. Furthermore, OCEAN is comprised of several security components that enable the secure communication between two negotiation parties.

The proposed framework is implemented as a prototype and preliminary evaluated by means of a simulation. In the simulation, the authors test the applicability and performance of their applied discovery and matching algorithms. Unfortunately, they do not analyze the communication effort that is required for realizing the bilateral bargaining process. This effort is, however, assumed to become very high with an increasing number of participating nodes. Furthermore, the authors do not measure economic metrics such as efficiency, incentive compatibility, and the efficiency of the applied information propagation algorithm. As the information propagation in decentralized systems plays an important role for achieving economically efficient results, detailed studies of the propagation performance are crucial for the application of the system. As such, OCEAN is rather seen as a proof-of-concept of applying economic algorithms to Grids.

4.3.2.4 CATNETS

CATNETS is a project that aims to determine the applicability of a decentralized economic self-organization mechanism for resource allocation in Grids (Eymann et al. 2005). The project investigates a *free market* economic self-organization approach on the basis of the work proposed by Hayek (1945).

The project addresses different types of trading objects: On the one hand, standardized and non-standardized application services are supported by the system and are denoted as basic services. On the other hand, the resources required by the basic services to execute a job are called resource services. In order to trade basic services and resource services, the environment is divided into two layers: the application layer and the resource layer. In these two layers, the authors contemplate three different traders: (1) complex services such as workflows that require specific application services, (2) basic services that provide a particular application service to the complex services, and (3) resource services that provide the required computational resources (Eymann et al. 2006).

The partitioning of interdependent logical areas into two different markets is depicted in Figure 4.2. The service market involves the trading of application services; the trading objects in the resource market are computational and data resources, such as processors, storage, and memory. In case a complex service requires a basic service to perform an

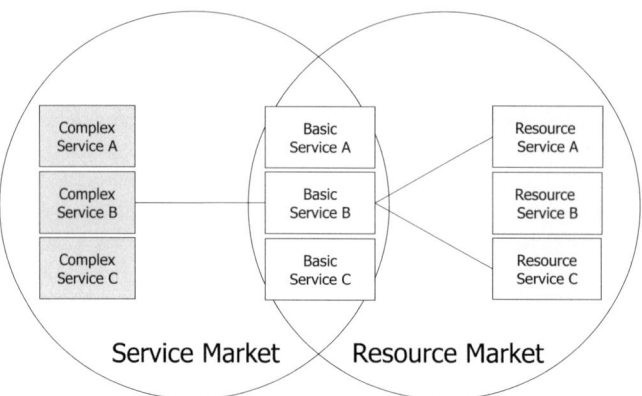

Figure 4.2: CATNETS scenario: Service market and resource market

application job, e.g., a PDF conversion tool, the basic service provides this logical service and is responsible for purchasing the required computational resources to perform the job. The logical service is traded on the service market, whereas the resources are traded on the interdependent resource market.

In CATNETS, the free market economy is realized by an agent-based bilateral bargaining strategy. In case an agent wants to purchase a service, the agent starts to discover relevant counterparts. This step is supported by Peer-to-Peer discovery strategies and matchmaking algorithms. In the instance that potential counterparts are discovered, the agent starts to negotiate the required resources. The decision process of the agents is supported by different learning algorithms.

The proposed bilateral bargaining strategies are compared to auction-based mechanisms: For the service market, a double-auction serves as a benchmark. In addition, an extended combinatorial exchange is implemented for the resource market[13]. The bargaining strategies and the auctioneers are both implemented in a simulation environment and compared according to technical and economic metrics (Reinicke et al. 2006). Furthermore, the bargaining strategies are integrated into a generic economic Grid middleware (Ardaiz et al. 2005). Unfortunately, no empirical results exist at the moment. The work is, however, a promising approach for applying economic based mechanisms to the Grid.

4.3.2.5   Grosu and Das Approach

Grosu and Das (2006a) study the applicability of different types of auction mechanisms for allocating resources in the Grid. They compare the FPSB auction, the Vickrey Auction, and a double auction call market with respect to their applicability in a Grid setting.[14] The trading objects in the proposed markets are computational power, data storage, computer networks, and all kinds of software services. As such, they comprise all trading object layers outlined in Section 4.1.1.

---

[13]The auction applied in the resource market is a simplified adaption of the mechanism presented in this work (cf. Chapter 5).

[14]A comparable approach of evaluating different economic based resource allocation models is proposed by Gomoluch and Schroeder (2003).

Their general model of auction based resource allocation consists of three basic entities: *User Brokers*, *Grid Service Providers*, and a *Local Market for Auctions*.

User Brokers: A user broker represents any user that needs computational resources or software services to execute a predefined set of jobs. In the applied model, a job is characterized by its execution time, its required resources, and the available budget for executing it. The user broker is responsible for discovering auction instances, selecting suitable instances, and bidding for the required resources.

Grid Service Providers: Grid service providers represent computing nodes that offer computational resources. A provider of a resource can specify three parameters that are used to select a particular auction instance: the processing rate of the underlying machine, the reservation price for offering the resource, and the costs that arise to use the resource. By means of a local market for auctions, a Grid service provider can instantiate new instances of a single sided auction and propagate it to user brokers. Alternatively, the provider can join an existing instance of a double auction that is also provided by the local market for auctions component.

Local Market for Auctions: The local market for auction provides functionality to support service providers in instantiating and propagating their auction instances. Furthermore, user brokers can use this component to discover relevant auction instances, i.e., auctions that offer the required resources in the required processing rate.

The proposed model and the applied auctions are evaluated by means of a simulation. As basis for their simulation environment, the authors extend the SimGrid[15] package. As a result, the experiments show that the FPSB favors sellers due to higher prices compared to the Vickrey auction. Similarly, the Vickrey auction is advantageous for buyers, as the expected prices are lower than in the FPSB. This result is obvious and in line with the theoretical results: A winner in a FPSB has to pay the highest bid, whereby a winner in a Vickrey auction only has to pay the second highest bid. From an economic point of view, however, these empirical results are limited, as the authors assume truthful bidding in their experiments. The FPSB is not incentive compatible and, as a consequence, it is not a dominant strategy for users to bid truthfully.

In addition, the experiments emphasize that the double-auction is advantageous for both buyers and sellers. As such, the authors can transfer the results obtained from former studies that propose double sided mechanisms for distributed systems to the Grid.

In Grosu and Das (2006b), the authors extend their framework to single sided combinatorial mechanisms. They apply a first price combinatorial auction for trading multiple heterogenous jobs.[16] This solves the problem of receiving only a subset of resources that are required to perform a set of jobs. In a simulation they analyze the profits of resource providers and the utilization of the computing infrastructure. Unfortunately, they do not compare their results to non-combinatorial markets or traditional schedulers. Furthermore, the complexity of the applied combinatorial mechanism is not evaluated.

---

[15]SimGrid is a framework that provides functionalities for simulating distributed applications in heterogeneous distributed environments such as Grids (Casanova 2001).

[16]Among others, Gradwell and Padget (2005) and Schwind et al. (2006) also propose the use of combinatorial auctions for the resource management in Grids.

The work proposed in Grosu and Das (2006a) and Grosu and Das (2006b) seeks towards the requirements proposed in Section 4.2. Moreover, the application of different auction schemes may even qualify to trade both standardized services and non-standardized services. For standardized services, however, the applied auction mechanisms do not meet all requirements. For instance, the proposed mechanisms neglect the existence of quality and time attributes. Although the application of a combinatorial mechanism solves the exposure problem, the single sided nature of the auction does not provide competition on both sides, which may lead to inefficient outcomes.

4.3.2.6   The tsfGrid Auction

Bapna et al. (2007) propose a family of single sided combinatorial call auctions for allocating Grid services. Following Wolski et al. (2001), they focus on trading CPU cycles and storage space.

Bidders who want to purchase computational resources can specify their requirements by means of a market bidding language. Bapna et al. (2007) propose an extension of RSL in order to express operational parameters and constraints of the required resources. Buyers can specify the earliest time slot for starting the job and the latest possible time slot for finishing it. Furthermore, they can specify the amount of CPU cycles and storage space needed. The authors consider two different types of storage space: A static amount of space that is required to upload a file before the job is started and a dynamic amount of space that becomes larger, the longer the job takes. This dynamic value is parameterized by means of a linear growing factor. Sellers, that have idle resources, can offer a time interval during which they can provide their computational resources. Furthermore, they can specify the amount of available CPU cycles and the maximum size of available storage space.

The authors assume that sellers are price-takers, i.e., sellers participate in the market if their per unit reservation price for selling their resources is not greater than a given reservation price. This reservation price is set exogenously and is publicly known. As a result, the authors can aggregate the submitted bids of the sellers into one virtual order.

For determining an allocation and corresponding prices, the authors propose three different mechanisms: an *efficient auction*, a *fair auction*, and the *tsfGrid auction*.

Efficient Auction: The efficient auction is as an extension of a single sided combinatorial auction that incorporates the CPU cycles and storage space restrictions as additional constraints. As pricing rule, Bapna et al. (2007) propose a VCG schema. As such, the auction requires discriminatory prices to achieve efficient outcomes (Bikhchandani and Ostroy 2000). An auction determines discriminatory prices if a distinct unique price is determined for each winning bid (Ströbel and Weinhardt 2003).

Fair Auction: As the provisioning of discriminatory prices may be disadvantageous in cases where market prices should be considered, Bapna et al. (2007) leverage the efficiency property by introducing an optimal fair mechanism that computes uniform market prices. In a uniform price setting, every originator of a winning bid has to pay the same price (Ströbel and Weinhardt 2003). The fair auction schema is still determined optimally which requires a staggering amount of computation, as the problem is $\mathcal{NP}$-complete.

tsfGrid Auction: Finally, the third proposed type of auction is called tsfGrid[17] and applies a greedy heuristic to approximate the winner determination problem. Thus, the problem of determining the winners of the auction becomes computationally tractable. However, desirable economic properties such as incentive compatibility and economically efficiency can no longer be achieved by the heuristic.

The authors propose the use of the efficient auction in small scaled settings that require optimal economic properties. In settings in which a market operator requires uniform commodity prices, the optimal fair mechanism should be used. Finally, the tsfGrid auction qualifies for markets that require real-time fast solution techniques for determining an outcome.

The auction mechanisms are evaluated by means of a stochastic simulation. As a result, the authors show that the welfare loss of the tsfGrid auction is significantly high compared to both other auction types. This is a result of the greedy heuristic that is applied to compute an outcome. However, the incentive compatibility violations in the tsfGrid are fairly mild. As such, it is reasonable to believe that buyers will not strongly deviate from their true valuations. Furthermore, the simulations show that the overall revenue of the tsfGrid auction does not significantly differ from the efficient outcome. Thus, the heuristic is a practical alternative to exact solutions and is highly relevant for further research on combinatorial mechanisms.

In summary, the proposed mechanisms achieve fairly well economic properties. The auctions do, however, not fulfill all requirements upon a market mechanism for trading standardized services: First, the authors restrict their trading object space to two types of services: CPU cycles and storage. In some scenarios, this may be insufficient as also standardized application services may be required by Grid participants. Second, the mechanism does not incorporate for co-allocation restrictions. Finally, the assumption that all sellers are price takers may be inadequate in some cases. This restriction assumes that the production and management costs of computational and application resources are equal for all providers. Such settings, however, can only be rarely found in practice.

4.3.2.7 Reflection

Most of the reviewed auction based mechanisms achieve desirable economic properties as outlined in Section 3.2.1.4. The applied auctions are theoretically well-studied and are known to achieve (approximate) efficient outcomes. Unfortunately, the bargaining strategies as introduced by Nimrod/G, OCEAN, and CATNETS are currently not evaluated according to their economic characteristics in a Grid setting. It is, however, hard to consider, whether the decentralized bargaining strategies may result in economically efficient outcomes. This is reasoned by the lessons learnt from former decentralized information propagation techniques such as implemented in Spawn (Waldspurger et al. 1992).

While complying with the desired economic properties, the analyzed systems lack of fulfilling the Grid specific requirements as elicited in Section 2.3.1. This obstacle is illustrated in Table 4.4 which denotes whether or not each particular domain specific requirement is fulfilled.

When reviewing the related mechanisms, it becomes obvious that no market mechanism fulfills the current domain specific requirements upon a resource allocation manager for the

---

[17]This abbreviation stands for *time sensitive fair Grid*.

System	Trading Object	Market Mechanism	Computational Tractable	Automated Selection	Double sided	Heterogenous Resources	Different Characteristics	Bundling	Co-Allocation	Usage Time	Advanced Reservation	Substitutabilities	Network Quality
Nimrod/G	No	Bargaining	○	●		●							
(Buyya et al. 2000)	restriction	English Auction	●	●		●							●
G-Commerce	CPU cycles,	Commodity Market	●	●	●								
(Wolski et al. 2001)	Storage	Vickrey Auction	●	●									
OCEAN	CPU, Memory,	Bargaining	○	●		●							●
(Padala et al. 2003)	Network												
CATNETS	No	Bargaining	○	●		●		●	○	○			●
(Eymann et al. 2005)	restriction												
		FPSB	●	●		●							
(Grosu and Das 2006a)	No	English Auction	●	●		●							
	restriction	Double Auction	●	●	●	●							
(Grosu and Das 2006b)		Combinatorial Auction	○	●		●		●				●	
tsfGrid	CPU cycles,	Efficient, Fair		●				●			●	●	
(Bapna et al. 2007)	Storage	tsfGrid	●	●				●			●	●	

● denotes that the requirement is fulfilled, ○ denotes that the requirement is not yet evaluated/implemented, an empty cell denotes that the requirement is not fulfilled.

Table 4.4: Summary of market mechanisms for the Grid

Grid.[18] Reasons for this stem from recent changes in the technical Grid infrastructures and the emergence of complex auction mechanisms: On the one hand, past systems such as G-Commerce had to deal with limitations in infrastructures that mostly based on allocating physical resources without proper service level agreements. As such, the support for multiple attributes that characterize different services and the integration of time attributes that guarantee a predefined usage time were useless. On the other hand, most of the proposed mechanisms apply simple market mechanisms such as Vickrey auctions. These mechanisms, however, cannot attain economic efficiency, as they are unable to support complementarities or substitutability of resources. During the last years, advances have been made in theory and practice of more complex market mechanisms. For instance, combinatorial auctions can be successfully applied to achieve efficient outcomes when resources are complementarities. Table 4.4 further suggests the application of such complex auctions for Grids, as both combinatorial mechanisms fulfill several of the requirements upon a resource allocation manager.

The direct application of the combinatorial mechanisms to a real Grid system – such as proposed by Grosu and Das (2006b) and Bapna et al. (2007) – is still hampered. The combinatorial auction proposed by Grosu and Das (2006b) does neither support multiple resource characteristics, nor time attributes. The support of such properties is, however, indispensable in a Grid environment. Furthermore, the mechanism does not provide sufficient incentives for agents to bid truthfully. This is reasoned by the implementation of a pay-as-you bid pricing schema which is known to be not incentive compatible. Counteractively, the work proposed by Bapna et al. (2007) supports time characteristics and is approximately incentive compatible. The auction is restricted to two different types of resources. Thus, the potential application area of the mechanism is limited to scenarios that only require CPU and storage. Furthermore, both propositions neglect co-allocation guarantees. Moreover, they are

---

[18]Moreover, none of the proposed mechanisms made it into practice.

single sided and, thus, do not install competition on both sides. This fact may lead to further economically inefficient outcomes.

In summary, none of the proposed mechanisms is directly applicable to the Grid. The work at hand intends to address these deficiencies by engineering a market-based resource management system that addresses the requirements outlined before.

4.4 Summary

This chapter outlined the environmental analysis of a Grid market. In the first step, Section 4.1 performed an environment definition: Potential trading objects in a Grid were identified and classified as standardized services and non-standardized services. Based upon this classification, potential market segments were outlined for each class of the trading objects. A market for trading standardized services was targeted, as its number of different application areas is assumed to be high. Subsequently, the number of potential participants in such a market was determined by means of an empirical analysis. In Section 4.2, the requirements upon the target market were elicited. The resulting requirement specification was a conflation of desirable economic properties and general requirements upon a resource allocation manager.

Section 4.3 reviewed existing market implementations for traditional distributed systems and Grids with regard to their requirement satisfaction. The result of the analysis was that currently none of the proposed mechanisms fulfills all requirements outlined in this work. Furthermore, the analysis evinced that classical auction mechanisms and bargaining strategies are not adequate for efficiently allocating resources in the Grid. Rather, the application of complex market mechanisms, such as combinatorial auctions, is seen as a promising basis for designing a Grid market.

This chapter served as a basis for the further design, implementation, and evaluation of a Grid market. Chapter 5 outlines the design of a market mechanism that is applicable for trading standardized services and fulfills most of the elicited requirements.

Part II

Design and Implementation

Chapter 5

Design of a Grid Market Mechanism

It is useful to think of the VCG theory as a lovely and elegant reference point – but not as a likely real-world auction design. Better, more practical procedures are needed.

(Ausubel and Milgrom 2006, p. 37)

The previous section reviewed existing market mechanisms for the Grid according to the requirements presented in Section 4.2. It is turned out that no market mechanism installs competition on both sides, includes combinatorial bids, allows for time constraints, manages quality constraints, and considers co-allocation restrictions. This chapter addresses these deficiencies by outlining the design of a Multi-Attribute Combinatorial Exchange (MACE) for allocating and scheduling Grid resources.

The contributions of MACE are the following: It is the first auction mechanism that simultaneously addresses several Grid specific requirements such as quality characteristics, time attributes, and co-allocation restrictions. MACE allows agents to bid on bundles rather than on single items. This results in more efficient outcomes compared to traditional auctions, as Grid resources are complementarities. The mechanism applies a new pricing schema for combinatorial exchanges. In contrast to VCG payments, the proposed k-pricing rule is feasible and computationally more efficient. In summary, the derivation of MACE is a step towards an engineered market mechanism for the Grid that accounts for economic and domain specific requirements.

MACE relies on the principles of combinatorial mechanisms. As such, the design space of combinatorial auctions and exchanges is introduced in Section 5.1. After that, Section 5.2 outlines the conceptual design of MACE. This includes (i) the definition of a rich bidding language that accounts for the characteristics of Grid resources, (ii) the formulation of a winner determination model that can attain efficient allocations, and (iii) the derivation of a pricing schema as an incentive mechanism for agents to bid truthfully. Finally, Section 5.3 summarizes the chapter.

5.1 Design Space for Combinatorial Auctions

In the Grid context, a combinatorial auction allows an agent to bid on a bundle[1] of Grid resources. For instance, an agent can bid on a bundle that consists of a database service

---

[1] A bundle is understood as a set of resources that are concatenated by the logical AND operator.

and a computation service. In contrast to traditional auctions, the combinatorial mechanism ensures that the agent is allocated to either both resources or none of them. As such, agents avoid the *exposure risk* of obtaining only a subset of resources that may be useless for them.

Aside from bundle bids, an agent can also bid on several bundles simultaneously that substitute each other. The mechanism ensures that at most one of the bundles is allocated to the agent. For instance, the agent can bid on a storage service with 200 GB that can be used for 2 hours and on another storage service with 100 GB for 5 hours. In this case, the mechanism allocates at the most one of the services to the agent.

Combinatorial auctions are suitable for agents that have complex preference structures with respect to substitutability and complementarity (Boutilier and Hoos 2001). By expressing preferences for bundles and substitutes, agents can reflect their desired valuations for combinations of resources. Engineering a mechanism for the Grid on the basis of a combinatorial auction is practicable, as the Grid resource allocation mechanism should support the expression of complements and substitutes (cf. Section 2.3.1).

Beside their qualification for Grids, there are further examples of applying combinatorial auctions in practice: Rassenti et al. (1982) propose them for allocating airport arrival and departure slots, Schmidt (1999) applies them to coordinate transportation routes, Ausubel and Milgrom (2002) suggest them for auctioning electromagnetic spectrum licenses, and Bichler and Kalagnanam (2006) use them for procurement scenarios.

Although combinatorial auctions have a high variety of application areas, the designer of such an auction faces several challenges (de Vries and Vohra 2003): First, agents require a comprehensive bidding language to express their complex preference structures. Next, the designer must solve the problem of allocating bundles of resources with respect to a given performance criteria. According to the market engineering approach, sufficient incentives are required that influence agents to reveal their true preferences to the auctioneer (Weinhardt et al. 2003). In the following subsections, several models are discussed that address these challenges. Section 5.1.1 describes how logical constraints over resources can be expressed by means of bids. After that, allocation rules and price schemes are outlined for single sided combinatorial auctions (Section 5.1.2) and combinatorial exchanges (Section 5.1.3). Finally, Section 5.1.4 argues why current concepts found in literature cannot be directly applied for allocating Grid resources.

5.1.1 Combinatorial Bidding Languages

Agents in a combinatorial auction must be able to express their preferences over interdependent resources in form of bids. Following common auction theory, bids are abstract elements drawn from the space of strategies defined by the auction (Nisan 2006). The designer of a combinatorial auction has to decide which bids are allowed to be submitted by the agents, i.e., the designer has to define the strategy space of the auction.

In combinatorial auctions, the strategy space has to be carefully designed, as the number of submitted bids may grow immensely. For instance, suppose there are 20 resources to be auctioned by a seller and 20 agents that are interested in bidding on them. Allowing each agent to bid on each combination of resources would result in $20 \cdot (2^{20} - 1) = 20.971.500$ bids. Assuming that a bid on a bundle can be encoded using 8 bytes[2], the submission of all

---

[2]3 bytes are required to encode the ID of the bundle, 1 byte for the ID of the agent, and 4 bytes are used to encode the valuation.

bids requires more than 159 MB to be communicated. The objective is to define a bidding language that restricts the message space in order to become tractable for communication systems, but allows the formal specification of common bids. Agents can use this language to encode their bids and, subsequently, to submit them to the auctioneer.

The following notation serves as a basis for the definition of different bidding languages: Let $\mathcal{I}$ be a set of I agents, where $i \in \mathcal{I}$ defines an arbitrary agent. Furthermore, there are G discrete resources $\mathcal{G} = \{g_1, \ldots, g_G\}$ with $g_k \in \mathcal{G}$ to be auctioned. Agents can bid on a set of D bundles $\mathcal{S} = \{S_1, \ldots, S_D\}$ with $S_j \in \mathcal{S}$ and $S_j \subseteq \mathcal{G}$ as a subset of resources. For example, the term $S_j = \{g_k, g_j\}$ denotes that the bundle S_j consists of two resources g_k and g_j. Finally, let $v_i(S_j)$ be the valuation of agent i for bundle S_j. For instance, the formulation $v_i(S_j) = 10$ with $S_j = \{g_1, g_2\}$ denotes that agent i is willing to pay 10 for receiving the bundle S_j which consists of the two resources g_1 and g_2.[3] Without loss of generality, the following notation assumes that the reported valuation $\tilde{v}_i(\cdot)$ of an agent i is truthful, i.e., $\tilde{v}_i(\cdot) = v_i(\cdot)$. Settings in which this assumption is violated are discussed separately.

For the introduction of different bidding languages, a clear distinction between buyers and sellers is not necessary. The concepts that are presented in the following are valid for both, buyer as well as seller bids.

Based on the aforementioned notation, the most fundamental types of bidding languages are introduced based upon the work by Nisan (2000, 2006). The presented types comprise *atomic* bids, *OR* bids, and *XOR* bids:

Atomic Bids: An atomic bid is a pair $(S_j, v_i(S_j))$, where $S_j \in \mathcal{S}$ is a bundle on which an agent i bids with a valuation of $v_i(S_j)$. The use of atomic bids allows agents to place one single bid. As such, the language intensely restricts the strategy space which can lead to a reasonable communication effort. In some cases, however, atomic bids are insufficient to represent common preferences. For instance, even simple additive valuations cannot be represented by atomic bids.

OR Bids: OR bids allow agents to submit several atomic bids to the auctioneer. This is useful if agents have additive valuations concerning several atomic bids. In formal terms, OR bids are represented as $((S_j, v_i(S_j)) \vee \cdots \vee (S_k, v_i(S_k))$ where the total number of atomic bids can be restricted by the auctioneer. Consequently, the required communication effort can be controlled according to the number of available resources. OR bids are equivalent to the submission of multiple atomic bids, each from a different agent. They can represent all bids that do not have any substitutes.

XOR Bids: The use of XOR bids allows agents to submit multiple atomic bids that are concatenated by the logical XOR operator. By means of such bids, agents can express that they are interested in at most one of the atomic bids. A XOR bid is defined as $((S_j, v_i(S_j)) \oplus \cdots \oplus (S_k, v_i(S_k))$, where the number of atomic bids can be limited by the auctioneer to control the maximum communication effort. XOR bids can represent additive, sub-additive, and super-additive valuations. However, the length that is required to encode all valuations may become tremendous. For instance, some valuations that can be represented by OR bids shortly may require exponential size by the use of XOR bids (Nisan 2006).

---

[3]It is abstracted from currencies, i.e., valuations and reservation prices are denoted without any currency unit.

Beside these basic bidding languages, Nisan (2000) further proposes combinations of the OR and the XOR language. Furthermore, he proposes the OR^* language which simulates the XOR operator by means of an OR operator combined with dummy variables. For instance, the XOR bid $((S_j, v_i(S_j)) \oplus (S_k, v_i(S_k)))$ can be represented by $((S_j \cup \{d\}, v_i(S_j)) \vee (S_k \cup \{d\}, v_i(S_k)))$, where d is a dummy resource that can be allocated at most once. This allows a more compact representation of most bids compared to the XOR language.

The decision of which bidding language is supported by the auction depends on the requirements by the agents and the objectives of the market engineer. For instance, the objective of the market engineer can be the minimization of the communication complexity caused by the bidding language.

After the bids are formulated by means of the selected type of bidding language, they are submitted to the auctioneer that computes an allocation and corresponding prices. In the following subsections, state of the art of allocation and pricing rules for single sided combinatorial auctions and combinatorial exchanges are outlined.

5.1.2   Single Sided Combinatorial Auctions

Single sided combinatorial auctions are mechanisms in which either buyers or sellers can submit bids on multiple heterogenous resources. The following discussion focuses on single-unit combinatorial auctions in which an auctioneer offers a set of heterogeneous resources $\mathcal{G}$ to a set of agents $\mathcal{I}$ that act as buyers.[4] An agent $i \in \mathcal{I}$ with quasi-linear utility functions submits a set of XOR concatenated bundle bids $(S_j, v_i(S_j))$ to the auctioneer, where $S_j \subseteq \mathcal{G}$ is a bundle of resources and $v_i(S_j) \geq 0$ is the valuation for the bundle S_j. Assume that $v_i(\emptyset) = 0$ and that the valuation function $v_i(\cdot)$ satisfies *free disposal*. Free disposal of resources implies that agents have weakly increasing values for bundles with more resources, i.e., $v_i(S_j) \leq v_i(S_j \cup T)$ with $S_j \subseteq \mathcal{G}$ and $T \subseteq \mathcal{G}$ (Parkes 2001).

5.1.2.1   Winner Determination

Solving the winner determination problem means selecting a set of bids so that a predefined objective can be achieved. Following the discussion outlined in Section 3.2.1.4, an efficient allocation is the objective that a mechanism designer wants to attain.

The conventional way of formulating the winner determination problem – also called the combinatorial allocation problem (CAP) – is the use of integer programming. This is advantageous, as standard operations research algorithms and diverse solver packages can be applied for solving it (Andersson et al. 2000). For this purpose, let $x_i(S_j)$ be a binary decision variable with $x_i(S_j) = 1$ if the bundle S_j is allocated to buyer i and $x_i(S_j) = 0$ otherwise. Consequently, CAP can be formulated as follows (de Vries and Vohra 2003):

---

[4]Sandholm et al. (2002) and de Vries and Vohra (2003) outline formulations for combinatorial multi-unit and reverse auctions.

$$\max \sum_{i \in \mathcal{I}} \sum_{S_j \in \mathcal{S}} v_i(S_j) x_i(S_j) \tag{5.1}$$

$$\text{s.t.} \sum_{S_j \in \mathcal{S}} x_i(S_j) \le 1, \ \forall i \in \mathcal{I} \tag{5.2}$$

$$\sum_{i \in \mathcal{I}} \sum_{S_j \ni g_k} x_i(S_j) \le 1, \ \forall g_k \in \mathcal{G} \tag{5.3}$$

$$x_i(S_j) \in \{0, 1\}, \ \forall i \in \mathcal{I}, S_j \in \mathcal{S} \tag{5.4}$$

The objective function 5.1 maximizes the total value over all agents. By construction, this objective function attains an efficient allocation if agents bid truthfully. Constraint 5.2 ensures that no bidder receives more than one bundle (XOR constraint). Constraint 5.3 ensures that any resource is allocated at most once. Finally, Constraint 5.4 defines the decision variables of the optimization problem.

The value of the optimal solution is further denoted as V^*, the corresponding allocation is denoted as $\mathcal{S}^* = (S_1^*, \ldots, S_I^*)$, where S_i^* represents the bundle that is allocated to agent i in the optimal allocation.[5] Furthermore, *ties* – different allocations that both maximize the objective function – are broken according to a predefined rule. For instance, ties can be broken in favour of maximizing the number of agents in the allocation or randomly.

Beside their economic attractiveness, combinatorial auctions have also technical shortcomings. For instance, the winner determination problem belongs to the $\mathcal{NP}$-complete problems.

Theorem 5.1: CAP Complexity
The combinatorial allocation problem (CAP) is $\mathcal{NP}$-complete (Rothkopf et al. 1998).

Sketch of proof. CAP is equivalent to the set packing problem (SPP) on hypergraphs (Rothkopf et al. 1998, p. 1136), which is known to be $\mathcal{NP}$-complete (Karp 1972, p. 94). □

As a consequence, solving a combinatorial auction optimally may not be feasible in large-scale scenarios. For a description of algorithms that can be applied to solve CAP, refer to Chapter 6.

Example 5.1: CAP Problem Set
As an example of the winner determination problem, consider the bids given in Table 5.1. The auctioneer sells 3 different goods g_1, g_2, g_3 and 3 agents submit XOR bids on each resource combination. For instance, agent 1 values the bundle $S_2 = \{g_2\}$ with $v_1(S_2) = 5$, agent 2 the bundle $S_5 = \{g_1, g_3\}$ with $v_2(S_5) = 9$, and agent 3 the bundle $S_7 = \{g_1, g_2, g_3\}$ with $v_3(S_7) = 22$. The optimal solution is to allocate the bundle $S_1 = \{g_1\}$ to agent 1 ($x_1(S_1) = 1$) and to allocate the bundle $S_6 = \{g_2, g_3\}$ to agent 3 ($x_3(S_6) = 1$). The value of the allocation is $V^* = 26$.

The allocation determined by CAP is efficient as long as agents report their preferences truthfully. It is the objective of the price system to provide sufficient incentives to reveal some of the agents' private information in order to attain an efficient allocation. In the following paragraphs, common pricing schemes for combinatorial auctions are discussed.

---

[5]If no bundle is allocated to agent i, then $S_i^* = \emptyset$ with $v_i(\emptyset) = 0$.

Agent	$S_1 = \{g_1\}$	$S_2 = \{g_2\}$	$S_3 = \{g_3\}$	$S_4 = \{g_1, g_2\}$	$S_5 = \{g_1, g_3\}$	$S_6 = \{g_2, g_3\}$	$S_7 = \{g_1, g_2, g_3\}$
1	8*	5	4	12	10	11	21
2	6	3	5	15	9	12	19
3	7	4	10	12	10	18*	22

Table 5.1: Valuations of bidders in the CAP problem set

5.1.2.2 Generalized Vickrey Auction

The Generalized Vickrey Auction (GVA) is an application of the VCG mechanism (cf. Section 3.2.2.2) to combinatorial auctions. The auction process is as follows (Varian 1995; Parkes 2001): All agents $i \in \mathcal{I}$ submit their XOR bundle bids to the auctioneer by communicating (not necessarily truthfully) their types $\hat{\theta}_i$. Subsequently, the auctioneer solves the choice function $k^*(\hat{\theta})$ that maximizes the total reported preferences over all agents. This is achieved by solving CAP optimally to obtain $\mathcal{S}^*$. Next, the auctioneer determines prices for each agent i by solving the VCG payment rule

$$p_i(\hat{\theta}) = \sum_{j \neq i} v_j(k^*_{-i}(\hat{\theta}_{-i}), \hat{\theta}_j) - \sum_{j \neq i} v_j(k^*(\hat{\theta}), \hat{\theta}_j),$$

where $k^*_{-i}(\hat{\theta}_{-i})$ denotes the choice rule with all agents except agent i. Let $(V_{-i})^*$ be the value of the allocation without agent i and let $(\mathcal{S}_{-i})^*$ be the corresponding allocation. Then, the auctioneer has to determine the following payment function for each agent i:

$$p_{VICK,i}(S_i^*) = (V_{-i})^* - \sum_{j \neq i} v_j(S_j^*) = v_i(S_i^*) + (V_{-i})^* - V^* \qquad (5.5)$$

In words, prices agents have to pay for allocated bundles do not only depend on their valuations. The price of each agent gets further influenced by the difference between the value of the allocation without his own participation $(V_{-i})^*$ and the sum of the valuations $v_j(S_j^*)$ of all other agents in the optimal solution. As such, the price reflects the impact of agent i's participation. An agent i must not necessarily pay the value of the bid as he receives a discount $\Delta_{VICK,i} \geq 0$ in form of a transfer payment (Parkes 2001). This discount is computed as the difference between the value of the optimal solution and the value of the solution without agent i, i.e.,

$$\Delta_{VICK,i} = V^* - (V_{-i})^*. \qquad (5.6)$$

As a consequence, the payment rule of the GVA can be reformulated to

$$p_{VICK,i}(S_i^*) = v_i(S_i^*) - \Delta_{VICK,i}.$$

Thus, the discount $\Delta_{VICK,i}$ represents the utility $u_i(S_i^*)$ of agent i, i.e.,

$$u_i(S_i^*) = v_i(S_i^*) - p_{VICK,i}(S_i^*) = \Delta_{VICK,i}.$$

Example 5.2: GVA Problem Set
The GVA payments for the problem set given in Example 5.1 are computed as follows: First, an allocation is computed without agent 1. This means, that the auctioneer computes $(\mathcal{S}_{-1})^*$ to obtain $(V_{-1})^*$. Given the bids in Table 5.1, the optimal solution $(\mathcal{S}_{-1})^*$ is to allocate bundle $S_4 = \{g_1, g_2\}$ to agent 2 and bundle $S_3 = \{g_3\}$ to agent 3. The value of $(\mathcal{S}_{-1})^*$ is accordingly $(V_{-1})^* = 25$. Thus, agent 1 has to pay $p_{VICK,1}(S_1^*) = 8 - (26 - 25) = 7$ for

the bundle $S_1 = \{g_1\}$. As the discount is computed as $\Delta_{VICK,1} = 26 - 25 = 1$, the impact of agent 1 on the allocation is assessed with the value 1. Likewise, the payment of agent 3 is computed as $p_{VICK,3}(S_3^*) = 15$ with $(V_{-3})^* = 23$ and $\Delta_{VICK,3} = 3$. As agent 2 is not part of the allocation, his payment sums up to $p_{VICK,2}(S_2^*) = 0$.

The GVA is an instance of a VCG mechanism. As such, it is efficient, incentive compatible, and individually rational for agents with quasi-linear utility functions. Furthermore, the GVA is budget-balanced. This means, that the auction does not have to be subsidized from outside sources. It is to note, that the Myerson-Satterthwaite theorem (cf. Section 3.2.2.3) does not hold for the GVA due to its single sided nature.

Aside from the attractiveness due to its economic properties, a practical application of the GVA has several drawbacks: The first and most commonly discussed weakness of the GVA is the low (and sometimes even zero) revenue of a seller (Ausubel and Milgrom 2002). Suppose the bids of the two agents shown in Table 5.2. The optimal solution is to allocate $S_2 = \{g_2\}$ to agent 1 and $S_1 = \{g_1\}$ to agent 2. The value of the allocation is $V^* = 4$. The payment of agent 1 is $p_{VICK,1}(S_1^*) = 2 - 2 = 0$, as his impact on the allocation is denoted with the same value as his bid. The same conclusion applies to agent 2, thus making the revenue of the auctioneer zero. As a consequence, such a deficit of the GVA "*is decisive to reject it for most practical applications.*" (Ausubel and Milgrom 2006, p. 23). Another weakness of the GVA is its vulnerability to collusion. Agents can improve their own utility by entering joint deviations with other agents in the auction. Furthermore, they can lower their payments by shill bidding, as agents can improve their utility by the use of multiple identities (Ausubel and Milgrom 2002).

Agent	$S_1 = \{g_1\}$	$S_2 = \{g_2\}$
1	0	2*
2	2*	0

Table 5.2: Valuations of bidders that lead to zero payments in a CAP setting

Most theoretical analyses neglect the computational complexity of the GVA: CAP belongs to the $\mathcal{NP}$-complete problems. In a setting with I agents, this problem has to be solved $I + 1$ times in the worst case.[6] In several practical application areas, an outcome of the GVA cannot always be found within a reasonable time frame (Parkes 2001; Dash et al. 2003).

In summary, the GVA has strong and unique economic properties. However, due to the aforementioned weaknesses, its practical application is hampered. For this reason, Milgrom (2006, p. 39) suggests the use of alternative designs: "*Vickrey auctions, long the darling of theoretical mechanism designers, are impractical even for auction applications mainly because the seller's revenues are too low. There are flexible new designs [...] that attractively compromise the incentive properties of the Vickrey auction with the need to avoid low revenues and that seem to correspond well with mechanisms that are reported to have good success in economic laboratories.*"

---

[6]One instance has to be solved to determine an allocation and I instances have be computed for the payments.

5.1.2.3   Pricing Per Column

One drawback of the GVA is the computational effort that is required to determine an outcome. In the worst case, $I+1$ instances of CAP must be solved. This is a consequence of the underlying VCG pricing rule: It values the impact of each agent on the allocation. In contrast to the GVA, the Pricing Per Column (PPC) mechanism attempts to reduce this computational effort (Schmidt 1999; Gomber et al. 2000). The mechanism implements an alternative payment function that is computationally more efficient. The choice rule of the PPC remains the same as in the GVA. This means the auctioneer first solves CAP to determine an allocation.

The payment rule for agent i with S_i^* depends on the valuations of other agents that bid for the same bundle. The price agent i has to pay for S_i^* is simply the highest valuation for S_i^* if i would not be present. Formalizing the payment rule, let $\mathcal{S}^* = (S_1^*, \ldots, S_I^*)$ be the optimal allocation determined by CAP. The price rule is defined as

$$p_{PPC,i}(S_i^*) = \begin{cases} \min(\max_{k \neq i} v_k(S_i^*), v_i(S_i^*)) & \text{if the number of bids on } S_i^* \geq 2 \\ 0 & \text{otherwise.} \end{cases} \quad (5.7)$$

In words, the function determines the second highest bid for a particular bundle S_i^*. If there is an unsuccessful bidder that bids more than $v_i(S_i^*)$, the price is set to $p_{PPC,i}(S_i^*) = v_i(S_i^*)$ in order to ensure individual rationality. In case agent i is the only bidder on S_i^*, his payment is $p_{PPC,i}(S_i^*) = 0$.

Example 5.3: PPC Problem Set

As an example of the PPC, reconsider the valuations given in Table 5.1. According to the PPC pricing rule, agent 1 has to pay the second highest bid for $S_1 = \{g_1\}$, i.e., the agent has to pay $p_{PPC,1}(S_1) = 7$. Likewise, agent 3 pays $p_{PPC,3}(S_6) = 12$.

The PPC is budget-balanced and individually rational. From a computational viewpoint, the auction is less complex than the GVA. However, one instance of CAP has still to be solved optimally. As the PPC does not implement a Groves mechanism, it is not incentive compatible. For example, consider the setting given in Table 5.1: For the bundle $S_4 = \{g_1, g_2\}$, assume agent 2 does not bid the valuation $v_2(S_4) = 15$ but overbids up to $\hat{v}_2(S_4) = 17$. As a consequence, agent 2 is part of the allocation. The bid, together with the bid from agent 3 on $S_3 = \{g_3\}$, maximizes the objective function of CAP. Agent 2 bids more than his valuation and has a positive utility from this transaction. The agent has only to pay the second highest bid for S_4 with $p_{PPC,2}(S_4) = 12$. Moreover, the utility due to overbidding is greater than the utility for telling the truth. As such, the agent does not have an incentive to reveal the true valuation.

In a numerical experiment, Neumann et al. (2007) show that deviating from the true valuations does not always improve the individual utility of agents. If the number of competing agents is sufficiently high with respect to the available resources, agents profit more by revealing their true preferences. This property is lost if the number of available resources is increased. The authors conclude that if the size of the auction is very large, strategic manipulations of bids do not pay off. Competition drives the bidders to reveal their true valuations. As a consequence, the application of the PPC in such settings may be a practical alternative to the GVA.

5.1.2.4   Iterative Combinatorial Auctions

Iterative combinatorial auctions such as iBundle (Parkes 1999), AkBA (Wurman and Wellman 2000), or the Clock-Proxy auction (Ausubel et al. 2006) allow agents to submit multiple bundle bids to the auctioneer. Such auctions do not require that agents submit their valuations at once. Rather, they allow them to reveal their preferences in regard to the information feedback they get.

One can differentiate between two types of iterative auctions: quantity based and price based auctions (de Vries and Vohra 2003). In each round of a quantity based auction, agents submit their bids to the auctioneer. On the basis of these bids, the auctioneer computes a provisional allocation and propagates the outcome to the agents. Subsequently, agents can resubmit their adjusted bids to the auctioneer. The auction ends after a predefined stop rule. For instance, the auction may end after 5 minutes have passed without any new bid. In contrast to quantity based mechanisms, the auctioneer sets the price for each bundle in a price based auction. Agents announce which bundles they want to acquire for the given price. After that, the auctioneer may rise prices according to the number of requests received for each bundle. Agents in price based settings are usually characterized as *myopic best response bidders*. They bid for the bundles that maximize their utility with respect to the announced prices (Parkes 2001). The intuition behind price based auctions is a Walrasian auctioneer that announces prices so that supply equals demand for a resource (Hurwicz 1972). Most iterative combinatorial auctions rely on a price based mechanism.

Price based auctions can be interpreted as primal-dual algorithms. Given a problem that is represented as a primal and a dual linear program, such algorithms try to find feasible primal and dual solutions that satisfy complementary slackness conditions[7]. If both solutions satisfy these conditions, they are optimal due to the strong duality theorem (Wolsey and Nemhause 1999). A primal-dual auction problem is now interpreted as follows: The provisional allocation is a feasible primal solution and the current prices are feasible dual solutions. The winner determination problem uses the bids to compute a feasible primal solution that minimizes the violations of the complementary slackness conditions. Price updates adjust the dual solution towards an optimal solution (Parkes 2006). If the announced prices and the allocation satisfy the complementary slackness conditions, the auction is terminated.

A popular example of a primal-dual auction algorithm is the English auction where the auctioneer announces prices (dual problem) and determines an allocation on the basis of the bids (primal problem). Agents bid myopically by raising their hands for a given price (de Vries and Vohra 2003). An implementation of a primal-dual algorithm as an iterative combinatorial auction is given by iBundle (Parkes 1999; Parkes and Ungar 2000).

Iterative combinatorial auctions are advantageous in settings in which agents cannot reveal all of their preferences at once. This can be the case if agents do not know their valuations correctly or if the submission of all valuations at once requires too much communication. Due to their multi-round game form, iterative auctions may be disadvantageous if the underlying resources are time-critical. For instance, an agent may not use an iterative auction if he wants to sell a storage service from now on for 5 hours. In this case, a one-shot auction is superior, as the agent gets informed about the allocation decision more quickly.

5.1.3   Combinatorial Exchanges

Combinatorial exchanges are generalizations of combinatorial auctions. They allow multiple buyers and sellers to bid on a set of heterogeneous resources simultaneously. Analogous to

---

[7]Complementary slackness conditions are logical connections between constraints in a primal problem and its corresponding variables in the dual problem and vice versa (Wolsey and Nemhause 1999).

the previous discussion, the focus lies on single-unit combinatorial exchanges with agents that have quasi-linear utility functions and have valuation functions that satisfy $v_i(\emptyset) = 0$ and free disposal. For a discussion on multi-unit combinatorial exchanges, refer to Kothari et al. (2003) and Xia et al. (2005). Furthermore, the focus lies on one-shot (direct) mechanisms. For an iterative implementation of a combinatorial exchange refer to Parkes et al. (2005).

For simplicity, it is assumed that there are either buyer agents or seller agents. This means, that no agent can simultaneously act as buyer and seller. Let $\mathcal{N}$ be a set of buyers with $n \in \mathcal{N}$ as an arbitrary buyer and let $\mathcal{M}$ be a set of sellers with $m \in \mathcal{M}$ as a particular seller. Both types of agents can submit XOR bids on any bundle S_j with $S_j \subseteq \mathcal{G}$. It is assumed that resources $g_k \in S_j$ are indivisible. A buyer n expresses his valuation for a bundle S_j with $v_n(S_j) \geq 0$ which denotes the maximum price for which buyer n is willing to purchase the item. The reservation price for selling a bundle S_j is denoted by $r_m(S_j) \geq 0$ which represents the minimum price for which seller m is willing to sell the item.

The design and analysis of combinatorial exchanges mainly affects two phases: clearing and pricing. Clearing an exchange means solving a winner determination problem with a given objective. The result of this problem is an allocation of resources from sellers to buyers. The pricing mechanism determines the net payments to the agents after the exchange cleared.

5.1.3.1   Winner Determination

In an exchange, the common objective of the winner determination problem is either the maximization of surplus or the maximization of trade volume (Kothari et al. 2003). The first objective maximizes the difference between the valuations of buyers and the reservation prices of sellers. This objective is equivalent to maximizing social welfare in an economy as the resources are allocated in a way that maximizes the value of the participants. Under the assumption that agents are risk neutral and have quasi-linear utility functions, the corresponding allocation is efficient if social welfare is maximized (Kothari et al. 2003). The second objective maximizes the number of traded resource units. Following the argumentation outlined in Section 3.2.1.4, the discussion focuses on the maximization of surplus in order to attain an efficient allocation.

The clearing interval – i.e., the timing of determining the winners – can be either periodically or continuously. In a periodical clearing, agents are given a specific length of time for posting their bids. After that period, the auctioneer clears the market and calculates prices. In a continuous exchange, the auctioneer immediately matches compatible bids and tries to clear whenever a new bid is sent to the market. Parkes et al. (2001) state that a larger number of bids can be aggregated in periodically cleared combinatorial exchanges. As a consequence, periodical clearing may increase the value of the allocation. However, the use of periodical clearing is inferior to continuous clearing in terms of immediacy. For simplicity, this question is not further addressed, as the presented winner determination problem is applicable for both, periodical and continuous clearing.

Similar to CAP, the winner determination problem of a combinatorial exchange (combinatorial exchange problem, CEP) is also formulated as an integer program: Let $x_n(S_j)$ be a binary decision variable with $x_n(S_j) = 1$ if the bundle S_j is allocated to buyer n and $x_n(S_j) = 0$ otherwise. Likewise, let the binary decision variable $d_m(S_j)$ denote whether the seller m allocates the bundle S_j ($d_m(S_j) = 1$) or not ($d_m(S_j) = 0$). On the basis of these decision variables, the corresponding integer program is formulated as follows (Kothari et al. 2003):

$$\max \sum_{n \in \mathcal{N}} \sum_{S_j \in \mathcal{S}} x_n(S_j) v_n(S_j) - \sum_{m \in \mathcal{M}} \sum_{S_j \in \mathcal{S}} d_m(S_j) r_m(S_j) \tag{5.8}$$

$$\text{s.t.} \sum_{S_j \in \mathcal{S}} x_n(S_j) \leq 1, \ \forall n \in \mathcal{N} \tag{5.9}$$

$$\sum_{S_j \in \mathcal{S}} d_m(S_j) \leq 1, \ \forall m \in \mathcal{M} \tag{5.10}$$

$$\sum_{S_j \ni g_k} \sum_{n \in \mathcal{N}} x_n(S_j) \leq \sum_{S_j \ni g_k} \sum_{m \in \mathcal{M}} d_m(S_j), \ \forall g_k \in \mathcal{G} \tag{5.11}$$

$$x_n(S_j) \in \{0,1\}, \ \forall n \in \mathcal{N}, S_j \in \mathcal{S} \tag{5.12}$$

$$d_m(S_j) \in \{0,1\}, \ \forall m \in \mathcal{M}, S_j \in \mathcal{S} \tag{5.13}$$

The objective function 5.8 maximizes the surplus which is defined as the difference between the sum of the buyer's valuations and the sum of the seller's reservation prices. The objective function reflects the goal of maximizing social welfare. The first and second constraints guarantee that neither a buyer n (Constraint 5.9) nor a seller m (Constraint 5.10) are part of the allocation with more than one bundle S_j (XOR constraints). Constraint 5.11 ensures that for each good, demand is less or equal than its supply. It is to note that the free-disposal constraint can be amplified to full market clearing by formulating Constraint 5.11 as an equation. Ties are broken according to a predefined rule such as maximizing number of trades, or at random.

In the same way as CAP, CEP also belongs to the group of $\mathcal{NP}$-complete problems.

Theorem 5.2: CEP Complexity
The combinatorial exchange problem (CEP) is $\mathcal{NP}$-complete.

Proof-Sketch. CAP can be reduced to CEP. Obviously, any CAP instance (multiple buyers, one seller with a zero reservation price) can be solved by CEP. As such, CEP is also $\mathcal{NP}$-complete. $\square$

Buyer	Bundle	Valuation	Seller	Bundle	Reservation
1	$S_4 = \{g_1, g_2\}$	12	1	$S_2 = \{g_2\}^* \oplus$	3
2	$S_1 = \{g_1\} \oplus$	6		$S_4 = \{g_1, g_2\}$	9
	$S_7 = \{g_1, g_2, g_3\}^*$	13	2	$S_5 = \{g_1, g_3\}^*$	5

Table 5.3: Valuations and reservation prices in the CEP problem set

Example 5.4: CEP Problem Set
As an example for CEP, consider the valuations and reservation prices given in Table 5.3. There are two buyers and two sellers that can bid on any combination of the resources g_1, g_2, and g_3. For instance, buyer 2 submits a XOR bid on the bundles $S_1 = \{g_1\}$ and $S_7 = \{g_1, g_2, g_3\}$. The valuation for S_1 is given by $v_2(S_1) = 6$ and the valuation for S_7 by $v_2(S_7) = 13$. Seller 2 submits an atomic bid on $S_5 = \{g_1, g_3\}$ with a reservation price of $r_2(S_5) = 5$.

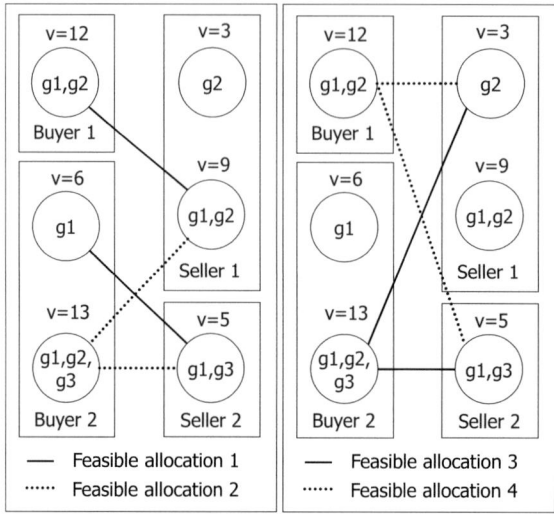

Figure 5.1: Potential allocations in the CEP example

The objective of CEP is now to find a feasible allocation that maximizes the total surplus. An allocation is feasible if the constraints of CEP are satisfied. Figure 5.1 depicts four feasible allocations:[8] For instance, the feasible allocation 1 allocates bundle $S_4 = \{g_1, g_2\}$ from seller 1 to buyer 1 and bundle $S_5 = \{g_1, g_3\}$ from seller 2 to buyer 2. The surplus of this allocation is $V_{f1} = 12 + 6 - 9 - 5 = 4$. Analogously, the surplus of feasible allocation 2 is $V_{f2} = 13 - 9 - 5 = -1$ and the surplus of feasible allocation 4 is $V_{f4} = 12 - 3 - 5 = 4$. The optimal allocation is given by feasible allocation 3: Buyer 2 gets allocated the bundle $S_7 = \{g_1, g_2, g_3\}$ from seller 1 $(d_1(S_2) = 1)$ and seller 2 $(d_2(S_5) = 1)$. The surplus of this allocation is $V_{f3}^* = 13 - 3 - 5 = 5$.

Similar to CAP, CEP determines an efficient allocation as long as agents bid truthfully. As such, a pricing schema is required that provides sufficient incentives that agents reveal their private information.

5.1.3.2 Pricing

The question how to determine payments of the agents to the exchange, and vice versa after the mechanism has cleared, is referred to as pricing problem (Parkes et al. 2001). With respect to the objective of achieving an efficient allocation, a pricing scheme based on a VCG mechanism would attain this objective. However, Myerson and Satterthwaite (1983) proved that it is impossible to design an exchange that is incentive compatible, (interim) individually rational, budget-balanced, and efficient in equilibrium (cf. Section 3.2.2.3). Hence, the VCG pricing scheme is briefly illustrated to serve as a benchmark. Subsequently, an approximated VCG pricing schema is introduced that achieves fairly efficient allocations and is budget-balanced. Both mechanisms are applicable for CEP, i.e., they support atomic bids and XOR bids. For alternative pricing mechanisms that are restricted to atomic bids, the reader is referred to Fan et al. (1999).

---

[8]This figure is not an enumeration of all feasible allocations.

VCG Pricing: The VCG pricing mechanism for combinatorial exchanges is a generalization of the GVA. Agents submit their bids to the auctioneer who computes an allocation by solving CEP and subsequently determines prices. Analogues to the GVA, payments for buyers and sellers are computed as follows: Let V^* denote the surplus of the optimal allocation $\mathcal{S}^*$. Furthermore, let $(V_{-n})^*$ be the value of the optimal allocation $(\mathcal{S}_{-n})^*$ without buyer n and let $(V_{-m})^*$ be the value of the allocation $(\mathcal{S}_{-m})^*$ without seller m. The discounts of agents are formalized as $\Delta_{VICK,n}^N = V^* - (V_{-n})^*$ for a buyer n and $\Delta_{VICK,m}^M = V^* - (V_{-m})^*$ for a seller m. The payment of a buyer n is computed as

$$p_{VICK,n}^N(S_n^*) = v_n(S_n^*) - \Delta_{VICK,n}^N = v_n(S_n^*) - V^* + (V_{-n})^*, \tag{5.14}$$

where $v_n(S_n^*)$ denotes the valuation of buyer n for the bundle S_n^*. Likewise, the payment of a seller m is computed as

$$p_{VICK,m}^M(S_m^*) = r_m(S_m^*) + \Delta_{VICK,m}^M = r_m(S_m^*) + V^* - (V_{-m})^*, \tag{5.15}$$

where $r_m(S_m^*)$ is the reservation price of seller m for the bundle S_m^*. For buyers, the discount is subtracted from their valuations. They have to pay less (or equal) than their maximum willingness to pay. For sellers, the discount is added. They get more (or equal) than their minimum price for which they want to trade.

The application of a VCG mechanism requires to restrict attention to periodical clearing known as call markets. The reason for this is intuitive: A continuous market tries to clear, whenever a new bid is submitted to the auctioneer. If adequate counterparts can be found for the bid, they are directly cleared. Otherwise, the bid is stored in the order book. This means that CEP could not find any matchable bid in the order book. Now, suppose an agent i submits a new bid that matches with some of the other bids in the order book. Accordingly, an allocation is determined with a value V^*. The VCG price that agent i has to pay is $p_i(\cdot) = 0$, as $(V_{-i})^* = 0$. The impact of agent i equals the value of the bid. As such, all new bids that can be directly cleared have a zero price.

The VCG mechanism for a combinatorial exchange is efficient and individually rational. According to the Myerson-Satterthwaite theorem (cf. Section 3.2.2.3), it is not budget-balanced. This means, that the auctioneer has to endow the exchange, which is practically not realizable. In addition, the drawbacks of the VCG as outlined in Section 5.1.2.2 may further hamper its practical application. Hence, the VCG pricing schema can only serve as an economic benchmark.

Example 5.5: VCG Pricing for CEP Problem Set
Applying the VCG mechanism to Example 5.4 ($V^* = 5$) results in the payments shown in Table 5.4. Buyer 2 with $v_n(S_7) = 13$ has to pay $p_{VICK,2}^N = 13 - (5 - 4) = 12$, as the impact on the allocation is 1. Seller 1 gets $p_{VICK,1}^M = 3 + (5 - 1) = 7$ for allocating bundle S_2; this is 4 money units more than the reservation price. Likewise, the payment of seller 2 is computed as $p_{VICK,2}^M = 5 + (5 - 3) = 7$. Summing up the payments from buyers to sellers results in $12 - 7 - 7 = -2$, meaning that the total budget runs in a deficit. As mentioned above, this is not realizable in practice.

Approximated VCG Pricing: Retaining most of the VCG properties, a possible implementation of a budget-balanced pricing scheme for a combinatorial exchange is the so-called *approximated VCG pricing* mechanism introduced by Parkes et al. (2001). The idea is to

Buyer	$(V_{-n})^*$	$\Delta^N_{VICK,n}$	$p^N_{VICK,n}$	Seller	$(V_{-m})^*$	$\Delta^M_{VICK,m}$	$p^M_{VICK,m}$
2	4	1	12	1	1	4	7
				2	3	2	7

Table 5.4: VCG discounts and prices in the CEP problem set

cleave the budget-balance and individually rational constraints and approximate the VCG discounts resulting in a relaxation of incentive compatibility.

The goal of the approximated VCG mechanism is to minimize a function L which denotes the distance between an original VCG discount Δ_{VICK} and an approximated discount $\bar{\Delta}$. Let Θ_{VICK} be the set of the buyers' and sellers' VCG discounts and let $\bar{\Theta}$ denote the set of the approximated discounts with $\bar{\Delta}^N_n \in \bar{\Theta}^N$ as a buyer discount, $\bar{\Delta}^M_m \in \bar{\Theta}^M$ as a seller discount, and $\bar{\Theta} = \bar{\Theta}^N \times \bar{\Theta}^M$. The minimization problem of the distance function L is formulated as a linear program (Parkes et al. 2001):

$$\min \ L(\bar{\Theta}, \Theta_{VICK}) \tag{5.16}$$

$$\text{s.t.} \ \sum_{n \in \mathcal{N}} \bar{\Delta}^N_n + \sum_{m \in \mathcal{M}} \bar{\Delta}^M_m \leq V^* \tag{5.17}$$

$$\bar{\Delta}^N_n \leq \Delta^N_{VICK,n}, \ \forall n \in \mathcal{N} \tag{5.18}$$

$$\bar{\Delta}^M_m \leq \Delta^M_{VICK,m}, \ \forall m \in \mathcal{M} \tag{5.19}$$

$$\bar{\Delta}^N_n \geq 0, \ \forall n \in \mathcal{N} \tag{5.20}$$

$$\bar{\Delta}^M_m \geq 0, \ \forall m \in \mathcal{M} \tag{5.21}$$

The objective function 5.16 minimizes a distance function L between the original VCG discounts and the approximated ones. Constraint 5.17 guarantees the budget-balance property which ensures that the exchange never has to transfer net payments to the agents. Constraints 5.18 and 5.19 ensure that no agent gets more than the original VCG discount. The constraints 5.20 and 5.21 guarantee the individual rationality property of agents.

Parkes et al. (2001) indicate among others the following distance functions $L(\bar{\Theta}, \Theta_{VICK})$ for this problem: The quadratic error function

$$L_2(\bar{\Theta}, \Theta_{VICK}) = \sum_{i \in \mathcal{N} \cup \mathcal{M}} (\Delta_{VICK,i} - \bar{\Delta}_i)^2,$$

a squared relative error function

$$L_{RE2}(\bar{\Theta}, \Theta_{VICK}) = \sum_{i \in \mathcal{N} \cup \mathcal{M}} \frac{(\Delta_{VICK,i} - \bar{\Delta}_i)^2}{\bar{\Delta}_i},$$

and a product error function

$$L_\Pi(\bar{\Theta}, \Theta_{VICK}) = \prod_{i \in \mathcal{N} \cup \mathcal{M}} \frac{\Delta_{VICK,i}}{\bar{\Delta}_i}.$$

On the basis of these approximations, the approximated Vickrey payments (AV) for buyers are computed as

$$p^N_{AV,n}(S^*_n) = v_n(S^*_n) - \bar{\Delta}^N_n, \tag{5.22}$$

where $v_n(S_n^*)$ denotes the valuation of buyer n for the bundle S_n^* and $\bar{\Delta}_n^N$ denotes the approximated discount. Likewise, the sellers' payments are computed as

$$p_{AV,m}^M(S_m^*) = r_m(S_m^*) + \bar{\Delta}_m^M, \tag{5.23}$$

where $r_m(S_m^*)$ is the reservation price of seller m and $\bar{\Delta}_m^M$ the approximated discount. For the given distance functions, Parkes et al. (2001) show that the resulting linear programm can also be formulated as an analytic expression using the Lagrange relaxation.

Applying these approximations in order to determine prices, the exchange does not have to endow the participants. In contrast to VCG pricing, the approximation fulfills the weak budget-balance property. Numerical simulations show, that the overall efficiency loss is fairly mild (Parkes et al. 2001).

Example 5.6: Approximated VCG Pricing Exchange
For this example, the quadratic error function (also called *threshold function*) is applied as a distance function. Table 5.5 shows the approximated discounts and the corresponding prices for the problem set of the previous Example 5.4. It is obvious that all discounts get decreased by the same factor as the quadratic error is minimized. As a result, the payment of buyer 2 is higher than in the VCG case; respectively, the payments of the sellers are smaller than in the VCG case. The exchange is weak budget-balanced, i.e., the payments sum up to $12.67 - 6.33 - 6.33 \geq 0$.

Buyer	$(V_{-n})^*$	$\Delta_{VICK,n}^N$	$\bar{\Delta}_n^N$	$p_{AV,n}^N$	Seller	$(V_{-m})^*$	$\Delta_{VICK,m}^M$	$\bar{\Delta}_m^M$	$p_{AV,m}^M$
2	4	1	0.33	12.67	1	1	4	3.33	6.33
					2	3	2	1.33	6.33

Table 5.5: Approximated VCG discounts and prices in the CEP problem set

5.1.4 Reflection

The previous paragraphs outlined state of the art of combinatorial auction design. First, bidding languages are introduced that allow the formalization of bundle bids including OR and XOR operators. Second, the discussion reflected the two basic types of combinatorial auction mechanisms in practice: single sided combinatorial auctions and combinatorial exchanges.

However, both types of auction mechanisms cannot be directly applied for trading Grid resources. With regard to the requirements elicited in Section 4.2, neither auction types support bids on multiple attributes and time intervals. They further neglect Grid specific allocation requirements such as resource dependencies and network quality.

In summary, the outlined work builds the basis for the design of MACE that reverts to the principles of a combinatorial exchange.

5.2 MACE: A Multi-Attribute Combinatorial Exchange

The previous section reviewed basic concepts of combinatorial auctions and exchanges. On the basis of this exploratory work, this section tailors a Multi-Attribute Combinatorial Exchange (MACE) that attains most of the specified requirements for trading standardized Grid resources.

The design of MACE follows common assumptions of mechanism design and auction theory: Agents are assumed to be risk neutral, have quasi-linear utility functions as well as independent private valuations and reservation prices. The valuation functions of agents satisfy free-disposal and $v_i(\emptyset) = 0$. The valuation functions of sellers allow a linear transformation in case of partial executions. For instance, if a seller values a storage service with 300GB capacity with 10, he values a partial execution of the service with 150GB with 5. In contrast, buyers do not accept partial executions of their requests or their applications. Furthermore, it is assumed that buyers can specify their resource requirements in terms of quality characteristics and job duration. For instance, it is assumed that a buyer can specify the amount of storage space that is required for executing a job. In addition, the buyer can specify how long the job has to be executed. Likewise, a seller of resources can specify the characteristics of those resources that he can offer in the future. The elicitation of the resource characteristics can be supported by prediction models such as proposed by Smith (2004). In addition, it is assumed that jobs can be paused and be resumed at a later time.

Resource allocations are interpreted as contracts. This means, that a seller has to provide the allocated resources. In case of failure, the seller has to offer alternative resources or compensate the buyer for the failed allocation.

As in any combinatorial auction, the design of MACE mainly affects three components: (i) the communication language which defines how bids can be formalized, (ii) the winner determination problem, and (iii) the pricing scheme to determine net payments. As such, the following description of MACE is structured as follows: First, a bidding language is introduced which supports multi-attribute combinatorial bids including co-allocation constraints. Second, a winner determination model (allocation rule) is proposed that attains an efficient allocation if agents bid truthfully. Finally, a family of pricing schemes is outlined to incentivize agents to reveal their private information.

5.2.1 Bidding Language

The design of an auction that meets the requirements specified in Section 4.2 requires an expressive bidding language. The following notation is used to define such a language:

Let $\mathcal{N}$ be a set of N buyers and $\mathcal{M}$ be a set of M sellers, where $n \in \mathcal{N}$ defines an arbitrary buyer and $m \in \mathcal{M}$ an arbitrary seller. There are G discrete resources $\mathcal{G} = \{g_1, \ldots, g_G\}$ with $g_k \in \mathcal{G}$ and a set of D bundles $\mathcal{S} = \{S_1, \ldots, S_D\}$ with $S_j \in \mathcal{S}$ and $S_j \subseteq \mathcal{G}$ as a subset of resources. For instance, $S_j = \{g_k, g_l\}$ denotes that the bundle S_j consists of two resources g_k and g_l, where g_k could be a computation service and g_l a storage service.

A resource g_k has a set of A_k cardinal quality attributes $\mathcal{A}_{g_k} = (a_1^k, \ldots, a_{A_k}^k)$ where $a_i^k \in \mathcal{A}_{g_k}$ represents the $i.th$ attribute of the resource g_k. For instance, in the context of a Grid resource, a quality attribute can be the $size$ of a storage service.

A buyer n can specify the minimal required quality characteristics for a bundle $S_j \in \mathcal{S}$ with $q_n^N(S_j, g_k, a_i^k) \geq 0$, where $g_k \in S_j$ is a resource of the bundle S_j and $a_i^k \in \mathcal{A}_{g_k}$ is an attribute of the resource g_k. For instance, the minimal required size of a storage service $g_k \in S_j$ can be denoted by $q_n^N(S_j, g_k, a_i^k) = 200\,GB$. Accordingly, a seller m can specify the maximum offered quality characteristics with $q_m^M(S_j, g_k, a_i^k) \geq 0$. The quality attributes are assumed to be cardinal numbers. The characteristics have to satisfy $q_n^N(\cdot) \geq \overline{q_n^N}(\cdot)$ if the first quality characteristic $q_n^N(\cdot)$ satisfies at least the second one $\overline{q_n^N}(\cdot)$. These quality characteristics are also used to specify a value for the agent's network connection. For instance, this can be used to denote the uplink and downlink rates of the given network connection.

Parameter	Meaning
$n \in \mathcal{N}, m \in \mathcal{M}$	Buyers and sellers
$g_k \in \mathcal{G}, \mathcal{G} = \{g_1, \ldots, g_G\}$	Resources
$S_j \in \mathcal{S}, S_j \subseteq \mathcal{G}, \mathcal{S} = \{S_1, \ldots, S_D\}$	Bundles
$a_i^k \in \mathcal{A}_{g_k}, \mathcal{A}_{g_k} = (a_1^k, \ldots, a_{A_k}^k)$	Attributes of a resource
$q_n^N(S_j, g_k, a_i^k) \geq 0, q_m^M(S_j, g_k, a_i^k) \geq 0,$ $q_n^N(S_j, g_k, a_i^k), q_m^M(S_j, g_k, a_i^k) \in \mathbb{R}$	Quality characteristics
$\gamma_n(S_j, g_k) \geq 0, \gamma_n(S_j, g_k) \in \mathbb{N}$	Number of co-allocations
$\varphi_n(S_j, g_k, g_l) \in \{0, 1\}$	Coupling of resources
$t \in \mathcal{T}, \mathcal{T} = (0, \ldots, T-1), t \in \mathbb{N}$	Time slots
$s_n(S_j) \geq 0, s_n(S_j) \in \mathbb{N}$	Required slots
$e_n^N(S_j), e_m^M(S_j) \geq 0, e_n^N(S_j), e_m^M(S_j) \in \mathbb{N}$	Earliest time slot
$l_n^N(S_j), l_m^M(S_j) \geq 0, l_n^N(S_j), l_m^M(S_j) \in \mathbb{N}$	Latest time slot
$v_n(S_j) \geq 0, v_n(S_j) \in \mathbb{R}$	Valuation of a buyer per slot
$r_m(S_j) \geq 0, r_m(S_j) \in \mathbb{R}$	Reservation price of a seller per slot

Table 5.6: Notation of the bidding language of MACE

For each resource $g_k \in S_j$, a buyer n can specify the maximum number of co-allocations in each time slot with $\gamma_n(S_j, g_k) \geq 0$. This means, that a buyer n can limit the number of sellers that provide the required resource g_k. Let $\gamma_n(S_j, g_k) = K$ if the resource g_k has no divisibility restrictions, where K is a large enough constant[9]. The coupling of two resources in a bundle is represented by the binary variable $\varphi_n(S_j, g_k, g_l)$ where $\varphi_n(S_j, g_k, g_l) = 1$ if resources g_k and g_l have to be allocated from the same bundle bid of a seller and $\varphi_n(S_j, g_k, g_l) = 0$ otherwise. It is assumed that all resources offered in a bundle are located on the same machine.

Resources in the form of a bundle S_j can be assigned to a set of maximal T discrete time slots $\mathcal{T} = (0, \ldots, T-1)$, where $t \in \mathcal{T}$ specifies one single time slot. A buyer n can specify the minimum required number of time slots $s_n(S_j) \geq 0$ for a bundle S_j. The earliest time slot for any allocatable bundle S_j can be specified by $e_n^N(S_j) \geq 0$ for a buyer n and $e_m^M(S_j) \geq 0$ for a seller m; the latest possible allocatable time slot by $l_n^N(S_j) \geq 0$ for a buyer n and by $l_m^M(S_j) \geq 0$ for a seller m.

A buyer n can express the valuation for a single slot of a bundle S_j by $v_n(S_j) \geq 0$, whereat $v_n(S_j)$ denotes the maximum price for which the buyer n is willing to buy. The reservation price for allocating a single slot of a bundle S_j is denoted by $r_m(S_j) \geq 0$. This price represents the minimum price for which the seller m is willing to sell.

Table 5.6 summarizes this notation. On the basis of these parameters, an atomic bid of a buyer is defined as follows:

Definition 5.1: MACE Atomic Buyer Bid
In MACE, an atomic bid B_n of a buyer n is defined as

$$B_n(S_j) = \Big(v_n(S_j), s_n(S_j), e_n^N(S_j), l_n^N(S_j),$$
$$\big(q_n^N(S_j, \bar{g}_1, a_1^1), \ldots, q_n^N(S_j, \bar{g}_l, a_{A_{\bar{g}_l}}^l) \big), \big(\gamma_n(S_j, \bar{g}_1), \ldots, \gamma_n(S_j, \bar{g}_l) \big),$$
$$\big(\varphi_n(S_j, \bar{g}_1, \bar{g}_2), \varphi_n(S_j, \bar{g}_1, \bar{g}_3), \ldots, \varphi_n(S_j, \bar{g}_1, \bar{g}_l), \ldots, \varphi_n(S_j, \bar{g}_{l-1}, \bar{g}_l) \big) \Big),$$

---

[9]The constant K has to be greater than the total number of seller bids.

where $\mathcal{G}_{S_j} = \{\bar{g}_1, \ldots, \bar{g}_l\}$ are the resources of the bundle S_j.

It is to note that the atomic bid can also be represented in a more compact way. For instance, the encoding of the coupling conditions $\varphi_n(\cdot)$ can be restricted to cases with $\varphi_n(\cdot) = 1$. For a better readability, however, the atomic bid is formalized in this detailed way.

An example for a practical application of an atomic bid is given in the following Example 5.7.

Example 5.7: MACE Atomic Buyer Bid
As an example, consider the bid $B_n(S_1) = (1, 4, 2, 10, (3000, 30), (2, 4), 0)$ with $S_1 = \{g_1, g_2\}$. Agent n wants to buy a bundle S_1 that consists of a computation service g_1 with one attribute $A_{g_1} = (Speed)$ and a storage service g_2 with one attribute $A_{g_2} = (Space)$. The bid expresses that a buyer n wants to buy the bundle S_1 and has a valuation of $v_n(S_1) = 4$ per slot for it. The requested computation service g_1 should at least be capable of providing 3000 MIPS[10], and the storage service g_2 should have at least 30 GB of available space. The computation service g_1 can be split in 2 parts at the most, while storage service g_2 can run on 4 different machines simultaneously. Furthermore, neither of the services have coupling requirements. The buyer requires 4 slots of this bundle which must be fulfilled within a time range of slots 2 and 10.

In order to allow buyers to express substitutes over a set of resources, MACE supports the submission of XOR concatenated atomic bids.

Definition 5.2: MACE XOR Buyer Bid
A XOR bid of a buyer n is defined as

$$\mathcal{B}_n = \big(B_n(S_j) \oplus \ldots \oplus B_n(S_k)\big).$$

The total number of atomic bids that are concatenated by the XOR operator can be restricted by the auctioneer.

The sellers' bids are formalized in a similar way to those of the buyers. However, they do not include maximum divisibility and coupling properties and assume that the number of time slots is equal to the given time range. An atomic bid for a seller is defined as follows:

Definition 5.3: MACE Atomic Seller Bid
An atomic bid B_m for a seller m is defined as

$$B_m(S_j) = \Big(r_m(S_j), e_m^M(S_j), l_m^M(S_j), q_m^M(S_j, \bar{g}_1, a_1^1), \ldots, \big(q_m^M(S_j, \bar{g}_l, a_{A_{\bar{g}_l}}^l)\big)\Big),$$

where $\mathcal{G}_{S_j} = \{\bar{g}_1, \ldots, \bar{g}_l\}$ are the resources that are part of the bundle S_j.

Example 5.8: MACE Atomic Seller Bid
Seller m's bid is given by $B_m(S_1) = (4, 2, 8, (4000, 20))$ with $S_1 = \{g_1, g_2\}$ that consists of a computation service g_1 with an attribute $A_{g_1} = (Speed)$ and a storage service g_2 with an attribute $A_{g_2} = (Space)$. The bid expresses that the seller m offers the bundle S_1 and has a reservation price of $r_m(S_1) = 4$ per slot for it. The offered computation service g_1 can perform 4000 MIPS and the storage service g_2 has 20 GB of free capacity. The seller offers the bundle between time slot 2 and time slot 8.

---

[10]Million instructions per second (MIPS) is a measure for a computer's processor speed.

For sellers as resource providers, a XOR operator is not necessary. Grid resources are non-storable commodities. For instance, a computation service currently available cannot be stored and used at a later time. As such, the bidding space for sellers is restricted to OR bids.

Definition 5.4: MACE OR Seller Bid
An OR bid of a seller m is defined as

$$\mathcal{B}_m = \left(B_m(S_j) \vee \ldots \vee B_m(S_k) \right).$$

The total number of atomic bids that are concatenated by the OR operator can be restricted by the auctioneer.

In the following subsections, it is assumed that the bid elicitation has already taken place. This means, buyers and sellers submitted their preferences by means of the bidding language to the auctioneer. For formulating bids, agents may use preference elicitation techniques to formalize their preferences (Conen and Sandholm 2001) or may use an autonomous bidding agent that takes over their bidding strategies.

5.2.2   Winner Determination

Based upon this bidding language, the winner determination problem of MACE (MACE allocation problem, MAP) can be formulated. Following the previous winner determination models, MAP is formulated as a linear mixed integer program.

5.2.2.1   Mixed Integer Program Formulation

For formalizing the model, the decision variables $x_n(S_j)$, $z_{n,t}(S_j)$, $y_{m,n,t}(S_j)$, and $d_{m,n,t}(S_j)$ have to be introduced. The binary variable $x_n(S_j) \in \{0,1\}$ denotes whether bundle S_j is allocated to buyer n $(x_n(S_j) = 1)$ or not $(x_n(S_j) = 0)$. Furthermore, the binary variable $z_{n,t}(S_j) \in \{0,1\}$ is assigned to a buyer n and is associated in the same way as $x_n(S_j)$ with the allocation of S_j in time slot t. For a seller m, the real-valued variable $y_{m,n,t}(S_j)$ with $0 \leq y_{m,n,t}(S_j) \leq 1$ indicates the percentage contingent of bundle S_j allocated to the buyer n in time slot t. For example, $y_{m,n,t}(S_j) = 0.5$ denotes that 50 percent of the quality characteristics of bundle S_j are allocated from seller m to buyer n in time slot t. Suppose a seller is offering a storage service $S_2 = \{g_2\}$ with 30 GB of free space. A partial allocation of 15 GB from seller m to buyer n in time slot t would lead to $y_{m,n,t}(S_2) = 0.5$. The binary variable $d_{m,n,t}(S_j) \in \{0,1\}$ is linked with $y_{m,n,t}(S_j)$ and denotes whether the seller m allocates bundle S_j to buyer n in time slot t $(d_{m,n,t}(S_j) = 1)$ or not $(d_{m,n,t}(S_j) = 0)$.

By means of these variables, MAP is formulated as follows (Schnizler et al. 2004; Schnizler et al. 2006b):

$$\max \sum_{n \in \mathcal{N}} \sum_{S_j \in \mathcal{S}} \sum_{t \in \mathcal{T}} v_n(S_j) z_{n,t}(S_j) - \sum_{m \in \mathcal{M}} \sum_{n \in \mathcal{N}} \sum_{S_j \in \mathcal{S}} \sum_{t \in \mathcal{T}} r_m(S_j) y_{m,n,t}(S_j) \qquad (5.24)$$

$$\text{s.t.} \sum_{S_j \in \mathcal{S}} x_n(S_j) \leq 1, \forall n \in \mathcal{N} \qquad (5.25)$$

$$\sum_{t \in \mathcal{T}} z_{n,t}(S_j) - x_n(S_j)s_n(S_j) = 0, \forall n \in \mathcal{N}, \forall S_j \in \mathcal{S} \qquad (5.26)$$

$$\sum_{n \in \mathcal{N}} y_{m,n,t}(S_j) \leq 1, \forall m \in \mathcal{M}, \forall S_j \in \mathcal{S}, \forall t \in \mathcal{T} \qquad (5.27)$$

The objective function 5.24 maximizes the surplus V^*, which is defined as the difference between the sum of the buyers' valuations $v_n(S_j)$ and the sum of the sellers' reservation prices $r_m(S_j)$. Assuming bidders are truthful, the objective function reflects the goal of maximizing social welfare. The first Constraint 5.25 guarantees that each buyer n can be allocated to one only bundle S_j. This constraint is necessary to fulfill the XOR constraint of a buyer bid. Constraint 5.26 ensures that for any allocated bundle S_j, a buyer n receives exactly the required slots within the time set $\mathcal{T}$.

For each time slot t, Constraint 5.27 ensures that each seller cannot allocate more than the seller possesses. The formulation of this constraint implicates that a seller cannot fully allocate two resources to two different buyers in time slot t. For instance, suppose a seller offers the bundle $S_j = \{g_k, g_l\}$. An allocation of the resource g_k to buyer 1 (with $y_{m,1,t}(S_j) = 1$) and an allocation of g_l to buyer 2 (with $y_{m,2,t}(S_j) = 1$) is not possible. This restriction is applied to simplify the model. However, the above mentioned allocation can be attained by submitting an OR concatenated bid on the bundles $S_n = \{g_k\}$ and $S_i = \{g_l\}$.

The constraints 5.25 – 5.27 consider the basic allocation functionality of the exchange. In designing an adequate mechanism for the Grid, quality characteristics and dependencies between resources must also to be addressed:

$$\sum_{S_j \ni g_k} z_{n,t}(S_j)q_n^N(S_j, g_k, a_i^k) - \sum_{S_j \ni g_k}\sum_{m \in \mathcal{M}} y_{m,n,t}(S_j)q_m^M(S_j, g_k, a_i^k) \leq 0,$$
$$\forall n \in \mathcal{N}, \forall g_k \in \mathcal{G}, \forall a_i^k \in \mathcal{A}_{g_k}, \forall t \in \mathcal{T} \qquad (5.28)$$

$$\sum_{S_j \ni g_k}\sum_{m \in \mathcal{M}} d_{m,n,t}(S_j) - \sum_{S_j \ni g_k} \gamma_n(S_j, g_k)z_{n,t}(S_j) \leq 0,$$
$$\forall n \in \mathcal{N}, \forall g_k \in \mathcal{G}, \forall t \in \mathcal{T} \qquad (5.29)$$

$$\sum_{S_j \ni g_k, g_l} \varphi_n(S_j, g_k, g_l)\left(\sum_{S_j \ni g_k} d_{m,n,t}(S_j) - \sum_{S_j \ni g_l} d_{m,n,t}(S_j)\right) = 0,$$
$$\forall n \in \mathcal{N}, \forall m \in \mathcal{M}, \forall g_k, g_l \in \mathcal{G}, \forall t \in \mathcal{T} \qquad (5.30)$$

$$\sum_{S_j \ni g_k, g_l} \varphi_n(S_j, g_k, g_l)\left(\sum_{S_j \ni g_k}\sum_{m \in \mathcal{M}} d_{m,n,t}(S_j) + \sum_{S_j \ni g_l}\sum_{m \in \mathcal{M}} d_{m,n,t}(S_j) - 2z_{n,t}(S_j)\right) \leq 0,$$
$$\forall n \in \mathcal{N}, \forall g_k, g_l \in \mathcal{G}, \forall t \in \mathcal{T} \qquad (5.31)$$

Constraint 5.28 guarantees that for any allocated bundle in an arbitrary time slot t, all required resources have to be fulfilled in the same slot in at least the demanded qualities.

Constraint 5.29 ensures that a resource will be provided by at most $\gamma_n(S_j, g_k)$ different suppliers. For simplicity, it is assumed that a resource g_k with restricted co-allocations is not part of further XOR concatenated bids of the buyer n. Furthermore, resources with co-allocations cannot be allocated as free-disposal items. As an example, suppose a buyer n values $S_j = \{g_k\}$ with $v_n(S_j) = 1$ and $S_i = \{g_l\}$ with $v_n(S_i) = 10$. For bundle S_j, the buyer has co-allocation restrictions with $\gamma_n(S_j, g_l) = 1$. A seller m that offers $S_t = \{g_k, g_l\}$ cannot allocate the resource g_l to buyer n as this would imply a free-disposal allocation of the restricted resource g_k.

Constraints 5.30 and 5.31 account for the coupling of two resources. Constraint 5.30 ensures that two resources must be provided by the same seller, in case they should be coupled. This constraint alone does not suffice the coupling requirements since it would be possible for two sellers to co-allocate a coupled computation service with 3000 MIPS and a storage service with 30 GB in different quality characteristics. For instance, MAP could allocate a computation service with 2998 MIPS and a storage service with 1 GB from one seller, and a computation service with 2 MIPS and a storage service with 29 GB from another. To exclude these undesirable allocations, Constraint 5.31 imposes the restriction that coupled resources cannot be co-allocated. Simplifying the model, this also includes free-disposal resources. For instance, if the computation service with 3000 MIPS and the storage service with 30 GB are allocated from one particular seller as a bundle, another seller cannot allocate a bundle containing a rendering service and another storage service to the same buyer. However, the seller may allocate any bundle without a storage and computation service to the buyer, e.g., the rendering service alone. Furthermore, it is assumed that coupled resources are only part of one particular atomic bid $B_n(S_j)$ in case a buyer submits two XOR concatenated bids containing coupled resources.

The time restrictions of the bids are given by:

$$\left(e_n^N(S_j) - t\right) z_{n,t}(S_j) \le 0, \forall n \in \mathcal{N}, \forall S_j \in \mathcal{S}, \forall t \in \mathcal{T} \tag{5.32}$$

$$\left(t - l_n^N(S_j)\right) z_{n,t}(S_j) \le 0, \forall n \in \mathcal{N}, \forall S_j \in \mathcal{S}, \forall t \in \mathcal{T} \tag{5.33}$$

$$\left(e_m^N(S_j) - t\right) \sum_{n \in \mathcal{N}} y_{m,n,t}(S_j) \le 0, \forall m \in \mathcal{M}, \forall S_j \in \mathcal{S}, \forall t \in \mathcal{T} \tag{5.34}$$

$$\left(t - l_m^M(S_j)\right) \sum_{n \in \mathcal{N}} y_{m,n,t}(S_j) \le 0, \forall m \in \mathcal{M}, \forall S_j \in \mathcal{S}, \forall t \in \mathcal{T} \tag{5.35}$$

Essentially, constraints 5.32 – 5.35 indicate that slots cannot be allocated before the earliest and after the latest time slot of either a buyer (Constraint 5.32 and 5.33) or a seller (Constraint 5.34 and 5.35).

Finally, the establishment of the relationship between the real valued decision variable $y_{m,n,t}(S_j)$ and the binary variable $d_{m,n,t}(S_j)$ needs to be addressed and the decision variables of the optimization problem have to be defined:

$$y_{m,n,t}(S_j) - d_{m,n,t}(S_j) \leq 0, \forall n \in \mathcal{N}, \forall m \in \mathcal{M}, \forall S_j \in \mathcal{S}, \forall t \in \mathcal{T} \qquad (5.36)$$

$$d_{m,n,t}(S_j) - y_{m,n,t}(S_j) < 1, \forall n \in \mathcal{N}, \forall m \in \mathcal{M}, \forall S_j \in \mathcal{S}, \forall t \in \mathcal{T} \qquad (5.37)$$

$$x_n(S_j) \in \{0, 1\}, \forall n \in \mathcal{N}, \forall S_j \in \mathcal{S} \qquad (5.38)$$

$$z_{n,t}(S_j) \in \{0, 1\}, \forall n \in \mathcal{N}, \forall S_j \in \mathcal{S}, \forall t \in \mathcal{T} \qquad (5.39)$$

$$y_{m,n,t}(S_j) \geq 0, \forall n \in \mathcal{N}, \forall m \in \mathcal{M}, \forall S_j \in \mathcal{S}, \forall t \in \mathcal{T} \qquad (5.40)$$

$$d_{m,n,t}(S_j) \in \{0, 1\}, \forall n \in \mathcal{N}, \forall m \in \mathcal{M}, \forall S_j \in \mathcal{S}, \forall t \in \mathcal{T} \qquad (5.41)$$

Constraints 5.36 and 5.37 incorporate an `if-then-else` constraint. If a seller m partially allocates a bundle S_j to a single buyer n ($y_{m,n,t}(S_j) > 0$), the binary variable $d_{m,n,t}(S_j)$ has to be $d_{m,n,t}(S_j) = 1$ (Constraint 5.36); otherwise, it has to be $d_{m,n,t}(S_j) = 0$ (Constraint 5.37). Finally, the constraints 5.38 – 5.41 specify the decision variables of the optimization problem.

As multiple solutions may exist that maximize the objective function, ties are broken in favor of maximizing the number of traded bundles and then at random. A special case of tie breaking occurs if the total surplus is zero. This can be the case if buyers and sellers balance their payments or no possible trade can be matched. In such a scenario, the allocation with the balanced traders is selected.

Following the discussion on combinatorial auctions and exchanges, the presented winner determination problem is also $\mathcal{NP}$-complete.

Theorem 5.3: MAP Complexity
The MACE allocation problem (MAP) is $\mathcal{NP}$-complete.

Proof-Sketch. CAP can be reduced to MAP. Obviously, any CAP instance (multiple buyers, one seller with a zero reservation price, no attributes and no coupling constraints) can be solved by MAP. As such, MAP is also $\mathcal{NP}$-complete. □

5.2.2.2 Example

Suppose there are two buyers $1, 2$ and two sellers $1, 2$ that can bid on any combination of a computation service g_1 and a storage service g_2. Both services each have single attributes, namely $a_1^1 = (Speed)$ and $a_1^2 = (Size)$. The buyers and sellers can submit bids on the bundles $S_1 = \{g_1\}$, $S_2 = \{g_2\}$, and $S_3 = \{g_1, g_2\}$. The bundles can be allocated within a time range $\mathcal{T} = (0, \ldots, 4)$ of $T = 5$ slots. Each buyer submits a set of XOR bids (shown in Table 5.7) and each seller a set of OR bids (see Table 5.8).

For instance, buyer 2 submits two XOR concatenated bids on the bundles S_1 and S_3. The buyer has a valuation of $v_2(S_1) = 3$ for the bundle S_1 which consists of the computation service g_1. The service must have at least 400 GB of free space and can be allocated between the slots $e_2^N(S_1) = 1$ and $l_2^N(S_1) = 4$. The buyer requires $s_2(S_1) = 3$ slots of the service and has no co-allocation restrictions.

$\mathcal{N}$	S_j	$v_n(S_j)$	$q_n^N(S_j, g_k, a_i^k)$	$e_n^N(S_j)$	$l_n^N(S_j)$	$s_n(S_j)$	$\gamma_n(S_j, g_k)$	$\varphi_n(S_j, g_i, g_j)$
1	S_3	2	$g_1 \to 500, g_2 \to 15$	0	4	2		$g_1, g_2 \to 1$
2	S_1	3	$g_1 \to 400$	1	4	3		
	S_3	2	$g_1 \to 300, g_2 \to 25$	0	4	2	$g_2 \to 1$	

Table 5.7: MACE example: XOR bids of the buyers

$\mathcal{M}$	S_j	$r_m(S_j)$	$q_m^M(S_j, g_k, a_i^k)$	$e_m^M(S_j)$	$l_m^M(S_j)$
1	S_3	1	$g_1 \to 500; g_2 \to 40$	0	4
2	S_1	2	$g_1 \to 1000$	0	3
	S_3	2	$g_1 \to 700; g_2 \to 20$	1	4

Table 5.8: MACE example: OR bids of the sellers

An optimal solution for the winner determination problem is an allocation of the bundles S_3 and S_1 to the buyers 1 and 2 with $x_1(S_3) = 1$ and $x_2(S_1) = 1$. Seller 1 is part of the allocation with bundle S_3 and seller 2 with bundle S_1. The maximized value V^* of the winner determination problem is $V^* = 8.6$. The corresponding schedule for this allocation is given in Table 5.9.

Buyer 1 receives bundle $S_3 = \{g_1, g_2\}$ from seller 1 in time slots 0 and 1. The bundle is allocated from one seller and, as such, the buyer's requested coupling property is satisfied. Buyer 2 receives requested computation service $S_1 = \{g_1\}$ in time slots 1, 2, and 3.

Although buyer 1 does not require the entire allocated space of the storage service g_2, a partial execution of the bundle is not possible due to the computation service g_1 requirements. Bundles can only be partially executed as a whole. If an isolated partial execution of single resources in a bundle would be possible, these single resources would also have to be valued. However, as resources may be complementarities or substitutes, valuation and reservation prices for a single resource of a bundle do not always exist (Milgrom 2004). As such, resources of a bundle cannot be partially executed.

5.2.3 Pricing

The outcome of MAP is allocative efficient as long as buyers and sellers reveal their valuations truthfully. The incentive to set bids according to the valuation is induced by an adequate pricing mechanism.

As outlined in Section 5.1.3.2, the design of a price mechanism for an exchange is a challenging problem. The VCG schema cannot be applied as it runs a deficit and requires outside subsidiary. On the other hand, the approximated VCG mechanism is budget-balanced and approximately efficient. However, the pricing scheme still requires $I + 1$ instances of MAP to be solved if I agents are part of the allocation. As a consequence, an alternative pricing scheme is designed that is computationally more efficient and still attains desirable economic properties.

$\mathcal{M}$	S	$t = 0$	$t = 1$	$t = 2$	$t = 3$
1	S_3	$n = 1 : g_1 \to 500, g_2 \to 40$	$n = 1 : g_1 \to 500, g_2 \to 40$		
2	S_1		$n = 2 : g_1 \to 400$	$n = 2 : g_1 \to 400$	$n = 2 : g_1 \to 400$

Table 5.9: MACE example: Allocation

In the following paragraphs, the VCG mechanism and the approximated VCG scheme are both adapted for MACE. These pricing mechanisms serve as an economic benchmark. After that, the k-pricing scheme is introduced as a novel and adequate pricing scheme for MACE.

5.2.3.1 VCG Pricing

The application of the VCG mechanism for MACE is derivated from single-unit combinatorial exchanges as outlined in Section 5.1.3.2.

Following the VCG formalism, let V^* be the surplus of the optimal allocation $\mathcal{S}^*$. Furthermore, let $(V_{-n})^*$ be the value of the allocation without buyer n and let $(V_{-m})^*$ be the value of the allocation without seller m. The VCG discounts of the agents are given as $\Delta_{VICK,n}^N = V^* - (V_{-n})^*$ for a buyer n and as $\Delta_{VICK,m}^M = V^* - (V_{-m})^*$ for a seller m. On the basis of these discounts, the price $p_{VICK,n}^N(S_j)$ for a bundle S_j and a buyer n is calculated as

$$p_{VICK,n}^N(S_j) = v_n(S_j)s_n(S_j) - \Delta_{VICK,n}^N, \tag{5.42}$$

and the price $p_{VICK,m}^M(S_j)$ for a bundle S_j and a seller m by

$$p_{VICK,m}^M(S_j) = \begin{cases} r_m(S_j) \sum_{n \in N} \sum_{t \in T} y_{m,n,t}(S_j) + \frac{\Delta_{VICK,m}^M}{\alpha} & \text{if } \alpha \neq 0 \\ 0 & \text{otherwise.} \end{cases} \tag{5.43}$$

The term $v_n(S_j)$ denotes the valuation of a buyer n for a single slot. As such, it has to be multiplied by total number of slots $s_n(S_j)$. Likewise, the term $r_m(S_j)$ denotes the reservation price of a seller m for fully allocating his bundle in a single time slot. As such, it has to be multiplied by $\sum_{n \in N} y_{m,n,t}(S_j)$ representing the partial allocation of a seller m in time slot t to all buyers. As sellers submit OR concatenated bids, they can participate in the allocation with multiple bundles. Because the Vickrey discount refers to the seller's overall impact, the discount has to be portioned among all of the seller's successful bids. Thus, the discount is divided by α, where α is the number of bundles with which a seller m is participating in the allocation.

It is to note that the bundle prices of a seller which has several bundles in the allocation may not reflect the VCG impact of each bundle exactly. However, the sum of the bundle prices of a seller represents the impact of his presence. As a result, the desirable economic properties of the VCG mechanism are still valid.

In contrast to the previous sections, it is refrained from using the notation S_m^* to denote a bundle that is allocated to an agent m in the optimal outcome. As sellers may allocate several bundles simultaneously (OR bids), the notation is not applicable anymore. As a consequence, the function $p_{VICK,m}^M(S_j)$ computes the price for any bundle $S_j \in \mathcal{S}$ that is allocated by seller m. In order to be consistent, the same notation is also applied for buyers.

Example 5.9: MAP VCG Pricing
The application of the VCG pricing scheme to the example presented in Section 5.2.2.2 ($V^* = 8.6$) results in the prices $p_{VICK,i}(S_i^*)$ and the discounts $\Delta_{VICK,i}$ shown in Table 5.10 with $\bar{v}_n(S_j) = v_n(S_j)s_n(S_j)$ and $\bar{r}_m(S_j) = \sum_{n \in N} \sum_{t \in T} y_{m,n,t}(S_j)r_m(S_j)$.

Aggregating the net payments of the example leads to a negative value with $2 + 2.4 - (3 + 6.25) = -4.85$. In this case, the auctioneer has to subsidize the exchange. Naturally, such a situation cannot be sustained for a long period of time, making the VCG mechanism unfeasible.

$\mathcal{N}$	$(V_{-n})^*$	$\bar{v}_n(S_j)$	$\Delta^N_{VICK,n}$	$p^N_{VICK,n}(S_j)$	$\mathcal{M}$	$(V_{-m})^*$	$\bar{r}_m(S_j)$	$\Delta^M_{VICK,m}$	$p^M_{VICK,m}(S_j)$
1	6.6	4	2	2	1	7.6	2	1	3
2	2	9	6.6	2.4	2	4.75	2.4	3.85	6.25

Table 5.10: MACE example: VCG discounts and prices

5.2.3.2 Approximated VCG Pricing

On the basis of the VCG pricing rule for MACE, the adaption of the approximated VCG schema is intuitive: Let $\bar{\Delta}^N_n$ be the approximated VCG discount of a buyer and let $\bar{\Delta}^M_m$ be the approximated VCG discount of a seller. Following the derivation of the pricing schema as outlined in Section 5.1.3.2, the payment for a buyer is computed as

$$p^N_{AV,n}(S_j) = v_n(S_j)s_n(S_j) - \bar{\Delta}^N_n, \qquad (5.44)$$

where $v_n(S_j)$ denotes the valuation and $s_n(S_j)$ the required slots for the bundle S_j. Likewise, the sellers' payments are computed as

$$p^M_{AV,m}(S_j) = \begin{cases} r_m(S_j) \sum_{n\in\mathcal{N}} \sum_{t\in T} y_{m,n,t}(S_j) + \frac{\bar{\Delta}^M_m}{\alpha} & \text{if } \alpha \neq 0 \\ 0 & \text{otherwise.} \end{cases} \qquad (5.45)$$

The term $r_m(S_j)$ denotes the reservation price of seller m, $\sum_{n\in\mathcal{N}} y_{m,n,t}(S_j)$ the partial allocation in a time slot t and α is the number of bundles with which a seller m is participating in the allocation.

Example 5.10: MAP Approximated VCG Pricing

Applying these approximations on the example presented in Section 5.2.2.2, the approximated discounts $\bar{\Delta}_i$ using the quadratic error function and the prices $p_i(S_j)$ can be determined as shown in Table 5.11. In this case, the exchange does not have to endow the agents as the net payments from the exchange are zero.

$\mathcal{N}$	$(V_{-n})^*$	$\bar{v}_n(S_j)$	$\Delta^N_{VICK,n}$	$p^N_{VICK,n}(S_j)$	$\mathcal{M}$	$(V_{-m})^*$	$\bar{r}_m(S_j)$	$\Delta^M_{VICK,m}$	$p^M_{VICK,m}(S_j)$
1	6.6	4	0.72	3.28	1	7.6	2	0	2
2	2	9	5.32	3.68	2	4.75	2.4	2.57	4.97

Table 5.11: MACE example: Approximated VCG discounts and prices

Although Parkes et al. (2001) show approximative efficiency for this pricing schema, the computational effort that is required to compute an outcome is still very high. The need of a more computationally efficient pricing scheme gave rise to the development of a k-pricing scheme which is presented in the next section.

5.2.3.3 K-Pricing

The underlying idea of the k-pricing scheme is to determine prices for a buyer and a seller on the basis of the difference between their bids (Satherthwaite and Williams 1993). For instance, suppose that a buyer n wants to purchase a storage service for $v_n(\cdot) = 5$ and a seller m wants to sell a storage service for at least $r_m(\cdot) = 4$. The difference between these bids is $\beta = 1$, where β is the surplus of this transaction that can be distributed among the participants.

For a single commodity exchange, the k-pricing scheme can be formalized as follows: let $v_n(S_j) = a$ be the valuation of a buyer n and $r_m(S_j) = b$ be the reservation price of the buyer's counterpart m. It is assumed that $a \geq b$, which implicates that the buyer has a valuation for the commodity that is at least as high as the seller's reservation price. Otherwise, no trade would occur. The price for a buyer n and a seller m can be calculated by $p(S_j) = ka + (1 - k)b$ with $0 \leq k \leq 1$.

The k-pricing schema can also be applied to a multi-attribute combinatorial exchange: In each time slot t in which a bundle S_j is allocated from one or more sellers, the surplus generated by this allocation is distributed among a buyer and the sellers. Suppose a buyer n receives a computation service $S_1 = \{g_1\}$ with 1000 MIPS in time slot 4 and values this slot with $v_n(S_1) = 5$. The buyer obtains the computation service $S_1 = \{g_1\}$ by a co-allocation from seller 1 (400 MIPS) with a reservation price of $r_1(S_1) = 1$ and from seller 2 (600 MIPS) with $r_2(S_1) = 2$. The distributable surplus of this allocation is $\beta_{n,4}(S_1) = 5 - (1 + 2) = 2$. Buyer n gets $k\beta_{n,4}(S_1)$ of this surplus, i.e., the price buyer n has to pay for this slot $t = 4$ is

$$p_{k,n,4}^N(S_j) = v(S_1) - k\beta_{n,4}(S_1).$$

Furthermore, the sellers have to divide the other part of this surplus, i.e., $(1 - k)\beta_{n,4}(S_1)$. This will be done by considering each proportion a seller's bid has on the surplus. In the example, this proportion $0 \leq o_{m,n,t}(S_j) \leq 1$ for seller 1 is $o_{1,n,4}(S_1) = \frac{1}{3}$ and for seller 2 is $o_{2,n,4}(S_1) = \frac{2}{3}$. The price a seller m receives for a single slot $t = 4$ is consequently calculated as

$$p_{k,n,4}^M(S_j) = r_m(S_1) + (1 - k)\beta_{n,4}(S_1)o_{m,n,4}(S_1).$$

Expanding this scheme to a set of time slots, co-allocations, and the allocation of different bundles to a buyer results in the following formalization: let $\beta_{n,t}(S_j)$ be the surplus for a bundle S_j of a buyer n with all corresponding sellers for a time slot t:

$$\beta_{n,t}(S_j) = z_{n,t}(S_j)v_n(S_j) - \sum_{m \in M}\sum_{S_l \in S} y_{m,n,t}(S_l)r_m(S_l) \qquad (5.46)$$

The iteration over $\sum_{S_l \in S} y_{m,n,t}(S_l)r_m(S_l)$ is required, as one seller may allocate a subset S_l of the required bundle S_j to a buyer. For instance, this is the case if a buyer requires $S_3 = \{g_1, g_2\}$ and two sellers allocate $S_1 = \{g_1\}$ and $S_2 = \{g_2\}$.

For the entire job (i.e., all time slots), the price for a buyer n is calculated as

$$p_{k,n}^N(S_j) = x_n(S_j)v_n(S_j)s_n(S_j) - k\sum_{t \in T}\beta_{n,t}(S_j). \qquad (5.47)$$

This means, that the difference between the valuation for all slots $v_n(S_j)s_n(S_j)$ of the bundle S_j and the k-th proportion of the sum over all time slots of the corresponding surpluses is determined.

The price of a seller m is calculated in a similar way: First of all, the proportion $o_{m,n,t}(S_j)$ of a seller m allocating a bundle S_j to the buyer n in time slot t is given by

$$o_{m,n,t}(S_j) = \begin{cases} y_{m,n,t}(S_j)r_m(S_j)/ \displaystyle\sum_{m \in MS_l \in S}\sum y_{m,n,t}(S_l)r_m(S_l) & \text{if } y_{m,n,t}(S_j)r_m(S_j) > 0 \\ 0 & \text{otherwise.} \end{cases}$$

$$(5.48)$$

$\mathcal{N}$	S_j	$\bar{v}_n(S_j)$	$p_{0.5,n}^N(S_j)$	$\mathcal{M}$	S_j	$\bar{r}_m(S_j)$	$p_{0.5,n}^M(S_j)$
1	S_3	4	3	1	S_3	2	3
2	S_1	9	5.7	2	S_1	2.4	5.7

Table 5.12: MACE example: Prices using the k-pricing schema with k=0.5

The formula computes the proportion of a seller's allocation compared to all other allocations made by any seller to the particular buyer n. In case a buyer is allocated a bundle S_j, it is ensured that it is not allocated any other bundle (XOR constraint). As a consequence, any allocation of a seller to buyer n correlates with this bundle S_j.

Having computed $\beta_{n,t}(S_j)$ and $o_{m,n,t}(S_j)$, the price a seller receives for a bundle S_j is calculated as:

$$p_{k,m}^M(S_j) = \sum_{n \in \mathcal{N}} \sum_{t \in \mathcal{T}} y_{m,n,t}(S_j) r_m(S_j) + (1-k) \sum_{n \in \mathcal{N}} \sum_{S_l \in \mathcal{S}} \sum_{t \in \mathcal{T}} o_{m,n,t}(S_j)\beta_{n,t}(S_l). \quad (5.49)$$

Example 5.11: MAP k-Pricing

Applying this pricing scheme with $k = 0.5$ to the example presented above results in the prices given Table 5.12 with $\bar{v}_n(S_j) = v_n(S_j)s_n(S_j)$ and $\bar{r}_m(S_j) = \sum_{t \in \mathcal{T}, n \in \mathcal{N}} y_{m,n,t}(S_j)r_m(S_j)$. For instance, buyer 2 with a valuation of $\bar{v}_2(S_1) = 9$ has to pay $p_{0.5,2}^N(S_3) = 5.7$. The utility from this transaction is $u_2(S_1) = 9 - 5.7 = 3.3$. The exchange does not run in a deficit which makes it practically feasible.

Using the k-pricing schema, the exchange does not have to subsidize the participants, since it fulfills the budget-balance property in a way that no payments towards the mechanism are necessary. Hence, the k-pricing schema qualifies as a candidate pricing schema for the Grid. On the basis of the k-pricing schema, the MACE mechanism can now be defined as follows:

Definition 5.5: MACE Mechanism
MACE is an auction that implements MAP to determine an allocation and that uses the k-pricing schema to compute net payments.

Based upon this definition, desirable economic properties such as outlined in Section 3.2.1.4 can be analyzed.

Theorem 5.4: MACE Budget-Balance and Individual Rationality
MACE is budget-balanced and individually rational.

The proof is given in Appendix A.

Following the Myerson-Satterthwaite theorem (Myerson and Satterthwaite 1983), it is obvious that MACE cannot be incentive compatible. As a simple example, suppose one buyer n and one seller m. The buyer requires S_j and has a valuation of $v_n(S_j) = 10$ for it. The seller offers S_j with a reservation price of $r_m(S_j) = 5$. For the seller, the price is given by $p_{0.5,m}^M(S_j) = 7.5$ using $k = 0.5$ which results in a utility of $u_m(S_j) = 10 - 7.5 = 2.5$. However, the seller could increase his utility by bidding more than the reservation price, such as $r_m(S_j) = 9$. In this case, the seller increases the payment to $p_{0.5,m}^M(S_j) = 9.5$, which results in a higher utility. In this setting, truth-telling is not a dominant strategy. In practical settings, however, overbidding also raises the risk of non-execution. In order to evaluate these implications of the pricing schema in different settings, further analyses need to be investigated (refer to Chapter 7). The assumption is that competition among several agents and the risk of not getting allocated drive them in most cases to reveal their true preferences.

5.3 Summary

This chapter proposed the derivation of MACE, a multi-attribute combinatorial exchange for allocating and scheduling resources in the Grid. In contrast to other approaches, the proposed mechanism accounts for the variety of Grid resources by incorporating time and quality as well as co-allocation constraints.

MACE relies on the principles of combinatorial mechanisms that are outlined in Section 5.1. Although the reviewed mechanisms account for combinatorial bids, they neglect Grid specific requirements, such as time attributes or co-allocation restrictions. The design of MACE as outlined in Section 5.2 addresses these deficits by extending the allocation model of a combinatorial exchange by time attributes, co-allocation restrictions, and multiple attributes.

The mechanism provides buyers and sellers with a rich bidding language, allowing for the formulation of bundles expressing either substitutabilities or complementarities. The winner determination problem maximizes social welfare for the submitted bids. The winner determination scheme alone, however, is insufficient to guarantee an efficient allocation of the services. The pricing scheme must be constructed in a way that motivates buyers and sellers to reveal their true valuations and reservation prices. This is problematic in the case of combinatorial exchanges, since the only efficient pricing schedule, the VCG mechanism, is not budget-balanced and must be subsidized from outside the mechanism. Although an approximation of the VCG mechanism results in budget-balanced results, the computational effort that is required to compute the payments is high.

This chapter developed a new pricing family for a combinatorial exchange, namely the k-pricing rule. In essence, the k-pricing rule determines the price such that the resulting surpluses to the buyers and sellers divide the entire surplus being accrued by the trade according to the ratio k. The k-pricing rule is budget-balanced but cannot retain the efficiency property of the VCG payments. Further evaluations must be investigated to analyze the behavior effects of agents that do not have an incentive to bid truthfully. In most cases, however, it is assumed that competition in the market drive the agents to reveal their true preferences.

Following the market engineering process, the next step is to implement the conceptual model into a software system. This step is processed in the next chapter.

Chapter 6

Implementation of the Market Mechanism

Hikers encountering a fallen tree blocking a trail can climb over it, cut a path through it, or walk around it. In general, obstacles can be overcome, reduced, or avoided. Often, reducing or avoiding the obstacle is a preferable choice.

(Pekěc and Rothkopf 2006, p. 395)

The previous chapter outlined the conceptual design of MACE, a multi-attribute combinatorial exchange for allocating and scheduling resources in the Grid. Following the structured lines of market engineering, the next engineering phase requires an implementation of the conceptual model into a software system.

An implementation of the proposed auction schema entails several challenges: First, efficient algorithms are required that determine an outcome of the auction within a meaningful time frame. However, the underlying winner determination problem of MACE is $\mathcal{NP}$-complete. Any optimal algorithm to determine an allocation will inherently be intractable with an increasing number of bids. As a consequence, algorithms are required that can solve the problem computationally efficient, if necessary with suboptimal outcomes. Second, the implementation of the auction mechanism has to provide open interfaces in order to be applicable in the Grid. Moreover, the implementation has to support Grid specific communication standards such as WS-Agreement for the establishment of service level agreements.

The aim of this chapter is to introduce algorithms and concepts that are required for a practical implementation of MACE. Section 6.1 discusses state of the art algorithms for solving the winner determination problem of combinatorial mechanisms. A discussion outlines which algorithms can be applied for realizing MACE. Subsequently, Section 6.2 introduces the MACE market service, a system that implements the proposed allocation and pricing schemes. After that, Section 6.3 analyzes whether or not the implemented auction mechanism fulfils the specified requirements (cf. Section 2.3.1). Finally, Section 6.4 concludes the chapter.

6.1   Solving the Winner Determination Problem

In theory and practice, several algorithms have been proposed to solve the winner determination problem of combinatorial auctions (among others Papadimitriou and Steiglitz (1998), Rothkopf et al. (1998) and Sandholm et al. (2005)). They can be classified as exact methods, algorithms for tractable special cases, and approximations. Exact methods guarantee feasible and optimal solutions at the expense of long runtime. In contrast, algorithms for tractable special cases find optimal solutions quickly as they make use of special structures of a problem. However, these algorithms require the restriction of the agents' bidding space in order to attain such special structures. A third way to solve the winner determination problem is the use of approximations. Such algorithms do not attempt to find optimal solutions, but rather to quickly compute feasible solutions near optimal. However, the use of suboptimal outcomes entails the risk of inefficient allocations and, thus, the loss of incentive compatibility.

The following paragraphs briefly outline the intuitions behind these algorithms and discuss their applicability to MACE. For a detailed survey on these algorithms, refer to Sandholm (2002, 2006), Müller (2006), and Lehmann et al. (2006).

6.1.1   Exact Methods

Exact methods optimally solve the winner determination problem of combinatorial mechanisms. They neither require restricting the bidding space of agents, nor result in suboptimal and inefficient allocations.

One way to obtain an optimal outcome is the exhaustive enumeration of the complete search space. This requires analyzing 2^B subsets of bids, where B is the number of bids (Lehmann et al. 2006). As a consequence, such a strategy is impractical for most settings. Modern search algorithms operate more efficiently as they only analyze a subset of the whole search space. This is supported by generating upper and lower bounds for a given problem instance. The boundaries indicate which parts of the search space should be processed in more detail and which parts can be neglected. Given a winner determination problem, the value of its linear relaxed solution indicates an upper bound.[1] Lower bounds are used to store the best feasible solution obtained at any given time (Papadimitriou and Steiglitz 1998).

A popular example of an intelligent search algorithm for any linear integer program is *Brach-and-Bound*. The algorithm tries to find a solution by partitioning the search space (*branch step*) and proves its optimality by means of the given bounds. Depending on the problem set, different branching und bounding strategies can be applied (Papadimitriou and Steiglitz 1998). Aside from branch-and-bound, similar search algorithms have been proposed, such as CASS (Fujishima et al. 1999) or CABOB (Sandholm et al. 2005).

Most exact algorithms for combinatorial problems are so-called *anytime* algorithms. In anytime algorithms approximate solutions are available at any time. Furthermore, the solution quality increases in execution time up to optimum (Garvey and Lesser 1994). This means that the best obtained solution is returned as an approximate outcome, whenever the algorithm is interrupted. Such a hybrid model with the objective of obtaining optimal solutions is deemed promising for an application in real-time auction settings.

---

[1]Alternatively, a Lagrange relaxation can also be used to find an upper bound (de Vries and Vohra 2003).

A practical implementation of an anytime algorithm for solving linear integer programs is the optimization engine CPLEX[2]. The engine is a commercial product and is currently the state of the art for solving optimization problems. It implements a branch-and-bound variant including different branching strategies.[3] The software has been successfully applied to different combinatorial auction settings and the system has been shown to be the fastest algorithm for solving the winner determination problem in a multitude of different settings (Andersson et al. 2000; Sandholm et al. 2005).[4]

Although the winner determination problem is $\mathcal{NP}$-complete, CPLEX can solve large instances within a few seconds. For instance, Sandholm et al. (2005) report that CPLEX solves combinatorial auction settings with 500 bids and 50 resources in less than 10 seconds. Given an initial feasible solution, the software can even determine good solutions near optimal for more complex scenarios. In regard to hard optimization problems, finding such feasible solutions may not always be possible within a meaningful time frame (Schnizler et al. 2006b). For such cases, alternative algorithms are required to determine an outcome.

6.1.2 Tractable Special Cases

A tractable case of a winner determination problem is an instance for which an algorithm exists that solves the problem optimally in polynomial time (Müller 2006). In practice, these problems can be solved by means of linear relaxations for which the decision variables remain integral. By means of linear programming techniques, the relaxed problem can be solved in polynomial time.

In literature, several conditions have been proposed under which the winner determination problem can be solved in polynomial time (Rothkopf et al. 1998). Given an integer program, one of the most discussed conditions is total unimodularity of the constraint matrix. A matrix is unimodular if the determinant of each square submatrix is 0, 1 or -1. As a practical example for such a case, suppose an auctioneer offers land areas along a shore line. The areas are ordered from north to south. If agents are only allowed to bid on combinations of contiguous areas, the resulting problem suffices total unimodularity and, thus, can be solved in polynomial time (de Vries and Vohra 2003).

The application of special case algorithms requires the auctioneer to restrict the bidding space of the agents. Such restrictions, however, may be too rigorous for some allocation problems. As a consequence, agents may be unable to express their complex preference structures which can lead to inefficient outcomes.

6.1.3 Approximations

A third approach for solving the winner determination problem is the use of approximations. The objective of an approximation is not to find an optimal solution, but rather a feasible solution that is near optimal (de Vries and Vohra 2003). The proposed approximations for combinatorial mechanisms comprise greedy algorithms (Lehmann et al. 2002), heuristic

---

[2]For details, see http://www.ilog.com/products/cplex/.

[3]Aside from CPLEX, alternative optimization engines can also be applied such as LINDO, XPRESS or lp_solve. For a comparison of these engines, refer to Atamtürk and Savelsbergh (2005) and Linderoth and Ralphs (2005).

[4]Sandholm et al. (2005) report that CABOB performs better than CPLEX in some single sided scenarios. Unfortunately, no analysis of the algorithm's performance in combinatorial exchanges currently exist.

search methods (Mito and Fujita 2004), hill climbing (Holte 2001), and evolutionary algorithms (Calegari et al. 1999).

An important characteristic of an approximation is how close its outcome is to the optimal solution (de Vries and Vohra 2003). This metric can be measured as follows: Let $k^*(\theta)$ be the optimal choice rule with a value of V^* and let $k(\theta)$ be the approximated outcome with a value of V. An algorithm is said to approximate an optimal outcome within $g(\rho)$ if it finds a feasible solution for every instance with $V^* \leq g(\rho)V$, where ρ denotes the encoding length of the instance and $g(\rho) : \mathbb{R}^+ \to \mathbb{R}^+$ is an arbitrary function (Lehmann et al. 2006).

The close relation of the winner determination problem to other combinatorial problems derived several impossibility theorems for approximations. An important theorem is adapted from Sandholm (2002) and is based on the inapproximability theorem by Håstad (1999). It states that it is impossible to design a polynomial algorithm that approximates CAP within $g(b, G, \epsilon) = \min(b^{1-\epsilon}, G^{1/2-\epsilon})$, where b is the number of bids, G is the number of resources, and ϵ is a fixed value with $\epsilon > 0$.[5] As an example, suppose a setting with 5 resources, 3 bids, and an optimal outcome of $V^* = 10$. Defining $\epsilon = 0.1$, the theorem states that it is impossible to design a polynomial algorithm for this setting that guarantees a higher welfare than $V = 5.26$. Although CAP is only a special case of MAP, this theorem emphasizes that the winner determination problem of MACE is hard to approximate.

Aside from these negative approximation results, the application of inexact outcomes may have further drawbacks. Approximations raise the risk of strategic interactions of agents. As the resulting outcome is usually not allocative efficient, agents may have an incentive to misrepresent their preferences (Nisan and Ronen 2000). They can exploit the approximation in order to increase their individual utility. Despite all drawbacks, the use of approximations is indispensable in complex scenarios where feasible solutions cannot be found quickly by means of an exact algorithm.

6.1.4 Discussion

The previous paragraphs outlined methods for solving the winner determination problem of combinatorial auctions. Although most of the proposed algorithms are designed for single sided combinatorial auctions, their advantages and disadvantages also apply to MACE.

With regard to the envisioned Grid setting, a restriction of the agents' bidding space to attain tractable special cases is seen as too rigorous. Agents may be unable to express their preferences by not being allowed to bid on their desired resource combinations. Although there may exist settings in which MAP can be solved in polynomial time, it is refrained from restricting the bidding language of MACE. Consequently, the focus for solving MAP lies on exact algorithms and approximations.

The advantage of exact algorithms is the determination of optimal outcomes. Desirable economic properties such as efficiency can be attained by the use of such algorithms. In contrast, approximations are able to determine suboptimal outcomes quickly. However, no fast algorithm can guarantee a solution close to optimum (Sandholm et al. 2005).

For a practical realization of MACE, an application of CPLEX in combination with its anytime property is deemed promising. CPLEX is applied with the objective of finding an optimal outcome. Whenever a predefined time limit is exceeded, CPLEX is interrupted and

---

[5]It is assumed that $\mathcal{NP} \neq \mathcal{ZPP}$, where $\mathcal{ZPP}$ is the class of problems that can be solved in polynomial time with a randomized algorithm and an error probability of zero (Sandholm 2002).

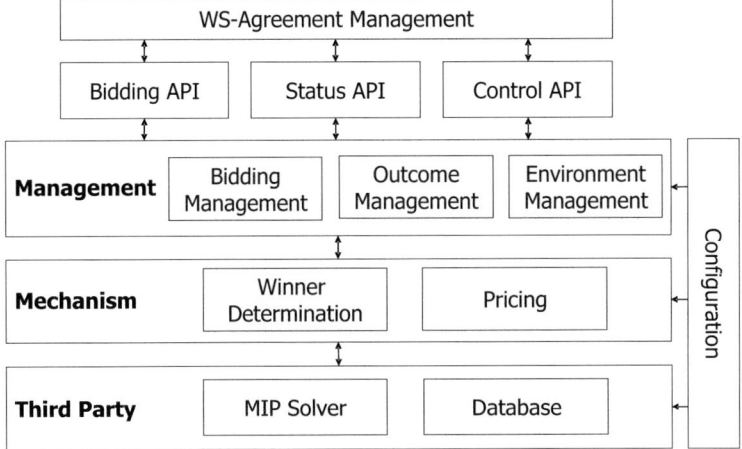

Figure 6.1: MACE market service architecture

returns the best feasible solution. Preliminary studies emphasize, that this procedure results in fairly well outcomes for the envisioned Grid market (Schnizler et al. 2006b). However, the determination of feasible solutions may be impossible in large-scaled settings. As a consequence, further evaluations have to identify an upper boundary of agents for which the problem is still computationally tractable within a meaningful time frame.

6.2 The MACE Market Service

The previous sections discussed conceptual models and algorithms that are required for building a Grid market mechanism. The objective of this section is to describe how these models are implemented into a software system. The following paragraphs briefly outline the architecture of the MACE market service that implements the proposed auction schema. After that discussion, two practical cases are outlined that apply the MACE implementation as a resource allocation manager.

6.2.1 Architectural Overview

The MACE market service fully implements the proposed auction schema as a Java based software system. The objective of the implementation is the provisioning of open interfaces and flexible components that can be easily exchanged. Figure 6.1 outlines the technical architecture of the market service.

Agents communicate with the market service by means of APIs or by a WS-Agreement interface. By means of the provided interfaces, they can submit bids, retrieve status information, and can control the market process. The underlying market service implements a three layered architecture: The *Management* layer is responsible for managing general market information such as bids and status information. The *Mechanism* layer offers an implementation of the allocation rule and the pricing schema. The *Third Party* layer encapsulates a set of third party components. In addition, specific parameters of each component can be configured from outside the system.[6]

6.2.1.1 External Interfaces

The service provides different interfaces through which agents can interact with the market. Agents can either submit WS-Agreement documents or directly access the APIs of the service.

In order to be compliant with current Grid middleware, the market service supports the submission of WS-Agreement encoded bids. The bidding language proposed in Section 5.2.1 is a subset of the WS-Agreement specification (Andrieux et al. 2005).[7] The specification in combination with a resource description language supports multiple attributes, time characteristics, and logical operators. Furthermore, additional XML-schemes allow the specification of coupling constraints as well as valuation and reservation prices.

The `WS-Agreement Management` component builds the interface between WS-Agreement documents and the APIs of the market service. The component receives bids and distributes outcome information as WS-Agreement documents. Whenever an agent submits a WS-Agreement bid, the component parses the bid's content and forwards it to the market service. Likewise, the component distributes allocation information whenever an outcome is determined.

In addition to the WS-Agreement interface, agents can also interact with the service by means of three different APIs. First, they can submit bids using the `Bidding API`. Second, they can receive status information such as allocation decisions and prices by means of the `Status API`. Finally, the service can be controlled from outside by means of the `Control API`. For instance, a market operator can use this API to trigger the outcome determination.

6.2.1.2 Management Layer

The management layer comprises of three basic components for managing bids, outcome information, and the economic environment. The `Bidding Management` component implements an order book that can be used to store and delete bids. The `Outcome Management` component is responsible for processing outcome related activities. It triggers the allocation process and receives relevant allocation and pricing decisions. Finally, the `Environment Management` component manages information concerning the economic environment. This includes information about the traded resources and the participating agents.

6.2.1.3 Mechanism Layer

The mechanism layer offers the winner determination model and the pricing schema. The `Winner Determination` component is responsible for computing an allocation, i.e., it implements the mixed integer program of MAP. After the computation of the allocation, prices can be computed by the `Pricing` component. Currently, this component supports the k-pricing schema, VCG payments, and the approximated VCG algorithm. According to the

---

[6]The verification of the service implementation is discussed in Section 7.5.

[7]The generic mapping from WS-Agreement into the bidding language is, however, not possible as some parts of the WS-Agreement specifications are not supported by MACE.

pricing schema, this component also makes use of the winner determination implementation. The particular models that are used for determining allocations and prices can be easily exchanged. Beside the proposed MACE mechanism, the service also implements winner determination problems for single sided combinatorial auctions and exchanges as well as the PPC schema for computing prices.

6.2.1.4 Third Party Layer

The third layer of the MACE market service comprises of third party components. This includes mixed integer program solvers that are required to determine an allocation and database components that are used to log relevant auction data.

The current implementation supports CPLEX and *lp_solve*[8] for solving the winner determination problem. As argued above, CPLEX is currently the state of the art optimization engine for mixed integer programs. The package lp_solve is an open source alternative to CPLEX and implements the branch-and-bound method for solving integer problems.[9] For performance reasons, lp_solve is only used for testing the service whereas CPLEX is applied for the evaluation.

6.2.2 Application Areas

The implementation of the MACE market service is currently applied in two independent projects. The following discussion introduces these projects and outlines the respective role of MACE as a resource coordination mechanism.

6.2.2.1 CATNETS

CATNETS is a research project funded by the European Union.[10] Its objective is the evaluation of the use of market mechanisms for coordinating resources in distributed systems (Eymann et al. 2005). For this purpose, decentral and central market mechanisms are developed to coordinate distributed resources economically efficient. These mechanisms are evaluated according to their technical and economical applicability by means of an agent based simulation and a proof-of-concept prototype.

A slightly modified version of MACE[11] serves as an auction based coordination mechanism for the CATNETS scenario. The mechanism is compared against a decentralized bargaining strategy with respect to technical and economical evaluation criteria. For this evaluation, the MACE market service is integrated into an agent-based Grid simulator called OptorSim (Bell et al. 2003; Calabrese et al. 2006). The simulator provides a Peer-to-Peer based communication infrastructure. Agents use this infrastructure to submit bids and to receive market information from the MACE auctioneer.

Aside from OptorSim, Chacin et al. (2006) describe how the MACE market service can be integrated into an economic based Grid architecture. The proposed architecture builds on top of existing Grid middleware such as GT 4 (Ardaiz et al. 2005).

---

[8]See `http://lpsolve.sourceforge.net/5.5/` for details (accessed 03.10.2006).

[9]The solvers are integrated by means of JOpt, a wrapper for integer programs. See `http://www.eecs.harvard.edu/econcs/jopt/` for details (accessed 04.10.2006).

[10]See `http://www.catnets.org/` for details.

[11]The MACE version applied in CATNETS does neither support time attributes nor co-allocation constraints.

Requirement	Description	Satisfied
R1	Efficient Allocation	○
R2	Incentive Compatible	○
R3	Individually Rational	●
R4	Budget-Balance	●
R5	Computational Tractable	○
R6	Automated Resource Allocation	●
R7	Double sided Mechanism	●
R8	Support for Heterogeneous Resources	●
R9	Support for Different Resource Characteristics	●
R10	Bundling of Resources	●
R11	Co-Allocation of Resources	●
R12	Guaranteed Resource Usage Time	●
R13	Advanced Reservation of Resources	●
R14	Substitutability of Resources	●
R15	Network Quality	⊙

● requirement is fulfilled, ⊙ requirement is partially fulfilled, ○ further evaluations are required

Table 6.1: Summary of the preliminary requirement satisfaction of MACE

6.2.2.2   Ontology-driven Markets

A scenario for trading Semantic Web Services by means of an ontology-driven market serves as a second case for the MACE implementation (Lamparter and Schnizler 2006). The proposed market allows semantically enriched bid formulation by means of ontologies. As a result, the matching of service providers and requesters is not realized on a syntactically but rather on a semantically level. As such, the market can be applied for allocating Semantic Web Services.

The proposed marketplace uses an ontology based communication language that is capable of representing semantically described requests, offers, and agreements. Agents use this communication language to submit their bids to the marketplace. In a transformation step, the ontology based messages are translated into syntactical bids and subsequently submitted to the MACE market service. The mechanism computes an allocation and prices and subsequently communicates the outcome to the market operator. After that, the market operator informs the bidding agents.

6.3   Preliminary Requirement Satisfaction

The previous sections outlined the design and implementation of MACE for allocating and scheduling resources in the Grid. In contrast to other approaches, the proposed mechanism accounts for a variety of Grid characteristics by incorporating time and quality, as well as coupling constraints.

This section analyzes which of the requirements specified in Section 4.2 are fulfilled by the proposed auction. Table 6.1 outlines the requirements and states whether or not they are satisfied by the MACE implementation. The following discussion aggregates these requirements and demonstrates how they are satisfied by the mechanism. As a consequence, this analysis reveals open issues that have to be further evaluated in Chapter 7.

Efficient Allocation (R1) and Incentive Compatibility (R2): MACE is efficient as long agents report their preferences truthfully. However, the k-pricing schema is not incentive compatible, as agents do not have an incentive to report their types truthfully to the mechanism. This may lead to inefficient allocations. For measuring the effects on the allocation, a numerical simulation is performed in Chapter 7 and 8.

Individual Rationality (R3) and Budget-Balance (R4): The mechanism is individually rational and budget-balanced (cf. Theorem 5.4).

Computational Tractability (R5): The winner determination problem of MACE is $\mathcal{NP}$-complete. Although modern search algorithms can solve many problem instances quickly, the auction schema is computationally intractable in some scenarios. Further evaluations are necessary to determine whether or not this requirement can be fulfilled with the estimated number of market participants. A detailed runtime analysis of the implementation will be performed with respect to the estimated number of agents in the envisioned Grid market (cf. Chapter 7).

Automated Resource Allocation (R6): The mechanism is fully implemented as a software system. This allows an automated resource allocation.

Double sided Mechanism (R7) and Support for Heterogeneous Resources (R8): MACE is a double sided mechanism that allows multiple buyers and sellers to trade heterogeneous resources simultaneously.

Support for Different Resource Characteristics (R9): Agents can account for different cardinal quality characteristics by means of the proposed bidding language. The winner determination guarantees that for each request all required resources are supplied in at least the demanded qualities. Although the quality characteristics are restricted to cardinal values, it is assumed that this is sufficient for most Grid resources. Furthermore, nominal attributes such as the operating system of a machine can be modelled by introducing additional resources. For instance, a computation service that runs on a Linux machine can be modeled as $g_k = CompService_{\text{Linux}}$. Likewise, a Windows computation service is modeled as $g_j = CompService_{\text{Windows}}$. Both resources will not match in the winner determination model.

Bundling of Resources (R10) and Substitutability of Resources (R14): MACE is an instance of a combinatorial exchange. As such, it allows buyers and sellers to submit bids on bundles. In addition, buyers can submit several bundle bids that substitute each others.

Co-allocation of Resources (R11): The bidding language and MAP support the specification of co-allocation constraints and the restriction of possible resource divisions. In addition, MACE allows the coupling of multiple resources so that they get allocated from the same provider.

Guaranteed Resource Usage Time (R12) and Advanced Reservation (R13): In case a buyer gets allocated a bundle, the mechanism guarantees that all of the required usage slots are allocated. In addition, MACE allows agents to specify their resource supply and demand in the future.

Network Quality (R15): The bidding language allows agents to specify a value for their network connections. This is limited to static values, such as the upstream or downstream of an agent's network connection. This attribute does not take the dynamics of the underlying network quality into account. As a result, this requirement is only partially fulfilled by the mechanism. Due to the central nature of the auctioneer component, a more realistic inclusion of the network quality is difficult. Counterparts in the model (i.e., a buyer that gets resources from a seller) do not know each other before an agreement is reached. As such, network latencies and network distance metrics cannot be measured before the auctioneer computed an outcome. One solution to this problem is to install a negotiation phase concerning network reservation after the outcome is determined. In addition, the performance of the currently applied method has to be evaluated by means of a field experiment.

In summary, the MACE implementation fulfills most of the requirements. However, the open issues such as efficiency, incentive compatibility, and computational tractability need further evaluations.

6.4 Summary

This chapter outlined the practical implementation of MACE into a software system. Section 6.1 discussed state of the art methods for solving winner determination problems in combinatorial auctions. As a result of the discussion, the use of an exact anytime algorithm in form of CPLEX is chosen for a practical implementation of MACE.

Section 6.2 discussed the implementation of the MACE market service and outlined practical application areas of the service. First, a flexible architecture is outlined that incorporates the proposed auction mechanism and algorithms. Second, two case studies are introduced that use the MACE implementation for their resource coordination.

An analysis whether or not the MACE market service satisfies the requirements upon a resource allocation manager for the Grid is given in Section 6.3. The discussion emphasizes that most requirements are fulfilled by the current implementation.

The implementation of the conceptual MACE model into a software system completes the second stage of the market engineering process. Consequently, the next chapter processes the testing stage. With respect to the previous work, the focus of this stage lies on the evaluation of the economic properties of the mechanism. This includes an evaluation concerning the efficiency, incentive compatibility, and computational tractability of the implemented mechanism.

Part III

Evaluation

Chapter 7

Simulation Design

Nature is capable of building [...] systems whose complexity lies far beyond the reach of our computers and supercomputers, present or prospective. [...] Modeling, then, calls for some basic principles to manage this complexity. We must separate what is essential from what is dispensable in order to capture in our models a simplified picture of reality.

(Simon 1990, p. 7)

The previous chapters outlined the design and implementation of MACE, a market mechanism for the Grid. The preliminary requirement satisfaction in Section 6.3 revealed open issues that need further evaluation. However, the complexities and interdependencies between these problems make it difficult to provide analytical solutions. As a consequence, alternative methodologies have to be applied to analyze the proposed auction.

The market engineering approach encompasses different techniques to evaluate market mechanisms. Due to the lack of large-scaled test-beds, simulations are applied to study the properties of MACE. Market simulations imitate the economic environment and the behavior of agents and allow a numerical evaluation of mechanisms. The application of simulations is seen as appropriate to evaluate the open issues of MACE.

The remainder of this chapter is structured as follows: Section 7.1 outlines the basic concepts of simulations and introduces a structured approach that assists in performing them. After that, Section 7.2 defines a set of questions the simulation has to answer. On the basis of these questions, Section 7.3 introduces a simulation model that imitates a Grid market system. Section 7.4 outlines a set of bidding scenarios that restrict the evaluation space, as an exhaustive enumeration of the system model is too complex. Section 7.5 discusses the derivation of a simulation framework that implements the proposed model and that is used to perform the simulation runs. Finally, Section 7.6 concludes the chapter.

7.1 Principles of Simulation

Simulation is a technique that uses computers to imitate a system and to evaluate a model numerically (Law and Kelton 2000). In the context of market engineering, the theory of simulation is an important building block to study the effects of market mechanisms (Weinhardt et al. 2006). The following subsections briefly outline the principles of simulations with a focus on those techniques that are required to simulate market systems.

7.1.1 Basic Concepts

The objective of a simulation is the imitation of a process or a system over a certain time interval (Banks 1998). Within this interval, state variables denote the collection of variables that are required to fully describe the system at any point in time (Law and Kelton 2000). In an auction scenario, the system comprises the economic environment, the strategies of the agents, and the market mechanism. State variables provide information about the status of the environment (e.g., behavior of agents) and the outcome of the mechanism.

The analysis of a system is usually performed to gain further information about the system's behavior (Schmidt 1980). For instance, a market engineer is interested in studying the effects that are caused by a modification of the institutional rules. One way to gather such information is to study the changes directly in the real system. However, such an analysis is impossible in many real life settings. If a market engineer wants to study the effects of a new pricing schema for a stock exchange, he hardly can do this using the productive trading system. Moreover, in some settings it is even impossible to study effects in the real system, as it has not yet been installed.

Aside from studying a real system, its behavior can also be analyzed by means of a system model that acts as a representation of the system and captures certain aspects of it (Banks 1998). If the model is designed properly, meaningful information can be obtained concerning the system's performance (Pritsker 1998). As a consequence, the model design and the degree of abstraction have to be carefully developed.

According to Law and Kelton (2000, p. 5–6), the characteristics of simulation models can be classified by three dimensions:

- *Static Model vs. Dynamic Model:* A static model represents the underlying system at a particular point in time. In contrast, dynamic models account for the evolution of a system over time.

- *Deterministic Model vs. Stochastic Model:* If a simulation model does not include any probabilistic component, it is said to be deterministic. A model is characterized as a stochastic model when the output is randomly biased and is only an estimate of the model's true characteristics.

- *Discrete Model vs. Continuous Model:* A model is discrete if the state variables change at particular points in time. In contrast, a model is continuous if the state variables change continuously and depend on time.

Theory and practice propose different types of simulations and offer tools that support their implementation. These types usually make assumptions upon the underlying model characteristics. For instance, a simulation type may require that the implemented model is static and stochastic. Popular examples for simulation types that are applied in market based settings are, among others, agent-based simulations and Monte Carlo simulations.

- *Agent-based Simulation:* The principle of an agent-based simulation approach is the design of a simple model in which agents interact on the basis of social rules (van Dinther 2006). The models are usually dynamic and stochastic. Such a simulation approach is applied in a variety of market settings (Gode and Sunders 1993; Veit et al. 2004; van Dinther 2006).

- *Monte Carlo Simulation:* In Monte Carlo simulations, random numbers are used to solve a stochastic or deterministic problem (Law and Kelton 2000). The underlying simulation model is rather static than dynamic. Monte Carlo simulations are usually applied to solve problems that are not tractable analytically. An example for such a simulation in a market setting is given by Cai and Wurman (2005). By means of a Monte Carlo approach, the authors determine equilibriums for which an analytical outcome cannot be computed.

The decision which dimension of a simulation model and, as a consequence, which type of simulation approach should be applied depends on the particular scenario and the effects that are to be studied.

7.1.2 Stages in a Simulation Study

The design and implementation of a simulation study follows a structured approach that assists the market engineer to perform a thorough simulation study. Figure 7.1 depicts the basic stages of a computerized simulation study for market scenarios and emphasizes their most important issues in each step (Banks 1998; Law and Kelton 2000; van Dinther 2006).

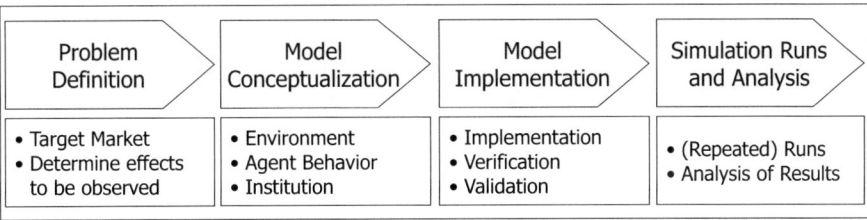

Figure 7.1: Steps in a simulation study of markets

Stage 1 – Problem Definition: In the first stage of the process, the market engineer defines the problem that is in the center of interest. In a market based setting, this includes the identification of the target market, the formalization of the effects to be observed, and a consideration if simulation is a reasonable approach to study the problem.

Stage 2 – Model Conceptualization: In the second stage, the conceptual simulation model is designed. With regard to market systems, this stage comprises the definition of the economic environment, the dynamics of the agent's behavior, and the applied institution.

In most cases, this stage requires an abstraction from the target system. For instance, if the market engineer wants to model human behavior, he has to make assumptions that restrict their decision space. In addition, complex characteristics of the economic environment (e.g., characteristics of resources) cannot always be modeled in a thorough detail. One way to tackle these complexities is the definition of different simulation scenarios that consider sub-aspects of the real system.

The result of this stage is a conceptual model that can be classified by the aforementioned three dimensions of simulation models. These characteristics further influence the type of simulation that can be applied for the given problem. For instance, if the model is static and discrete, the Monte Carlo method can be appropriate to simulate the market system.

Stage 3 – Model Implementation: After the design of the conceptual model, it is implemented into a software system. This stage can be supported by the use of existing and generic simulation frameworks such as Repast[1], JASA[2], or AMASE (van Dinther 2006). After the implementation of the model, it has to be verified and validated.

Verification denotes the process of proving the correctness of a system implementation with respect to the conceptual model specification. With regard to computerized simulations, this is supported by software engineering methods such as black box testing, unit testing, or dynamic program analysis (Hetzel 1993).

Validation is applied to substantiate that a model is an accurate representation of the real system (Banks 1998). Law and Kelton (2000) propose different techniques for increasing the validity and, as a consequence, the creditability of the implemented model: Validation starts with the collection of system relevant information and data. If no productive system exists for the proposed model, the engineer may rely on data of similar systems. Subsequently, one compares the implemented model with the real system by means of the collected data. In addition, validation can be supported by existing theories and expert interviews in order to compare the result of a simulation with its expected outcome. Furthermore, sensitivity analysis help to calibrate the model.

Stage 4 – Simulation Runs and Analysis: Having implemented the model, simulation runs can be performed. In many settings, the output data of a simulation is stochastically influenced. As a consequence, it is required to repeat the simulation runs to get an appropriate data basis for the evaluation.

The generated simulation data is evaluated by means of statistical methods such as computing means, variances, or by means of statistical test procedures (Law and Kelton 2000). A further step is to interpret the results and, if necessary, to repeat the simulation runs using different parameter settings.

Performing simulation studies is one way to analyze the effects of complex systems such as markets. The proposed process supports the market engineer in a thorough simulation study and, consequently, in obtaining creditable results.

7.1.3 Advantages and Disadvantages of Simulations

The previous sections outlined the basic concepts of simulations and introduced a structured approach that assists in performing them. Although simulations are an appropriate way to analyze market based systems, they also have shortcomings. In the following discussion, the advantages and disadvantages of applying simulations to study markets are briefly outlined.

Advantages of simulation: One advantage of a simulation approach is to study effects in a controlled environment (van Dinther 2006). The market engineer can control the

---

[1]See `http://repast.sourceforge.net/` for details.
[2]See `http://www.csc.liv.ac.uk/~sphelps/jasa/` for details.

model and the influences of single effects. Depending on the simulated market system, the approach allows a low cost evaluation of the system while performing a thorough exploration of possible conditions. With regard to a Grid market system, various effects can be analyzed although the productive system is not yet available. Simulations are particularly useful during the evolution of new technologies as they allow a comparison of different design alternatives.

Disadvantages of simulation: The approach only estimates outcome information for a given set of input parameters that are based on abstracted assumptions (Law and Kelton 2000). In addition, results obtained by a simulation cannot be generalized. Furthermore, the modeling and implementation stages are error prone. In complex simulation settings, it is often difficult to identify mistakes in the model or program errors in the implementation. Thus, wrong conclusions may be drawn from the obtained output data (van Dinther 2006).

In summary, simulations are useful in many market based settings. Although they have disadvantages, their application is often the only practical way to evaluate a system. However, it is not advisable to rely only on simulation results. The results may help to calibrate and tune a system. Often, the applicability of a proposed market mechanism has to be further evaluated by means of other approaches such as laboratory and field experiments.

7.2   Problem Definition

The first step in a simulation study is the definition of the target problem and the effects that are to be observed. For the work at hand, the target system is a Grid marketplace that comprises the economic environment, the agent's behavior, and MACE as a market mechanism. In addition to the standard pricing schema of MACE, the target system also comprises the VCG mechanism and the approximated VCG mechanism as benchmark implementations.

Section 6.3 emphasizes open issues of the MACE mechanism with respect to the proposed requirement specification. These issues are to be evaluated by means of the simulation study. This includes a detailed analysis of the mechanism's properties concerning allocative efficiency, incentive compatibility, and computational tractability.

The following paragraphs raise a set of questions that serve as a basis for the further evaluation. The questions are classified into problem sets that are either solved by an optimal winner determination algorithm or by approximations.

7.2.1   Optimal Winner Determination

The first set of questions relies on an optimal algorithm to solve the winner determination problem of MACE. On the basis of optimal solutions, computational and economical properties of the mechanism are to be analyzed.

7.2.1.1   Computational Tractability

The winner determination problem of MACE is $\mathcal{NP}$-complete. As a result, MACE is computationally intractable in large-scale scenarios. Ideally, an upper boundary of problem instances can be defined for which the problem is still computationally tractable within a meaningful time frame. In the context of trading Grid resources, a meaningful time frame is consistent with the maximum time limit that an allocation process may last. Experiences suggest that an allocation process shorter than 5 minutes is adequate (cf. Section 2.3.1).

Question 1: Upper boundary for optimal outcomes
What is the upper boundary for which the winner determination problem of MACE can be solved optimally within a meaningful time frame?

The resulting boundaries indicate which auction instances can be solved optimally and which instances have to be approximated.

7.2.1.2 Allocative Efficiency

The proposed k-price mechanism is not incentive compatible. Truthful bidding is not a dominant strategy as agents can improve their individual utility by misrepresenting their private information. If agents deviate from bidding their true valuation and reservation prices, the outcome of MACE is no longer efficient. This fact raises the second question to be answered by the numerical evaluation.

Question 2: Efficiency loss due to misrepresenting agents
What is the magnitude of efficiency loss due to misrepresenting agents?

In this case, *misrepresenting* means that buyers underbid their valuations and sellers over-bid their reservation prices. The benchmark for measuring efficiency loss is an incentive compatible mechanism in which all agents bid truthfully. For this benchmark setting, let V^* be the welfare of the allocation. In a second scenario it is assumed that some agents mis-represent their private information. Similar to the benchmark setting, let V_M be the welfare of the outcome with manipulating agents. The efficiency loss EL^O can be calculated as the percentage loss of the resulting welfare due to manipulating bidders:

$$EL^O = \frac{V_M}{V^*} \cdot 100\%, \tag{7.1}$$

where index O stands for an optimal winner determination algorithm.

7.2.1.3 Incentive Compatibility

The application of the k-pricing schema implicates that agents can gain a higher utility by misrepresenting their private information. This raises the question if this utility gain can be measured and if it can serve as a metric for the loss of incentive compatibility.

Question 3: K-Price incentive compatibility
Can agents gain a positive utility by manipulating their bids?

The utility gain is measured as follows: Let $\widetilde{\mathcal{I}}$ be a set of agents that can manipulate their valuations and reservation prices. In a benchmark scenario with an outcome o, all agents $\tilde{i} \in \widetilde{\mathcal{I}}$ honestly reveal their preferences. Consequently, their utility $u_{\tilde{i}}(o)$ from bidding truthfully can be calculated as $\sum_{\tilde{i} \in \widetilde{\mathcal{I}}} u_{\tilde{i}}(o)$. In a second setting with an outcome $\bar{o}$, agents $\tilde{i} \in \widetilde{\mathcal{I}}$ manipulate their bids, whereas the input parameters (i.e., the characteristics of the underlying bids) remain the same. The resulting utility due to manipulation is calculated as $\sum_{\tilde{i} \in \widetilde{\mathcal{I}}} u_{\tilde{i}}(\bar{o})$. Thus, the utility gained due to manipulation can be measured as

$$UG^O_{n,k}(S_j) = \sum_{\tilde{i} \in \widetilde{\mathcal{I}}} u_{\tilde{i}}(\bar{o}) - \sum_{\tilde{i} \in \widetilde{\mathcal{I}}} u_{\tilde{i}}(o), \tag{7.2}$$

where k stands for the k-pricing schema and O stands for an optimal winner determination algorithm.[3] The metric reflects the difference between the utility gained by manipulation and the utility gained in a truthful scenario. If this value is positive, agents have an incentive to manipulate their bids. In case the value is negative, agents do worse by manipulating.

A more profound statement concerning the incentive properties of the k-pricing schema requires a comparison with alternative pricing schemes. It is refrained from comparing the k-pricing schema with the VCG mechanism, as the VCG mechanism is incentive compatible. Moreover, due to the loss of the budget-balance property, the VCG is not applicable in practice. In contrast, a comparison of the k-price mechanism with the approximated VCG mechanism deems promising, as both are not incentive compatible but individual rational and budget-balanced.

Question 4: K-Price vs. approximated VCG pricing
Can misrepresenting agents gain a higher utility either by an application of the k-price schema or by use of the approximated VCG mechanism?

An answer to this question requires a comparison of the incentive properties of the k-price schema and the approximated VCG mechanism. This is achieved by comparing the utility gain of manipulating agents in both settings, i.e., by analyzing if the inequality $UG_{n,k}^O \leq UG_{n,AV}^O$ is true, where k stands for k-pricing, AV for approximated VCG pricing, and O for an optimal winner determination algorithm.

7.2.2 Approximated Winner Determination

Preliminary studies with the auction schema confirmed that solving the winner determination problem can become computationally intractable, even in settings with less than 100 agents (Schnizler et al. 2006b). This implies that exact solutions of the winner determination problem may require too much computation time. As a consequence, the problem cannot be solved optimally.

As discussed in Section 6.1, an application of CPLEX in combination with its anytime property deems promising. The solver is started with the objective of finding optimal outcomes. Whenever a meaningful time frame is elapsed, the solver is interrupted and returns the best feasible solution.

7.2.2.1 Allocative Efficiency

The application of approximations results in suboptimal allocations. This raises the question, how good the proposed procedure approximates the optimal outcome. One way to determine such a value is the measurement of the approximation's welfare loss compared to the optimal outcome.

Question 5: Efficiency loss due to an approximated allocation
What is the magnitude of welfare loss due to an approximated winner determination?

---

[3]An alternative technique for measuring loss of efficiency and incentive compatibility is given by Bapna et al. (2005). The authors propose a game in which all agents first submit their bids truthfully. After that, the bids of all agents are made public. Subsequently, each bidder is allowed to resubmit a bid based upon this information.

Following the discussion on approximations in Section 6.1.3, the quality of such algorithms is measured as follows: Let V^* be the value of the optimal outcome and let V be value of the approximation. A measure for defining the quality of the outcome is given by determining $g(\rho)$ with $V^* \leq g(\rho)V$, where ρ denotes the encoding length of the problem instance (Müller 2006).

7.2.2.2 Incentive Compatibility

An auction schema that implements an approximated winner determination schema cannot be incentive compatible (Nisan and Ronen 2000). Following the aforementioned problem definitions, this raises the question if agents can attain a positive utility by misrepresenting their bids. In order to isolate this effect, one requires an application of the VCG mechanism due to its incentive compatibility. If agents gain a higher utility by misrepresenting their valuations, it is only caused by the approximated allocation schema.

Question 6: Incentive compatibility of the VCG mechanism due to an approximated allocation
Can agents gain a positive utility by manipulating their bids with the application of an approximated winner determination algorithm and the VCG pricing schema?

This requires the computation of the utility gain UG_V^A for the VCG mechanism as defined in Equation 7.2. Index V stands for the VCG mechanism and A for an approximated winner determination algorithm. The value of this metric indicates the incentive loss due to an approximated winner determination. With respect to this benchmark, the effect of the approximation can be studied by the use of the k-pricing schema.

Question 7: Incentive compatibility of the k-pricing schema due to an approximated allocation
Can agents gain a positive utility by manipulating their bids if an approximated winner determination algorithm and the k-pricing schema is applied?

Following the previous definitions, this requires to determine UG_k^A, where index k stands for the k-pricing schema and A stands for an approximated winner determination. In order to compare the loss of incentive compatibility of the k-pricing schema, this procedure is also applied for the approximated VCG schema.

Question 8: K-Price vs. approximated VCG pricing using an approximated allocation
Can misrepresenting agents gain a higher utility by the use of the k-price schema or by the application of the approximated VCG mechanism if an approximated winner determination algorithm is applied?

Finally, this question requires an analysis if $UG_k^A \leq UG_{AV}^A$ is violated, where AV denotes the approximated VCG mechanism and A the approximated winner determination algorithm.

7.2.3 Reflection

The previous subsections defined a set of problems that are to be evaluated by the simulation study. Table 7.1 summarizes these problems and classifies them according to their underlying winner determination algorithm and the behavior of agents. For instance, question 2 analyzes

Solver	Agents	Nr	Question
Optimal	Truthful	1	Upper boundary for solving optimally
	Manipulation	2	Efficiency loss
		3	K-price incentive compatibility loss
		4	Incentive compatibility loss: K-Price vs. approximated VCG
Approximated	Truthful	5	Efficiency loss
	Manipulation	6	VCG incentive compatibility loss
		7	K-Price incentive compatibility loss
		8	Incentive compatibility loss: K-Price vs. approximated VCG

Table 7.1: Summary of problems to be studied by the simulation

the efficiency loss due to manipulating agents that occur by an application of an optimal winner determination algorithm.

After the review of these questions, the theory of simulation is seen as an appropriate technique for answering them. As a consequence, the next stage of the simulation study can be processed by designing the simulation model.

7.3 Simulation Model

A simulation model serves as a representation of certain aspects of a real system. Ideally, these aspects allow an isolated analysis of the effects to be studied. With regard to the envisioned Grid market, the model encompasses the economic environment including resource providers and consumers, the behavior of these agents, and MACE as a resource allocation manager.

At the present moment, no Grid market exists in real life. Moreover, there are only few test-beds that make use of state of the art Grid middleware. Consequently, the design of a simulation model is difficult as one cannot rely on existing systems. Although several computing platforms such as PlanetLab serve as related systems, they do not cover all characteristics of the envisioned Grid market. For example, PlanetLab does neither support prices as a coordination mechanism, nor the possibility of advanced reservations (Albrecht et al. 2006).

Figure 7.2 depicts the basic simulation model for the work at hand. It comprises resource consumers as buyers, resource providers as sellers, and MACE as a resource allocation manager. Buyers and sellers submit their resource requests and offers in the form of bids to the MACE service. Subsequently, the manager computes an allocation, determines prices, and logs the outcome data. The following subsections describe the model's components in more detail.

7.3.1 Economic Environment

Following the notation introduced in Section 5.2.1 and summarized in Table 5.6, the economic environment comprises a set of buyers $\mathcal{N}$ with $n \in \mathcal{N}$ and a set of sellers $\mathcal{M}$ with

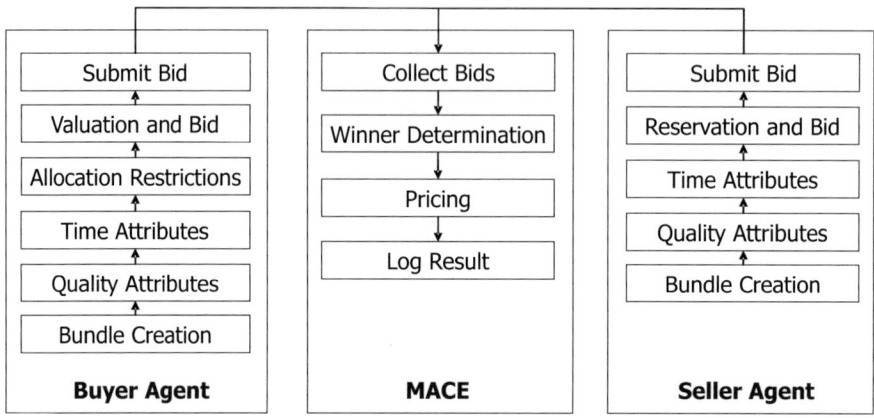

Figure 7.2: Sequence of the bid submission in the applied simulation model

$m \in \mathcal{M}$ that submit bids to the auctioneer. The bids reflect their resource requirements, respectively their offered resource endowments.

When generating a bid, a buyer first selects an appropriate bundle $S_j \in \mathcal{S}$. After this step, the agent describes the side-constraints of the required resources $g_k \in S_j$ by the definition of (i) the required quality characteristics $q_n^N(S_j, g_k, a_i^k)$, (ii) time attributes $e_n^N(S_j), l_n^N(S_j), s_n(S_j)$, and (iii) co-allocation restrictions $\gamma_n(S_j, g_k), \varphi_n(S_j, g_k, g_l)$. Finally, the agent computes his valuation $v_n(S_j)$ for the bundle and determines a bid $\tilde{v}_n(S_j)$ for it. In case the agent wants to submit several atomic bids, this process is repeated. Subsequently, the formalized bid is submitted to the auctioneer. For sellers, the bid formulation is processed in a similar way.

The bid formulation raises the question how particular resources and their characteristics are modeled. This requires, among others, the modeling of bundles, quality and time attributes, as well as valuation and reservation prices. Due to the fact that the model is not based on empirical data, the characteristics of these parameters are drawn from stochastic distributions. Literature proposes several distributions for generating bids in combinatorial auctions (Sandholm 2002; Leyton-Brown et al. 2006) and for modeling computer resources in a Grid context (Lu and Dinda 2003; Kee et al. 2004). For instance, Sandholm (2002) proposes a bundle generation technique that can be used to generate domain independent bids that are – in most cases – computationally hard to solve. However, no quality characteristics are supported by the distribution. Kee et al. (2004) propose a set of distributions for computer processors and hard disks. Although their model accounts for quality characteristics of both resources, it neglects further types of tradable resource and does not consider prices. Accordingly, none of the proposed distributions covers all aspects of MACE's bidding language. In order to generate bids, existing distributions have to be combined and adapted. Still, an exhaustive enumeration of all possible distribution combinations is impossible in a simulation study. Rather a set of bidding scenarios is defined in Section 7.4 that covers different aspects of the model.

Aside from their particular configurations, the characteristics of Grid resources are also influenced by their failure probability and the network topology. With respect to the proposed simulation questions, these characteristics are neglected for the work at hand. Grid simulation models and implementations that attempt to include these characteristics can be found in Casanova (2001) and Buyya and Murshed (2002).

7.3.2 Market Mechanism

The applied market mechanism is an instance of the MACE market service. The implementation is realized as a call market. This means that the auctioneer collects all bids and subsequently computes an outcome. This results in a one-shot game in which all agents can submit only one bid.

The CPLEX engine is applied to solve the winner determination problem. In cases an approximated outcome is required, CPLEX is interrupted after a predefined time frame. For the model at hand, an allocation time of 5 minutes appears as a meaningful time frame.

The model comprises three different pricing schemes: (i) the k-pricing schema as the standard mechanism for MACE, (ii) the VCG mechanism, and (iii) the approximated VCG mechanism with the threshold function as benchmark price schemes. For settings in which the k-price schema is applied, the parameter k is set to $k = 0.5$. This favors neither the buyers' nor the sellers' side.

7.3.3 Behavior of Agents

As a last step, the behavior of agents has to be modeled. Following the problem definition, this requires truthful and manipulating bidders. Truthful bidders submit their true valuations and reservation prices to the auctioneer, i.e., $v_n(S_j) = \tilde{v}_n(S_j)$ and $r_m(S_j) = \tilde{r}_m(S_j)$. Manipulating agents underbid their valuations ($v_n(S_j) \geq \tilde{v}_n(S_j)$), respectively overbid their reservation prices ($r_m(S_j) \leq \tilde{r}_m(S_j)$).

In order to model manipulating agents, simple misrepresentations by $\beta\%$ of the true valuations are considered, where $\lambda\%$ of the buyers reduce their reported values by $\beta\%$ and $\lambda\%$ of the sellers increase their reservation prices by bidding $\frac{100}{100-\beta} \cdot r_m(S_j)$. Instead of observing only symmetric Nash-equilibriums as in the analysis by Parkes et al. (2001), where agents either misrepresent their preferences by 0 or by $\beta\%$, the ratio of misrepresenting agents to the total number of participants varies as well. A ratio of $\lambda = 50\%$, for instance, denotes that 50% of the buyers and sellers misrepresent their preferences by $\beta\%$, while the other 50% report truthfully. By exploring the joint strategy space (i.e., varying the share of misrepresentative and truthful participants as well as the percentage of misrepresentation), the desired economic effects can be measured.

7.4 Bidding Scenarios

Understanding the effects of the proposed market mechanism requires the generation of representative resource configurations, workloads, and bidding strategies of agents. Until now, there exists no stochastic distribution for Grid configurations that is expressive enough for the proposed bidding language. As a result, one has to rely on alternative ways to generate resource configurations and bids.

In the combinatorial auction literature, several distributions have been proposed to generate bidding streams. These distributions generate bundles and valuations with regard to different objectives. Some distributions generate domain independent bids that lead to computationally hard problems (Sandholm 2002). Others attempt to imitate artificial bids that reflect some sort of real life scenarios (Leyton-Brown et al. 2000). However, the proposed distributions do not account for Grid specific characteristics such as multiple attributes or co-allocation constraints. In order to integrate these attributes into a bidding scenario, one can rely on studies that synthesize particular configurations of Grid resources (Kee et al. 2004). Although these studies do not include complementarities, substitutes, and prices of Grid resources, they can be combined with distributions for combinatorial bids to generate adequate test data.

With respect to the proposed simulation questions, a differentiation between bidding streams that generate domain independent bids and streams for generating realistic bids is deemed promising. On the one hand, domain independent bids serve as benchmark data that may amplify the observed effects. On the other hand, realistic bids are applied to study situations that may appear in a real Grid setting.

The following subsections outline the applied distributions for both bidding streams and introduce a set of parameter settings that are to be evaluated by the study.

7.4.1   Generating Domain Independent Bids

The first step when generating a bid of an agent concerns the bundle creation. For domain independent settings, a *decay* distribution is applied. The decay function has been recommended by Sandholm (2002) because it creates hard instances of the allocation problem in single sided combinatorial auctions.

At the beginning, a bundle S_j consists of one random resource g_k. Afterwards, new resources are added randomly with a probability of α. This procedure is iterated until resources are no longer added or the bundle already includes all resources. Following other combinatorial auction studies, the parameter α is set to $\alpha = 0.75$ as this leads to the hardest instances on average (Sandholm et al. 2005). In order to determine prices, one picks randomly a value between 0 and the number of resources in the bundle (Sandholm 2002). To avoid decimal values, the resulting valuation is multiplied by 1000 and then rounded (Andersson et al. 2000).

Quality characteristics $q_n(S_j, g_k, a_i^k)$[4] for each attribute a_i^k are integer values drawn from a uniform distribution between $[1, \ldots, 2000]$. The number of attributes of each resource g_k is a parameter that can be varied according to the applied scenario. Likewise to the quality characteristics, time attributes are also drawn from a uniform distribution. This includes (i) a uniformly distributed earliest time slot $e_n(S_j)$ within a range $[a_e, \ldots, b_e]$, (ii) a uniformly distributed latest time slot $l_n(S_j)$ within a range $[a_l, \ldots, b_l]$, and a uniformly distributed number of required slots $s_n(S_j)$ within $[a_s, \ldots, b_s]$.[5] The ranges of each distribution are varied according to particular bidding scenarios.

Subsequently, the distribution settings for co-allocation restrictions of buyer bids have to be defined. This includes the definition of a maximum number of co-allocations $\gamma_n(S_j, g_k)$ and the specification of coupling conditions $\varphi_n(S_j, g_k, g_l)$. The number of resources in a bundle and the number of buyers that have such restrictions is set by an external parameter.

---

[4]Index n is used to denote a buyer. Quality characteristics for sellers are modeled in the same manner by using index m.

[5]The number of slots are only required for buyer bids.

Bid Characteristics	Distribution	Varied Parameters
Bundle creation	Decay	Total number of goods G
Quality attributes	Uniform $[1, \ldots, 2000]$	Number of attributes A_k
Time attributes	Uniform $[a, \ldots, b]$	Time ranges a and b
Allocation restrictions	Fixed	Bids & goods with coupling restrictions
	Fixed, Uniform $[1, \ldots, c]$	Bids & goods with divisibility restrictions
Valuation	$1000 \cdot$ Uniform $[0, \ldots, \mathcal{G}_{S_j}]$	Truthful or manipulated bidding

Table 7.2: Distributions and parameters for generating domain independent bids

The maximum number of co-allocations is drawn from a uniform distribution within a range of $[1, \ldots, c]$, where c is a parameter that is varied in each bidding scenario. The percentage number of buyers that have these restrictions is also determined by an external parameter for each setting.

Finally, the number of buyers and sellers that trade on the market as well as the number of their atomic bids is determined by an external variable in each scenario. Table 7.2 summarizes the parameters and distributions for generating domain independent bids. Particular bidding scenarios that apply this technique are introduced in Subsection 7.4.3.

7.4.2   Generating Realistic Bids

The previous subsection introduced a technique for generating domain independent bids. An alternative technique that attempts to generate realistic bids serves as a second way to model bids.

The basis for generating realistic bids are distributions provided by the *combinatorial auction test suite* (CATS)[6]. The aim of this suite is the definition of bundles and valuations with respect to preferences found in real-world scenarios (Leyton-Brown et al. 2000; Leyton-Brown and Shoham 2006). Most of the distributions are based on a graph of resources that reflects their economical relationships.

CATS implements five different distributions for generating bundles and valuations. For instance, one distribution represents the problem of purchasing resources on a connection between two points. The aim of this distribution is to design path problems such as found in gas pipeline networks or bandwidth allocation problems (Leyton-Brown and Shoham 2006). Furthermore, a distribution is provided that accounts for complementarities of resources that arise due to their adjacency in a two-dimensional space (Leyton-Brown et al. 2000). A popular real-world example for such settings are spectrum auctions in which segments of spectrums are sold by means of an auction (Ausubel and Milgrom 2002).

For the model at hand, the *arbitrary relationships* distribution of CATS is applied. The basis of this distribution are relationships between single resources. The resulting bundles have the characteristic that particular pairs of resources have a high probability of being part of the same bundle. As a consequence, most bundles generated by this distribution include resources with arbitrary relationships. For the envisioned Grid market setting, such a way of modeling bundles of resources appears as appropriate. In practice, it is conceivable that bundles often contain related resources. For instance, if an agent requires a data-mining service, he most likely also requires a storage service.

---

[6]See http://cats.stanford.edu/ for details.

At the beginning, a bundle S_j consists of one resource g_k. New resources are added one by one. The probability of adding a new resource g_j depends on its relationship to other resources g_k in the bundle S_j. When the bundle is generated, a price is determined that depends on a common value component and a private value component of the bundle's resources.[7]

Having generated a bundle and a valuation, quality characteristics can be modeled. In order to model realistic bids, the quality attributes of resources have to be influenced by valuation and reservation prices. For instance, if a buyer 1 has a high valuation for bundle S_j and another buyer 2 has a low valuation for a bundle S_j, agent 1 has probably higher quality requirements than agent 2. This fact is taken into account by picking particular quality characteristics as integer values from a normal distribution $N(\mu, \sigma^2)$, where mean μ and variance σ^2 depend on the valuation or the reservation price as well as on the number of resources in the bundle. For the proposed model, μ is defined as $\mu = x \cdot v_i(S_j) \cdot (y + 0.5)$ and σ^2 is computed as $\sigma^2 = z \cdot v_i(S_j) \cdot G_{S_j}$, where $y \in \mathbb{R} | 0 \le y \le 1$ is a value picked from a uniform distribution. The parameters x and z are scaling factors that are set to $x = 4$ and $z = 0.1$. The use of normal distributions is in line with the synthesis of realistic Grid resources such as proposed by Kee et al. (2004). Likewise to the previous bid generation technique, the number of attributes is set by an external parameter.

Time attributes are drawn from a uniform distribution. The particular ranges of each distribution are varied with respect to the applied bidding scenario. Furthermore, the maximum number of co-allocations is drawn from a uniform distribution within a range of $[1, \dots, c]$, where c is a parameter that is varied in each scenario. In addition, the percentage number of buyers that have such restrictions is varied in each bidding scenario.

The number of buyers and sellers as well as the number of atomic bids is determined by an external variable in each scenario. Table 7.3 summarizes these distributions and parameter settings for generating realistic bids.

Bid Characteristics	Distribution	Varied Parameters
Bundle creation	Arbitrary relations	Total number of goods G
Quality attributes	Normal $N(\mu, \sigma^2)$	Number of attributes A_k, μ, σ^2
Time attributes	Uniform $[a, \dots, b]$	Time ranges a and b
Allocation restriction	Fixed	Bids & goods with coupling restrictions
	Fixed, Uniform $[1, \dots, c]$	Bids & goods with divisibility restrictions
Valuation	Arbitrary relations	Truthful or manipulated bidding

Table 7.3: Distributions and parameters for generating realistic bids

7.4.3   Simulation Settings

The previous subsections described two techniques for generating bids for the proposed Grid market model. The configuration of several parameters is externalized in order to allow the definition of different bidding scenarios. The complete enumeration of all potential configurations is not possible. As a consequence, a set of selected configurations is defined as target simulation settings. The parameter configurations for these settings are shown in Table 7.4. For simplicity, the number of atomic bids is set to 1. The economic influences of XOR and

---

[7]For the work at hand, prices are computed as integer values.

OR bids are assumed to be comparable to the effects observed with one atomic bid per agent. In addition, the number of available resources is set to $G = 5$.

Id	Attributes	Time	Coupling	Allocation
1	2	$[0..4], [1..3]$	0	0
2	5	$[0..4], [1..3]$	0	0
3	2	$[0..12], [1..3]$	0	0
4	2	$[0..4], [1..3]$	50%, 2	50%, 50%, $[1..3]$

Table 7.4: Parameters of different simulation settings

The first setting defines the baseline scenario. In this setting, each agent submits one atomic bid on a particular bundle. The bundle consists of at most 5 different goods that each have 2 different attributes. The earliest start time and the latest possible allocation time for the bundle are drawn from a uniform distribution within a range of $[0..4]$.[8] Likewise, the number of required slots for a buyer bid is uniformly distributed within a range of $[1..3]$. In the baseline setting, no agent has any coupling and co-allocation restrictions. The subsequent scenarios differentiate from this baseline scenario by varying one particular parameter. The number of attributes is varied in setting 2. In setting 3, the earliest and latest time slots are drawn from a uniform range within a range of $[0..12]$. Finally, setting 4 varies the coupling and co-allocation parameters. In this setting, 50% of the buyers have coupling constraints, where 2 different pairs of the bundle's resources are selected randomly. In addition, 50% of the buyers have maximal divisibility constraints for 50% of their resources. The maximum divisibility of each affected resource is picked randomly within a range of $[1..3]$.

The bundles for these settings are created either by the use of the technique for domain independent bids or by the technique for generating realistic bids. Thus, the evaluation space E for the study at hand is described by

$$E = <I_1, I_2, I_3, I_4, R_1, R_2, R_3, R_4>,$$

where I_i denotes an instance of setting i with the application of the domain independent bid generation technique. A scenario R_i is based on setting i and applies the technique for generating realistic bids. With respect to the particular simulation problem, the number of buyers and sellers is varied.

The definition of the bidding scenarios concludes the second stage of the simulation study. The proposed model can be characterized as a static, discrete, and stochastic imitation of a Grid market. Agents submit their bids as a one-shot game, i.e., they cannot dynamically adapt their strategies nor bid in a continuous manner. This results in a static and discrete simulation model. In addition, the agents' bids are stochastically influenced as values are picked from different stochastic distributions. Thus, the applied type of simulation can be based on the Monte Carlo approach.

---

[8]First, the earliest time slot is selected at random. Next, the latest time slot is computed by adding another random number to the value of the earliest time slot. In case the time frame is too small for the required slots ($l_n^N(S_j) - e_n^N(S_j) < s_n(S_j)$), the latest time slot is set to $l_n^N(S_j) = e_n^N(S_j) + s_n(S_j)$.

7.5   Model Implementation

The third stage of the simulation study is concerned with the implementation of the designed model. This comprises the process of transforming the model into a software system, verifying the implementation, and validating the model.

Different toolkits have been proposed for simulating market based settings. For instance, the Repast framework provides a generic platform for agent-based simulations. Furthermore, AMASE as proposed by van Dinther (2006) can be applied for simulating auction mechanisms within the meet2trade suite (Weinhardt et al. 2006). However, the proposed simulation toolkits neither implement combinatorial mechanisms nor support the proposed bid generation techniques.

In order to evaluate the mechanism, a new simulation tool was developed that accounts for the target model and that can be applied for the analysis of the simulation problems. The next section briefly describes this tool and demonstrates how simulations can be performed with it.

7.5.1   jCase – Java Combinatorial Auction Simulation Environment

The Java Combinatorial Auction Simulation Environment (jCase) is a toolkit for simulating combinatorial mechanisms.[9] jCase – shown in Figure 7.3 – is capable of generating different bidding streams with a varying number of participants, resources, and bundles. The simulator integrates the MACE market service (cf. Section 6.2) as an auction implementation. jCase can submit bids to the market service and can trigger allocation decisions by means of the service's APIs.

The simulation tool implements, among others, the proposed bidding techniques for generating stochastically influenced bids. It integrates the CATS 2.0 framework and provides a set of different bundle distributions. Different evaluation metrics can be measured and stored into a database for further analysis. Simulation settings are described using an XML based description language. Once a scenario is encoded by means of this specification, it can be executed using the graphical user interface or by means of a batch process. The bidding streams generated by jCase can also be stored as XML files on the local hard disk.

Figure 7.4 depicts a part of the simulation description for the above mentioned simulation setting I_1 with decay distributed bundles. By means of this description, 5 buyers and 5 sellers are generated that submit bids. The number of atomic bids which a buyer can submit is fixed to 1. Furthermore, the decay distribution is applied to create bundles. Attribute characteristics are drawn from a uniform distribution within a range of $[1..2000]$. The valuations are generated using the proposed technique for decay bundles and subsequently multiplied by 1000. In this exemplarily setting, 30% of the buyers manipulate their bids by underbidding their valuations by 20%. The time ranges (earliest start and latest deadline) are both drawn from a uniform distribution within a range of $[0..4]$. Furthermore, the number of slots is uniformly distributed within $[1..3]$.[10]

Aside from MACE, the simulator can also be applied to other combinatorial problems. The flexible description capabilities for simulation settings allow the analysis of a multitude

---

[9]See http://www.iw.uni-karlsruhe.de/jcase for details.

[10]Whenever a zero value is selected from the distribution, the random picking process is repeated. This is required due to practical reasons, as bids with 0 required slots are not valid.

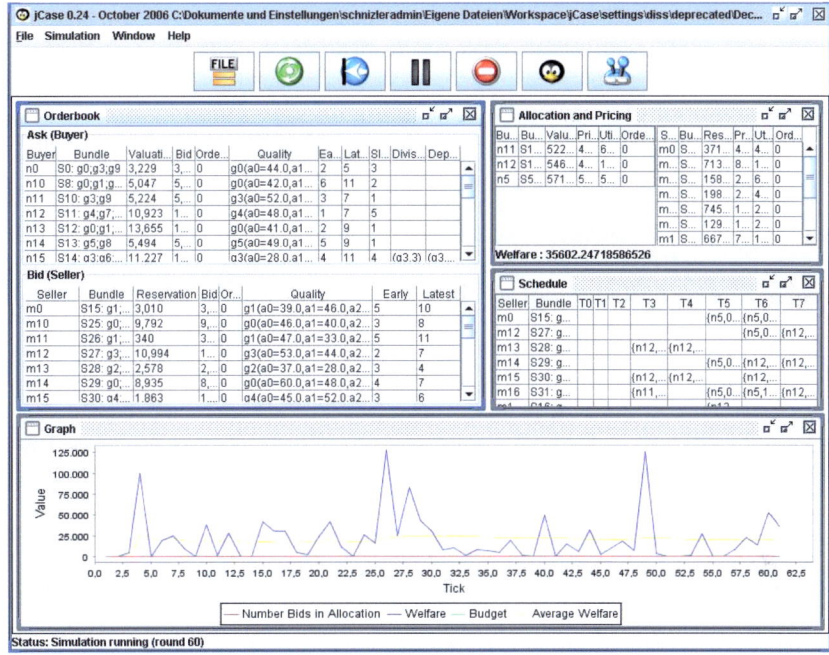

Figure 7.3: Screenshot of the user interface of jCase

```
<orderbook type="distribution">
 <buyerspertick distribution="Fixed" mean="5"/>
 <sellerspertick distribution="Fixed" mean="5"/>
 <buyerorder percentage="100">
   <maxbids distribution="Fixed" mean="1"/>
   <bundlecreator name="Decay">
     <attributes id="all">
       <distribution name="Uniform" multiplier="2000"/>
     <attributes>
   </bundlecreator>
   <valuation>
     <bundlepricing algorithm="Decay" multiplier="1000"/>
     <manipulation percentageAgents="30"
                   percentageManipulation="20"/>
   </valuation>
   <earlyrange distribution="Uniform" multiplier="4"/>
   <laterange distribution="Uniform" multiplier="4"/>
   <slot distribution="Uniform" multiplier="3"/>
 </buyerorder>
 [...]
</orderbook>
```

Figure 7.4: Part of a jCase simulation description

of different scenarios. In the context of market engineering, the tool is already successfully applied to simulate a single sided combinatorial mechanism and the PPC pricing schema (Neumann et al. 2007). As a consequence, jCase qualifies as a simulation environment that assists the market engineer in evaluating combinatorial auctions.

7.5.2 Verification and Validation

Having implemented the proposed simulation model, it is verified and validated. In the verification phase, one analyzes the correctness of the model transformation into a software system. In the validation phase, one determines that the conceptual model is an adequate representation of the real system (Banks 1998).

7.5.2.1 Verification

The implementation of the MACE market service and jCase was continuously supported by performing unit tests.[11] Such tests are performed to verify that particular modules of a software system work properly (Cheon and Leavens 2002). Unit tests call particular methods or modules with a predefined set of input data. Subsequently, the output of the method is compared to the expected outcome. For jCase and the MACE market service, such tests were implemented and performed for most methods and modules.

Aside from unit tests, the platform was verified by means of predefined bidding cases. Simple bidding settings were constructed manually, solved, and reexamined by the platform. Furthermore, different example sets found in literature served as additional test cases (Parkes 2001; Parkes et al. 2001).

7.5.2.2 Validation

A holistic validation of the model is difficult as no Grid marketplace or comparable system exists in practice. However, some of the proposed assumptions and characteristics of the model can be analyzed by means of existing validation techniques (Law and Kelton 2000).

The requirements upon the mechanism are based on experiences and propositions found in literature and expert forums such as the OGF. With regard to the work proposed within the Grid community, the elicited requirements are interpreted to be correct. The design of the bidding streams cannot be supported by existing theories derived from Grid technologies. However, the distributions used for the model are applied in several combinatorial auction studies to analyze similar effects as the ones proposed in this work (Parkes et al. 2001; Sandholm et al. 2005; Leyton-Brown et al. 2006). Finally, extreme condition tests have been performed to increase the creditability of the model. As an example, suppose that all agents manipulate their bids by a high value. As a result, none the of bids are successful, which leads to an empty allocation set. This observation corresponds with the expected outcome of the mechanism, as buyers pretend low valuations and sellers high reservation prices. Consequently, no potential buyer can be found that is willing to pay the reservation prices of sellers. In addition, an analysis of manipulating bidders and the VCG mechanism was performed. The effects observed by the simulation correspond with the theoretical findings. No agent can gain a positive utility by manipulating his bids.

---

[11]The testing framework jUnit was applied to perform the tests. See `http://www.junit.org/` for more details.

Although the applied validation of the model cannot be as comprehensive as models that are based on existing systems, the tests increase the validity and credibility of the model and its implementation.

7.6 Summary

This chapter introduced basic concepts of simulation, outlined the design of a Grid market model, and described its implementation into a software system. Section 7.1 outlined the theory of simulation and described a structured process that assists the market engineer in performing them. Based upon this process, Section 7.2 defined a set of simulation questions that are to be evaluated in the study. Subsequently, a simulation model was introduced in Section 7.3 that accounts for the defined simulation questions. Corresponding with the market model, Section 7.4 introduced a set of bidding scenarios that serve as input data for the MACE market mechanism. Finally, Section 7.5 outlined the implementation of a simulation framework that can be applied to study combinatorial market mechanisms.

The next chapter is concerned with the presentation and assessment of the obtained simulation results. The results reveal whether or not MACE fulfills the elicited requirements upon a Grid market mechanism.

Chapter 8

Simulation Results

Just as classic mechanism design introduces incentive-compatible constraints to restrict the space of feasible mechanisms, computational constraints further restrict the space of feasible mechanisms.
(Kalagnanam and Parkes 2004, p. 179)

The previous chapter introduced a simulation model that imitates agents submitting multi-attribute combinatorial bids in a Grid market. In addition, a simulation framework was proposed that is used to perform the simulation runs. Consequently, the aim of this chapter is to analyze and to interpret the obtained results.

All simulation runs were performed on a Pentium XEON with a single CPU (3.2GHz) and 2GB of main memory. The Windows 32-bit version of CPLEX 9.1 was used to solve the winner determination problem of MACE. Most of the standard parameters of CPLEX were not changed, except a set of settings that were set to emphasize the feasibility of solutions. The varied parameter settings are given in Table B.1 (Appendix B.1).

The obtained results are biased as the input bidding streams are influenced stochastically. In order to obtain meaningful data which, ideally, is not affected by stochastic processes, the simulation runs are replicated with different random seeds (van Dinther 2006).[1] As the particular random seeds are independent of each other, the results can be aggregated by means of statistical procedures such as computing means and variances. For each effect to be studied, the total number of repetitions is varied.[2]

With respect to the problem definition of the simulation study, the remaining of this chapter is structured as follows: First, Section 8.1 analyzes the technical and economical results obtained by the application of an optimal winner determination algorithm. After this step, Section 8.2 describes the results obtained by the use of approximated allocation decisions. Section 8.3 reflects the simulation results with respect to the open problems of the MACE mechanism and concludes the chapter.

---

[1] jCase uses the JET engine to compute pseudo random numbers. See `http://dsd.lbl.gov/ ~hoschek/colt/` for details.

[2] Among others, Law and Kelton (2000) propose different techniques to identify the number of required simulation repetitions. However, most of the procedures make strict assumptions upon the input data which may not be satisfied for the target bidding scenarios. In line with related combinatorial auction studies, a fixed number of repetitions is used (Parkes et al. 2001; Sandholm et al. 2005).

8.1 Optimal Winner Determination

The first set of treatments analyzes the effects obtained by the use of an optimal winner determination algorithm. First, Section 8.1.1 identifies an upper boundary of agents for which the problem is computationally tractable within a meaningful time frame. Subsequently, Section 8.1.2 analyzes the economic effects that occur if agents deviate from bidding truthfully.

8.1.1 Computational Tractability

The first analysis is concerned with the runtime of CPLEX that is required to solve the winner determination problem of MACE. In order to determine an upper boundary of problem instances that can be solved optimally, the solver is interrupted after 5 minutes. If no optimal solution is found within this time frame, the problem instance is marked as non solvable. The corresponding runtime of this instance is set to 5 minutes. As such, the measured runtime does not always reflect the true computational effort that is required to solve an instance. However, solving each instance optimally may require too much computation time.[3] Moreover, the simulation question at hand only requires the identification of problem instances that can be solved in less than 5 minutes.

The runtime of CPLEX is measured with a varying number of agents. In each setting, the number of buyers and sellers is equally distributed. For instance, a setting with 50 agents represents 25 buyers and 25 sellers each submitting one atomic bid to the auctioneer. The analysis is performed for all proposed simulation settings (cf. Section 7.4.3). In total, 50 problem instances are created with different initial random seeds for each sample set.

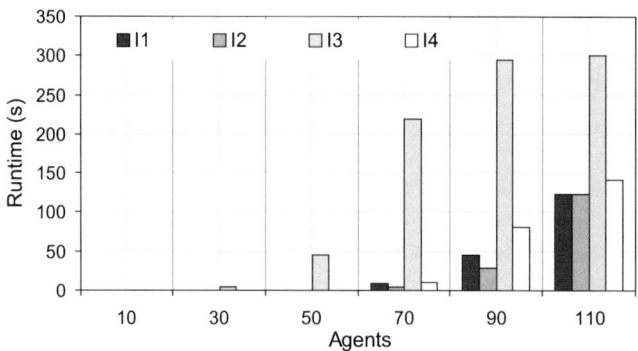

Figure 8.1: Runtime of CPLEX to solve settings $I_1 - I_4$ with independent domain bids

Domain Independent Bids: Figure 8.1 depicts the runtime of CPLEX for the domain independent bidding scenarios with a varying number of agents. On average, CPLEX requires more than 8 seconds to determine an allocation if 70 agents submit their I_1 distributed bids to the auctioneer. With I_3 distributed bids, the solver requires 3.92 seconds to compute an outcome for 30 agents.

---

[3]During preliminary studies, settings were identified that require more than 72 hours to get solved optimally.

The graph evinces that I_3 distributed bids lead to the hardest problem instances. This is reasoned by the fact that the earliest and latest allocation slots of the resources are greater than in other scenarios. Consequently, the decision space of potential solutions increases considerably.

The bars do not reflect the exponential runtime of the solver. As the solver is interrupted after 5 minutes, the runtime gets falsified with an increasing number of bids. There are already instances with 90 agents that cannot be solved optimally within 5 minutes in the I_1 bidding scenario.

Number	I_1			I_2			I_3			I_4		
of agents	μ	σ	max	μ	σ	max	μ	σ	max	μ	σ	max
10	0.0	0.0	0.2	0.0	0.0	0.0	0.0	0.0	0.0	0.0	0.0	0.0
30	0.0	0.0	0.1	0.0	0.0	0.2	3.9	25.5	180.8	0.0	0.0	0.2
50	0.4	0.7	4.1	0.6	1.4	10.1	44.7	87.0	300.0	0.4	0.9	6.3
70	8.5	21.3	114.3	4.2	8.5	52.6	219.8	119.3	300.0	9.9	29.1	193.3
90	44.4	78.8	300.0	28.5	60.8	300.0	295.0	29.7	300.0	81.3	108.1	300.0
110	123.6	119.4	300.0	123.4	124.4	300.0	300.0	0.0	300.0	141.4	125.1	300.0

Table 8.1: Mean, standard deviation, and maximum runtime to solve settings $I_1 - I_4$

Table 8.1 summarizes mean (μ), standard deviation (σ), and maximum runtime (max) for each processed data set in setting $I_1 - I_4$. The results show that the problem cannot be solved optimally within 5 minutes for settings with more than 30 agents (I_3 setting). Further, the high standard deviations indicate that the runtime fluctuates intensively for each setting. This means that two problem sets that are generated by equal distributions require very different computational effort to get solved. In line with other combinatorial studies, this result demonstrates that similarly generated bids may require different effort to get solved (Leyton-Brown et al. 2006; Sandholm et al. 2005).

Realistic Bids: In accordance with the previous analysis, the winner determination problem of MACE is also hard to solve for settings that are based on realistic bids. Figure 8.2 shows the computational runtime of CPLEX to solve the problem instances $R_1 - R_4$.

An interesting observation is that most realistic bid instances are slightly harder to solve than the domain independent settings. One reason for this could be the different approaches that are applied to generate quality characteristics. Domain independent quality attributes are distributed uniformly and neither depend on each other nor on the underlying price of the bundle. In contrast, quality characteristics of realistic bids reflect the bundle's characteristics as well as the valuation and reservation price. Due to the independent quality attributes in the domain independent settings, CPLEX may be able to find non-matchable bundles more quickly.

In contrast to the previous study, the computational runtime of the R_4 setting with coupling and co-allocation restrictions is also very high. This can be explained by the high number of overlapping bundles in R_4 distributed instances. In I_4 settings, most co-allocation restrictions cannot be considered, as there are not enough counterparts on the sellers' side that offer the required resources from the same machine. Due to the construction of realistic bids with arbitrary relationships, the number of potential sellers that can offer coupled resources is higher than in I_4 instances.

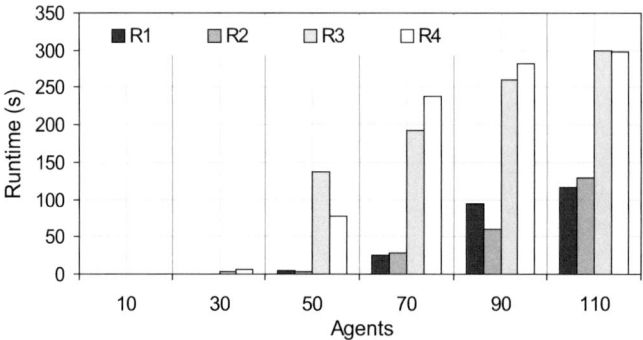

Figure 8.2: Runtime of CPLEX to solve settings $R_1 - R_4$ with realistic bids

Number	I_1			I_2			I_3			I_4		
of agents	μ	σ	max	μ	σ	max	μ	σ	max	μ	σ	max
10	0.0	0.0	0.0	0.0	0.01	0.0	0.0	0.0	0.0	0.0	0.0	0.0
30	0.1	0.5	3.4	0.1	0.17	1.1	3.1	16.0	113.6	6.06	38.4	272.5
50	3.9	17.5	123.8	3.9	15.6	109.8	137.6	137.7	300.0	77.5	114.5	300.0
70	24.6	65.1	300.0	28.8	72.8	300.0	192.7	137.65	300.0	238.6	111.6	300.0
90	95.1	119.5	300.0	59.4	103.4	300.0	260.2	93.66	300.0	281.7	59.8	300.0
110	117.4	127.9	300.0	129.2	131.2	300.0	300.0	0.01	300.0	297.9	11.8	300.0

Table 8.2: Mean, standard deviation, and maximum runtime to solve settings $R_1 - R_5$

Table 8.2 shows mean (μ), standard deviation (σ), and maximum runtime (max) for each processed data set. The results are similar to the ones obtained from the previous study. The problem cannot always be solved optimally with more than 30 agents. In addition, the small standard deviation of settings with 110 agents indicates that most of these problem instances require more than 5 minutes to get solved. In summary, the analysis shows that the winner determination problem of MACE is computationally intractable without the introduction of approximations.

8.1.2 Manipulating Agents

In the second treatment, it is assumed that $\lambda\%$ of all buyers and sellers misrepresent their true valuations and reservation prices. The remaining $(100 - \lambda)\%$ agents reveal their private information honestly. Manipulating buyers $\tilde{n} \in \widetilde{\mathcal{N}}$ underbid their true preferences by only revealing a valuation of $\tilde{v}_{\tilde{n}}(S_j) = \frac{100-\beta}{100} \cdot v_{\tilde{n}}(S_j)$ and sellers $\tilde{m} \in \widetilde{\mathcal{M}}$ overbid their reservation prices up to $\tilde{r}_{\tilde{m}}(S_j) = \frac{100}{100-\beta} \cdot r_{\tilde{m}}(S_j)$. Each generated bid stream is processed twice, once with truthful and once with manipulating agents. The differences between these outcomes serve as a basis for measuring the economic effects of the pricing schema.

In each simulated scenario, 12 buyers and 12 sellers submit their bids to the auctioneer. The low number of agents allows an expressive analysis of the economic effects caused by their behavior. The higher the competition is on the market, the lower the influences of single manipulating agents (Jackson 2002; Schnizler et al. 2006b).

The scenarios are analyzed for 4 different settings: In the first setting, only 1 buyer manipulates his bids (denoted as $1B$). In the second setting, 2 buyers and 2 sellers manipulate their preferences and the resulting utility of all agents is averaged (denoted as $2B, 2S$). In the third setting, half of the buyers and sellers manipulate (denoted as $6B, 6S$); in the fourth setting, all agents manipulate their bids (denoted as $12B, 12S$). In total, 350 samples are computed for each bidding scenario and the results are averaged.

8.1.2.1 Efficiency Loss

In the first treatment, the efficiency loss due to manipulating agents is measured for the baseline scenario I_1 with domain independent bids.

The left part of Figure 8.3 shows the percentage efficiency loss (cf. Equation 7.1) with a varying number of manipulating agents as a function of the manipulation factor. For instance, if half of the agents ($6B, 6S$) manipulate their valuations and reservation prices by $\lambda = 30\%$, the resulting efficiency loss is 46.65%. In case all agents manipulate their preferences by more than $\lambda = 90\%$, the resulting efficiency loss converges to 100%, i.e., the set of successful agents in the auction becomes empty. It is apparent that the efficiency loss is higher when more agents manipulate their bids.

If one agent ($1B$) manipulates by a factor greater than $\lambda = 40\%$, the efficiency curve stagnates. This stagnation results from the fact that the agent is not part of the allocation for settings with a manipulation factor higher than 40%. The reported valuation of the buyer is too low for being part of the allocation set. This means that none of his requests can be matched with any resource provider.

The graph evinces that an agent increases the risk of not getting allocated in the outcome if he manipulates his bids. This effect is supported by the right part of Figure 8.3 that depicts

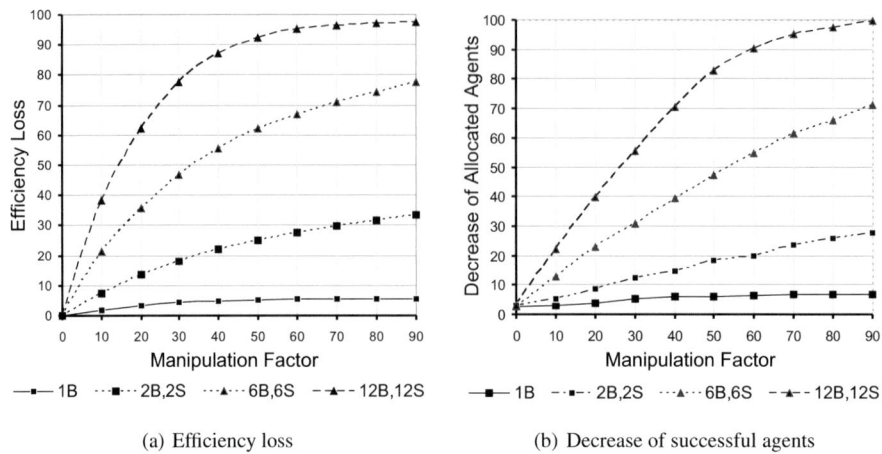

(a) Efficiency loss   (b) Decrease of successful agents

Figure 8.3: Efficiency loss and decrease of successful agents in setting I_1 with manipulating agents

the percentage loss of the number of successful bidders in the allocation. For instance, if half of the agents ($6B, 6S$) manipulate their bids by $\lambda = 30\%$, the number of allocated agents is 30% smaller than in the non-manipulating scenario. Furthermore, if all agents ($12B, 12S$) are manipulating by $\lambda = 40\%$, the size of the allocation set decreases by 70%.

Modification	1B		2B,2S		6B,6S		12B,12S	
Factor	μ	σ	μ	σ	μ	σ	μ	σ
5	0.97	3.05	4.05	8.00	12.16	14.25	21.73	17.21
10	1.91	6.01	7.49	11.97	21.36	19.11	38.13	21.85
15	2.77	8.73	10.63	15.65	29.03	22.34	51.46	23.81
20	3.40	10.25	13.44	18.55	35.67	24.59	62.16	24.09
30	4.37	12.61	18.12	22.38	46.65	27.32	77.46	22.07
40	4.94	13.80	21.98	25.23	55.55	29.28	86.97	19.39
50	5.28	14.48	25.03	27.18	62.03	29.99	92.40	17.41
60	5.46	14.79	27.52	28.53	67.09	30.35	95.19	16.41
70	5.57	15.00	29.87	29.99	71.01	30.10	96.50	16.01
80	5.62	15.09	31.69	30.88	74.25	29.35	97.12	15.86
90	5.63	15.13	33.60	31.94	77.62	28.94	97.39	15.85

Table 8.3: Mean and standard deviation of the percentage efficiency loss in setting I_1 with manipulating agents

Finally, Table 8.3 summarizes mean and standard deviation of these results.[4] The table shows that the results are partially unstable due to high standard deviations. This can be explained by the construction of the applied bidding scenarios which are subject to high degrees of freedom. For instance, the values for quality and time attributes are drawn from

---

[4]Means and standard deviations for the decrease of allocated agents are given in Table B.2 (Appendix B.2.1).

independent uniform distributions. Consequently, a bid with 5 different resources that each
has 3 different attributes is influenced by more than 15 independent distributions. Thus, it
is in the nature of the generated bids being characterized by a high standard deviation. In
contrast, an analysis that restricts all but one distribution to a fixed value would lead to stable
– but too simplistic – results.

8.1.2.2 K-Price Incentive Compatibility

In the second analysis, the individual utility gain of manipulating agents is measured. This
gives information on whether or not the utility of agents can be improved through manipulation. Following Equation 7.2, the measured metric reflects the difference between the
utility gained by manipulation and the utility gained in a truthful scenario. Consequently, the
following results reflect absolute values. In case a manipulating agent $\tilde{i}$ is neither part of the
allocation in the truthful scenario o nor in the manipulating scenario $\bar{o}$, the resulting utilities
$(u_{\tilde{i}}(o) = u_{\tilde{i}}(\bar{o}) = 0)$ are neglected.

Domain Independent Bids: Figure 8.4 depicts the utility gain of agents as a function
that depends on the manipulation factor $\beta\%$. The input data is generated using the baseline
setting I_1 for domain independent bids. The graph points out that agents can increase their
utility by manipulation. For instance, if one agent underbids his valuation by $\lambda = 20\%$,
his average utility gain is $UG_k^O = 394.15$. However, if the agent manipulates by more than
$\lambda = 20\%$, his average utility gain continuously decreases. This is reasoned by the fact
that he increases the risk of not getting allocated in the final outcome. In settings with a
manipulation factor greater than $\lambda = 40\%$, he has a negative utility gain. Consequently, he
has no incentive to underbid his valuation by more than $\lambda = 40\%$. Utility losses greater than
500 ($UG_k^O \leq -500$) are truncated in the graph.

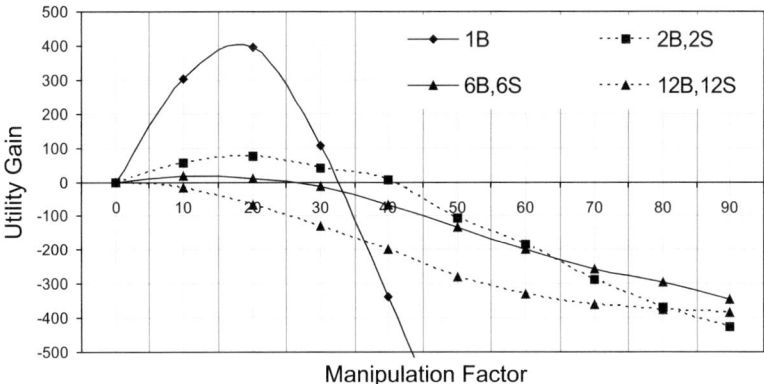

Figure 8.4: Utility gain of manipulating agents with the application of the k-pricing schema
and bidding scenario I_1

If more agents deviate from bidding truthfully, the average utility gain of each agent
decreases. In settings where half of the agents manipulate their bids by more than $\lambda = 30\%$,

no agent has a positive utility gain on average. Moreover, if all agents manipulate their bids, none of them can attain a positive utility. This can be explained by the fact that the total number of potential counterparts decreases as the price span between buyers and sellers increases.

Modification	1B			2B,2S			6B,6S			12B,12S		
Factor	μ	σ	CV	μ	σ	CV	μ	σ	CV	μ	σ	CV
5	163.0	165.2	1.0	28.5	101.6	3.5	12.7	40.0	3.1	-4.7	10.5	-2.2
10	304.1	356.3	1.1	54.4	141.8	2.6	16.7	65.6	3.9	-17.9	27.8	-1.5
15	354.3	651.6	1.8	70.2	198.0	2.8	13.9	88.1	6.3	-37.0	46.5	-1.2
20	394.1	866.1	2.2	76.8	250.3	3.2	10.0	106.9	10.6	-65.6	73.0	-1.1
30	108.0	1496.2	13.8	39.0	347.5	8.9	-15.1	161.1	-10.6	-128.5	122.2	-0.9
40	-337.2	1757.2	-5.2	4.2	416.6	97.3	-68.7	223.9	-3.2	-198.4	171.4	-0.8
50	-782.9	1715.5	-2.1	-106.8	489.5	-4.5	-132.0	261.4	-1.9	-280.9	239.8	-0.8

Table 8.4: Utility gain in setting I_1 with the application of the k-pricing schema for values $\lambda \leq 50\%$

Table 8.4 shows mean (μ), standard deviation (σ), and coefficient of variation ($CV = \sigma/\mu$) for the measured points with $\lambda \leq 50\%$. The high CV values with $CV > 1$ indicate that the utility gain fluctuates in most settings. Following the previous argumentation, the input data for the simulation is already characterized by a high standard deviation.[5] Consequently, the incentive properties of the k-pricing schema strongly depend on particular problem instances. The complete table representing all measured values can be found in Table B.3 (Appendix B.2.2).

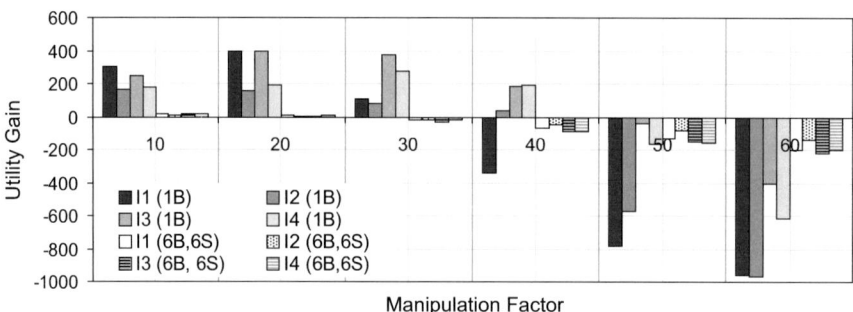

Figure 8.5: Utility gain of manipulating agents with the application of the k-pricing schema in setting $I_1 - I_4$

Figure 8.5 compares all domain independent bidding scenarios $I_1 - I_4$. It depicts scenarios in which one agent ($1B$) and half of the agents ($6B, 6S$) manipulate their bids up to a

---

[5]For this setting, an alternative study was performed with an increased number of repetitions. However, a repetition of 800 times with varying random seeds resulted in similar means that are also characterized by high standard deviations.

factor of $\lambda = 60\%$. If half of the agents manipulate, the results for the scenarios are comparable. A manipulation factor that is smaller than 30% leads to positive utility gains of agents. If agents manipulate by a higher factor, they have negative utilities.

In contrast, the results differ if only one agent manipulates ($1B$). The most conspicuous cases are I_3 distributed bids in which the number of allocatable time slots is increased. In this setting, the agent gains the highest utility. The increased number of allocatable slots decreases the degree of competition on single slots. Due to the lack of competition, the manipulating agent still finds counterparts, even if he manipulates by a high factor. In settings with $\lambda \geq 50\%$, however, the revealed valuation is too low to find any seller. This results in negative utility gains. In addition, the baseline setting I_1 is the only one in which the individual utility gain is negative for a manipulation factor of $\lambda = 40\%$. This indicates that I_1 distributed settings lead to higher competition than the remaining ones.[6]

In summary, the results show that agents can gain a positive utility by manipulating their bids. The gains, however, are restricted to settings in which only few agents manipulate their bids by a low factor.

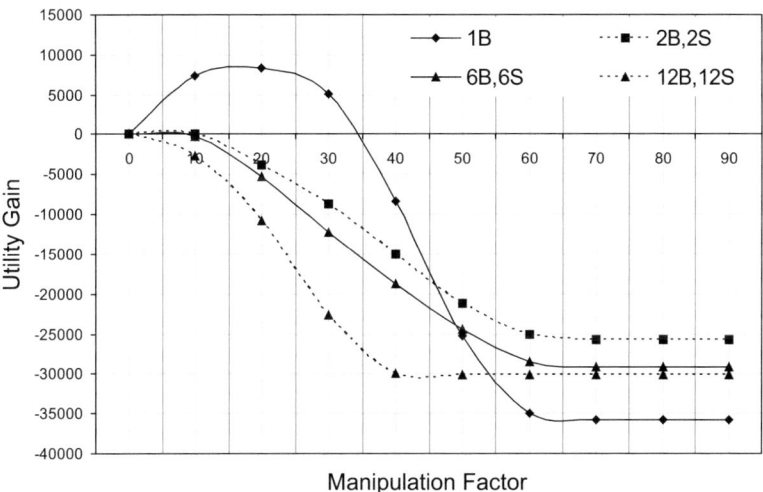

Figure 8.6: Utility gain of manipulating agents with the application of the k-pricing schema and bidding scenario R_1

Realistic Bids: Figure 8.6 shows the utility gain of agents for the baseline scenario R_1 with realistic bids. The trends of the curves are comparable to the previous study. The highest utility gain is attained if only one agent manipulates his bids by $\lambda = 15\%$ ($UG^O_{n,k}(o) = 8699.08$). In settings with a factor higher than $\lambda = 40\%$, the agent cannot gain a positive utility by manipulating. If more agents deviate from bidding truthfully, the average utility gains decrease considerably. In contrast to the domain independent bidding scenarios, negative utilities of

---

[6]Appendix B.2.2 (Table B.4–B.5) shows mean and standard deviation for settings $I_2 - I_4$.

agents are already attained by a smaller manipulation factor. For instance, if 2 buyers and 2 sellers manipulate their bids, they only have a positive utility with a manipulation factor of $\lambda \leq 10\%$. This fact supports the assumption that domain independent bids serve as worst case scenarios for the problem at hand.

Modification	1B			2B,2S			6B,6S			12B,12S		
Factor	μ	σ	CV	μ	σ	CV	μ	σ	CV	μ	σ	CV
5	3789	8950	2.36	710	6334	8.92	491	3007	6.13	-606	789	-1.30
10	7432	13321	1.79	45	10938	242.25	-265	5573	-21.04	-2734	2416	-0.88
15	8699	20378	2.34	-1459	15258	-10.46	-2234	8116	-3.63	-6034	4374	-0.72
20	8340	26394	3.16	-3820	17948	-4.70	-5307	10866	-2.05	-10727	6824	-0.64
30	5110	37499	7.34	-8717	23232	-2.67	-12275	14927	-1.22	-22706	12111	-0.53
40	-8368	45293	-5.41	-14994	25359	-1.69	-18768	18017	-0.96	-29964	15897	-0.53
50	-25259	43344	-1.72	-21229	26518	-1.25	-24392	19220	-0.79	-30090	15974	-0.53

Table 8.5: Utility gain in setting R_1 with the application of the k-pricing schema for values $\lambda \leq 50\%$

Table 8.5 shows mean, standard deviation, and CV for settings with $\lambda \leq 50\%$. In accordance with the previous studies, the results are characterized by a high standard deviation and a high CV. In particular, a high CV value can be found for the settings $2B, 2S$ and $6B, 6S$ with $\lambda = 10\%$. Although the individual utility gains are negative on average, the standard deviations are considerably high. This means that there are cases in which the average utility is strictly positive. The complete table that represents all measured values can be found in Table B.7 (Appendix B.2.2).

Figure 8.7 depicts the utility gains for realistic distributed bids $R_1 - R_4$. The graph is restricted to scenarios in which either one agent ($1B$) or half of the agents ($6B, 6S$) manipulate. The complete data for these settings is shown in Table B.8 – B.10 (Appendix B.2.2).

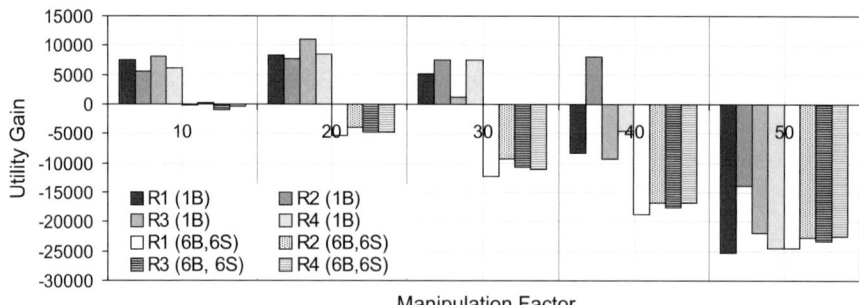

Figure 8.7: Utility gain of manipulating agents with the application of the k-pricing schema in setting $R_1 - R_4$

In analogy to domain independent bids, the highest utility gain is attained if one agent manipulates by $\lambda = 20\%$ in the R_3 setting, which includes the increased number of allocatable time slots. In contrast to the previous comparison, R_2 distributed bids favor most manipulating agents. A single agent can still gain a considerable high utility by underbidding his valuation by $\lambda = 40\%$. However, if the number of manipulating agents increases, the individual utility gains are fairly mild.

In summary, the analysis of the realistic bidding scenarios shows that the incentive properties of the k-pricing schema are better than in domain independent settings. Although a single agent can gain a positive utility by not revealing his true preferences, the gain decreases if more agents start to manipulate their bids. If only one agent manipulates by a low factor, the overall efficiency losses are small (cf. Section 8.1.2.1). Consequently, the application of the k-pricing schema for the Grid deems promising. However, a comparison of the incentive properties with other price mechanisms is still required.

8.1.2.3 Approximated VCG Incentive Compatibility

An assessment of the incentive properties of the k-pricing schema requires a comparison with an alternative pricing mechanism. For the work at hand, the approximated VCG pricing schema serves as benchmark (Parkes et al. 2001). In order to compare both pricing schemes, the analysis of the utility gain with the approximated VCG mechanism is performed on the same input data as for the k-price settings. Consequently, the results of both pricing mechanisms can be compared.

Domain Independent Bids: The first comparison is concerned with domain independent bids I_1. Figure 8.8 shows the utility gained by manipulating agents for both pricing mechanisms. The bars denote the results obtained by the approximated VCG mechanism; the lines represent the outcomes with the k-pricing schema. If the utility losses are higher than 500, they are truncated.

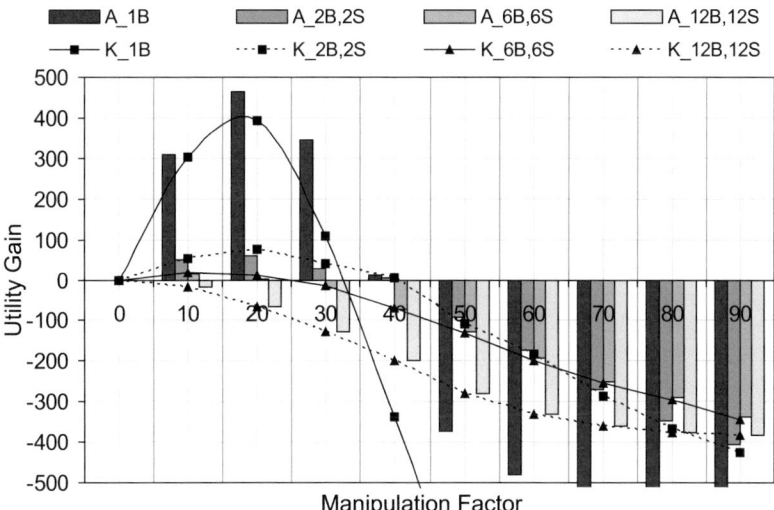

Figure 8.8: Utility gain of manipulating agents using the approximated VCG mechanism and the k-pricing schema in setting I_1

The graph indicates that the incentive properties of both pricing schemes are similar. With both mechanisms, the highest individual utility gain of one manipulating agent is attained by a factor of $\lambda = 20\%$. Higher manipulation factors continuously decrease the agent's utility. In cases with only one manipulating agent ($1B$), the k-pricing mechanism performs slightly better than the approximated VCG pricing. In addition, the agent still attains a positive utility using the approximated VCG schema by underbidding his valuation by $\lambda = 40\%$. In settings with the same manipulation factor, however, the agent gains a negative utility with the k-pricing schema. If 2 buyers and 2 sellers manipulate, no considerable difference between the utilities can be identified. Settings in which all agents manipulate their bids are equal in both pricing schemes. No individual agent can gain a positive utility by manipulation as the resulting net payments are equally distributed among all agents. A detailed overview of the means, standard deviations and CVs of the I_1 setting with approximated VCG pricing is given in Table B.11 (Appendix B.2.2).

Modification	1B			2B,2S		
Factor	μ_{AV}	μ_k	$\frac{\mu_{AV}}{\mu_k}$	μ_{AV}	μ_k	$\frac{\mu_{AV}}{\mu_k}$
5	150.33	163.07	0.92	26.39	28.53	0.92
10	307.64	304.11	1.01	48.98	54.49	0.90
15	399.72	354.34	1.13	58.43	70.21	0.83
20	465.95	394.15	1.18	61.41	76.84	0.80
30	343.29	108.03	3.18	28.38	39.07	0.73
40	10.21	-337.20	-0.03	4.25	4.28	0.99
50	-372.20	-782.98	0.48	-93.78	-106.81	0.88
60	-480.54	-957.00	0.50*	-172.57	-183.33	0.94
70	-747.96	-1251.33	0.60*	-271.50	-286.09	0.95
80	-915.92	-1431.37	0.64*	-348.86	-368.29	0.95
90	-979.31	-1496.45	0.65*	-406.38	-426.84	0.95

∗ denotes significant differences between the samples

Table 8.6: Comparison of utility gains attained by the approximated VCG mechanism and the k-pricing schema in setting I_1

Table 8.6 compares both pricing schemes for settings in which one buyer ($1B$) and 2 buyers and 2 sellers manipulate ($2B, 2S$). The table shows the mean of the utility gain for the approximated VCG mechanism (μ_{AV}) and for the $k-$pricing schema (μ_k). In addition, the fraction $\frac{\mu_{AV}}{\mu_k}$ compares the results of both mechanisms. If the value is greater than 1, agents gain a lower utility in the k-pricing schema. For these settings, the k-pricing schema has better incentive properties than the approximated VCG mechanism. If the value is positive and smaller than one, the approximated VCG mechanism is superior. The negative value denotes the setting in which the k-pricing schema results in negative utilities while the agent still attains a positive utility using the approximated VCG mechanism.

The data emphasizes that both pricing mechanisms have similar incentive properties for $\lambda < 40\%$. In case one agent underbids by a factor greater than 40%, the utility losses in the k-pricing schema are higher than in the approximated VCG schema. This means that the k-pricing penalizes manipulating agents higher than the approximated VCG schema.

In order to substantiate these suggestions, the measured samples of both mechanisms are tested upon equality by means of a statistical test. The underlying data is independent from

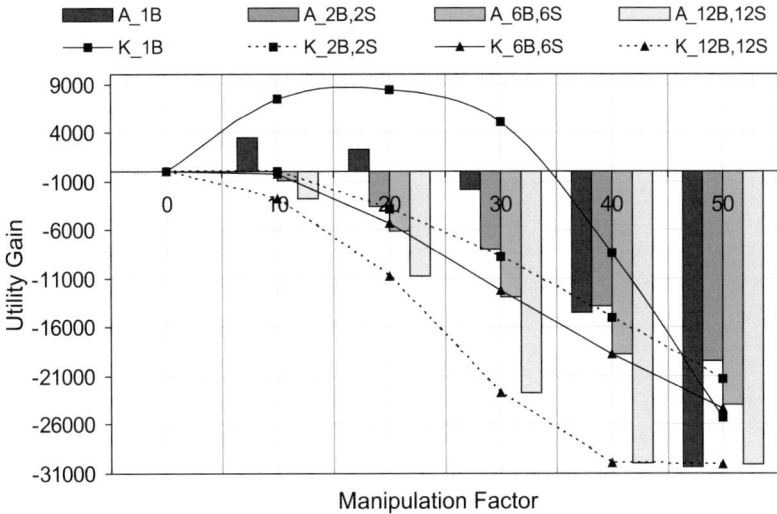

Figure 8.9: Utility gain of manipulating agents using the approximated VCG mechanism and the k-pricing schema in setting R_1

each other and can be characterized as a normal distribution.[7] Consequently, a paired t-test with unequal variances to test equality of both means can be applied. The corresponding H_0 hypothesis states that the curves are not different. For the data at hand, no significant difference can be determined except for values with one manipulating agent and $\lambda \geq 60\%$. Due to the high standard deviations of the samples, there may be further significant differences which cannot be detected by the test. For completeness, p-values for each sample are shown in Table B.12 (Appendix B.2.2).

The results for this setting show that the incentive properties of both mechanisms are comparable for small manipulation factors. As these factors denote the only situations in which agents can gain a positive utility, the mechanisms show comparable incentive properties. This fact strengthens the application of the k-pricing schema, as it is computationally more efficient than the approximated VCG mechanism.

Realistic Bids: In order to extend the obtained results, both mechanisms are compared for the bidding scenario R_1 with realistic bids in Figure 8.9. Likewise to the previous setting, bars represent the approximated VCG settings and lines denote utilities gained in the k-price setting. In addition, Table B.13 (Appendix B.2.2) shows means, standard deviations and CVs for the R_1 setting with approximated VCG pricing.

The graph evinces that the approximated VCG mechanism performs better than the k-pricing schema. These effects get confirmed by a comparison of the means of both mechanisms (μ_k and μ_{AV}) and the fraction $\frac{\mu_{AV}}{\mu_k}$ that are illustrated in Table 8.7. In settings where one agent manipulates, the approximated VCG mechanism outperforms the k-pricing schema. This is also the result of a Mann-Whitney U-test that tests whether two samples

---

[7]The one-sample Kolmogorov-Smirnov test was applied to test goodness of fit with a normal distribution.

are drawn from one population. The tests state that most of the samples are significantly different.[8] The corresponding p-values are given in Table B.14 (Appendix B.2.2).

Modification	1B			2B,2S		
Factor	μ_{AV}	μ_k	$\frac{\mu_{AV}}{\mu_k}$	μ_{AV}	μ_k	$\frac{\mu_{AV}}{\mu_k}$
5	1945	3789	0.51	502	710	0.71
10	3458	7432	0.47	-31	45	-0.69
15	3589	8699	0.41	-1309	-1459	0.90
20	2242	8340	0.27	-3551	-3820	0.93
30	-1863	5110	−0.36	-8024	-8717	0.92
40	-14511	-8368	1.73	-13800	-14994	0.92
50	-30342	-25259	1.20	-19448	-21229	0.92
60	-39644	-34996	1.13	-23123	-25075	0.92
70	-40448	-35825	1.13	-23736	-25695	0.92
80	-40448	-35825	1.13	-23835	-25772	0.92
90	-40448	-35825	1.13	-23847	-25761	0.93

Table 8.7: Comparison of utility gains attained by the approximated VCG mechanism and the k-pricing schema in setting R_1

This second comparison shows that the approximated VCG mechanism performs better than the k-pricing for settings in which only one agent manipulates. Likewise to the previous analysis, both mechanisms perform equally if more agents manipulate. Although the utility gain of one single agent is higher for most of the measured samples, the incentive properties of the k-pricing schema are sufficient for an application in the Grid. Due to the envisioned competition on the market, cases in which only one agent manipulates can be neglected.

8.1.2.4 Reflection

The previous results illustrate that both pricing rules do not rigorously punish inaccurate valuation and reservation price reporting. Buyers and sellers sometimes increase their individual utility by manipulating their preferences. This possibility, however, is limited to mild misreporting and a small number of strategic buyers and sellers. If the number of manipulating agents increases, the risk of not being allocated in the auction raises dramatically.

With regard to domain independent bids, no significant differences between both pricing schemes can be observed for settings with a manipulation factor smaller than 60%. In settings with realistic bids, the approximated VCG mechanism outperforms the k-pricing schema. However, on average the utility gains do not deviate too much from each other.

In summary, the simulation has shown it reasonable to believe that agents will not strongly deviate from revealing their true valuations and reservation prices. Although an agent's average utility gain can be improved through manipulation, he increases the risk of not being allocated in the auction. This risk increases the more agents use manipulation. The simulation results suggest that the k-pricing schema has accurate incentive properties resulting in fairly mild allocative efficiency losses. As such, the pricing schema is a practical alternative to the VCG and approximated VCG mechanism and is highly relevant for an application in the Grid.

---

[8]The Mann-Whitney U-test was applied as the realistic bid samples do not reflect a normal distribution.

8.2 Approximated Winner Determination

As denoted in Section 4.2, a computational tractable outcome determination of MACE is required. However, the previous runtime analysis emphasizes that the auction schema is computationally intractable in large-scaled scenarios. This implies that exact solutions of the winner determination problem require too much computation time. To remedy this obstacle, one has to rely on approximations. However, the application of approximations has impacts on the economic properties of the mechanism: Approximations result in suboptimal and inefficient outcomes. Consequently, approximated allocation decisions cannot be incentive compatible (Nisan and Ronen 2000).

The following subsections analyze the economic effects that occur due to approximations. Section 8.2.1 measures the resulting efficiency loss of the winner determination problem. Subsequently, Section 8.2.2 examines the impact of approximations on the incentive properties of the auction schema.

8.2.1 Efficiency Loss

The measurement of efficiency loss due to approximations requires a metric that reflects the differences between the optimal outcome V^* and the value of the suboptimal solution V. Following the problem definition in Section 7.2.2.1, one requires the determination of $g(\rho)$ with $V^* \leq g(\rho)V$, where ρ denotes the encoding length of the problem instance. However, preliminary simulation studies showed that the problem oftentimes cannot be solved optimally, even with a time limit of more than 72 hours. In order to measure the desired effect, the aforementioned metric has to be adapted.

Instead of comparing the approximated outcome with the optimal solution, one can also rely on upper boundaries of the problem. Oftentimes, an upper boundary denotes the maximum value of the linearly relaxed problem instance (cf. Section 6.1.1). Whenever the solver finished analyzing a sub-tree of the problem instance, this boundary is updated with respect to the unexplored decision space. CPLEX provides a method for determining such a boundary. The function computes the value of the maximization problem that comprises the unexplored nodes of the search tree (ILOG 2005).[9] Although this value may not reflect the optimal outcome of the problem, it provides a reasonable and practical way to measure efficiency loss.

The following simulation treatments assume truthful bidders in order to measure efficiency loss. The analysis is performed for the baseline settings I_1 and R_1 and for the settings I_3 and R_3, as they lead to the hardest problem instances in the previous runtime study. Likewise to the previous studies, the solver is interrupted after 5 minutes. The corresponding gap between the upper boundary and the obtained suboptimal outcome is computed as

$$gap = 100\% \cdot \frac{V_B - V}{V},$$

where V_B denotes the boundary and V represents the suboptimal outcome (Le 2006). Each sample is repeated 100 times with different initial random seeds and the results are averaged. The number of buyers and sellers in each treatment are equally distributed, i.e., a setting with 200 agents comprises 100 buyer bids and 100 seller bids.

---

[9]In CPLEX, this boundary is provided by the function `getBestObjValue()`.

Domain Independent Bids: Table 8.8 summarizes the gaps of the approximated outcomes compared to the upper boundaries for the domain independent settings I_1 and I_3. The table shows mean (μ), standard deviation (σ), maximum (max), and minimum (min) gap for the measured samples. In addition, the percentage number of infeasible outcomes is outlined, i.e., the percentage share of problem instances for which CPLEX could not determine a feasible solution within 5 minutes. The corresponding gap for these settings is set to 100%.

Setting	Agents	Gap (in %)				Infeasible
		μ	σ	max	min	Instances (in %)
I_1	100	0.11	0.22	0.65	0.00	0
	200	0.59	0.28	1.26	0.10	0
	300	0.56	0.20	1.00	0.24	0
	400	0.59	0.15	0.85	0.25	0
	450	0.53	0.13	0.78	0.24	0
	500	0.60	0.23	1.53	0.37	0
I_3	100	1.80	0.88	5.48	0.47	0
	200	1.51	0.46	2.50	0.65	0
	300	1.43	0.38	2.39	0.54	0
	400	1.41	0.35	2.19	0.79	0
	450	10.29	28.81	100.00	0.97	8
	500	88.38	32.15	100.00	0.64	88

Table 8.8: Optimality gap in settings I_1 and I_3 due to approximated allocation decisions

The measured gaps are fairly mild in the baseline settings I_1. If 200 agents submit their bids to the auctioneer, the average gap is 0.59%, the maximum gap is 1.26%, and the minimum gap is 0.1%. This means that the average value of the best feasible solution is 0.59% smaller than the upper boundary. With more than 200 agents, the resulting gaps are almost equal. In line with other combinatorial auction studies, this result states that CPLEX can find adequate solutions quickly (Andersson et al. 2000). However, the solver is not able to determine and to proof optimal solutions within the given time limit.

The gaps for the I_3 settings are higher than in the baseline scenarios. For 200 agents, the average gap is 1.51%, the maximum gap is 2.50%, and the minimum gap is 0.65%. With an increasing number of agents, the gap of the approximation becomes higher. On the one hand, this is reasoned by the fact that the problem instances become harder to solve within the given time frame. On the other hand, feasible solutions cannot always be determined. This results in a welfare loss of 100%. CPLEX could not find a feasible outcome for 8% of the instances in settings with 450 agents. Furthermore, the solver could not determine feasible solutions for most of the settings with 500 agents.

The analysis shows that the anytime algorithm achieves fairly efficient results. However, the applied time limits become useless for settings with more than 450 agents as CPLEX can oftentimes not find feasible solutions. For such cases, the use of other approximations has to be considered.

Realistic Bids: Table 8.9 shows the results for the realistic bidding scenarios R_1 and R_3. For instance, if 400 agents submit their R_3 distributed bids, the average optimality gap is

0.27%. Likewise to the previous analysis, the solver finds feasible solutions for all base-line settings R_1. In contrast to the I_3 setting, the total number of infeasible outcomes is considerably small.

Setting	Agents	Gap (in %)				Infeasible Instances (in %)
		μ	σ	max	min	
R_1	100	0.05	0.13	0.56	0.00	0
	200	0.10	0.10	0.37	0.00	0
	300	0.09	0.07	0.29	0.00	0
	400	0.11	0.09	0.39	0.00	0
	450	0.11	0.07	0.27	0.02	0
	500	0.10	0.07	0.27	0.01	0
R_3	100	0.31	0.39	1.55	0.00	0
	200	0.25	0.23	1.15	0.03	0
	300	0.32	0.34	2.05	0.02	0
	400	0.27	0.22	1.11	0.04	0
	450	9.36	29.11	100.00	0.04	3
	500	8.42	27.08	100.00	0.04	4

Table 8.9: Optimality gap in settings R_1 and R_3 due to approximated allocation decisions

The results emphasize that the average gap of realistic bids is smaller than the measured gaps in the domain independent scenarios. Furthermore, more feasible solutions can be determined for realistic bids, even with 500 agents. In contrast to the previous runtime analysis in Section 8.1.1, this suggests that realistic bids are easier to solve than domain independent bids with an increasing number of agents.

Likewise to the analysis of domain independent bids, the welfare losses are fairly mild with the application of the anytime algorithm. With regard to the envisioned Grid market with 340 agents (cf. Section 4.1.4), feasible and accurate efficient solutions can be found for both bidding scenarios. From a computational point of view, anytime algorithms make MACE suitable for allocating resources in the Grid.

8.2.2   Incentive Compatibility

The last treatments of the simulation study are concerned with the incentive properties of MACE with respect to approximated allocation decisions. The application of approximations raises several challenges for the study at hand:

First, the analysis cannot be performed under the same conditions as the previous incentive evaluation. Studying the same manipulation cases as described in Section 8.1.2.1 and terminating each allocation decision after 5 minutes is computationally very complex. Consequently, one has to adapt the scenario by setting the time limit of the solver to 30 seconds. In addition, the algorithm is terminated earlier whenever a solution is found with a gap smaller than 2%. This adaptation allows a worst case imitation of the efficiency results obtained in the previous study. In each setting, 100 agents submit their bids to the auctioneer. With regard to the specified termination conditions, the number of agents is seen as adequate to obtain worst case scenarios.

Second, the application of approximations biases the obtained economic effects. In VCG based mechanisms, the use of approximations can lead to violations of the individual rationality property. This problem can be illustrated by the following example: Suppose a setting with an approximated welfare of $V = 100$ and an allocated agent i. Assume that the optimal welfare of the problem is $V^* = 120$. Following the VCG based pricing schema, one has to compute an allocation without agent i. Suppose the solver finds a better solution for the problem without agent i more quickly. In this case, let the approximated value be $V_{-i} = 105$ with an optimal value of $V^*_{-i} = 107$. Here, the agent has a negative impact on the welfare, i.e., his resulting discount is negative. The welfare of such pricing allocations is set to $V_{-i} = V$ to avoid such violations.

Finally, the applied anytime solver is not deterministic. This means that some decisions of the algorithm are based on random numbers. As a consequence, it may lead to cases in which the resulting allocation of one and the same problem instance differs in the k-pricing study and the VCG study. Consequently, a comparison of these two mechanisms can lead to different utilities of the agents which are not caused by the pricing schemes. Due to simulation repetitions, however, it is assumed that these effects are on average negligible.

The following analysis is based on 4 different settings: In the first setting, only 1 buyer manipulates his bids (denoted as $1B$). In the the second setting, 4 buyers and 4 sellers manipulate ($4B, 4S$). In the third setting, 10 buyers and 10 sellers manipulate (denoted as $10B, 10S$) and 20 buyers and 20 sellers manipulate in the fourth setting (denoted as $20B, 20S$). Likewise to the previous study, each case is repeated 350 times with varying random seeds.

Domain Independent Bids: Figure 8.12 illustrates the utility gain of manipulating agents with the application of the VCG mechanism. As the underlying pricing schema is incentive compatible, positive utility gains are only caused by approximated allocation decisions. This indicates a value for the default loss of incentive compatibility due to the applied winner determination algorithm.

Although approximated allocation decisions are determined, manipulating agents cannot gain a positive utility on average. In the given simulation settings, the approximations do not affect considerably the incentive properties of the VCG mechanism. Consequently, agents have an incentive to reveal their preferences honestly.

The results obtained by the analysis of the VCG mechanism can partially be transferred to the k-pricing schema. Figure 8.11 illustrates the utility gain of agents with regard to different manipulation scenarios. The approximations do not have considerably an impact on the incentive properties of the mechanism. The obtained results are comparable to the previous study with 24 agents. Agents can attain a positive utility by manipulating their preferences. However, the cases are restricted to settings in which few agents manipulate by a small factor.

In contrast to the previous analysis of the k-pricing schema (cf. Section 8.1.2.2), the average utility gains decrease. For instance, if one agent underbids his valuation by $\lambda = 20\%$, his average utility gain is $UG^A_k = 171.0$. In the previous study, the agent gained a utility of $UG^O_k = 394.1$ by the same manipulation factor. The reason for this effect is the higher competition due to an increased number of agents on the market. Moreover, if more agents manipulate, the average utility gains decrease considerably. Consequently, it can be assumed that agents do best by submitting their bids truthfully when many agents submit bids to the auctioneer or the number of manipulating agents is high.

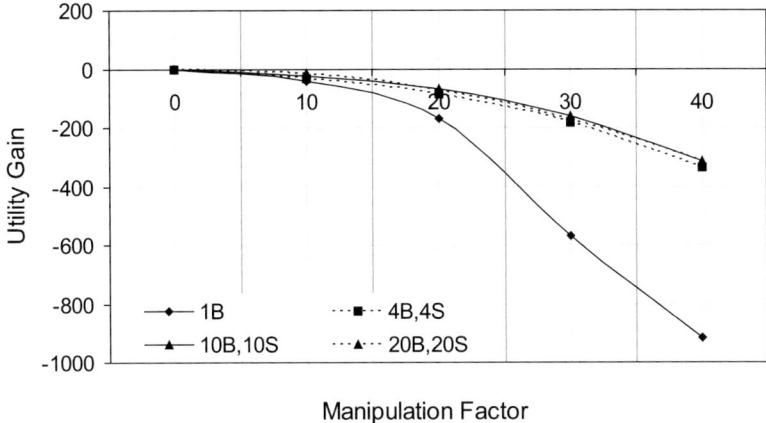

Figure 8.10: Utility gain of manipulating agents using the VCG mechanism in setting I_1 with approximated allocation decisions

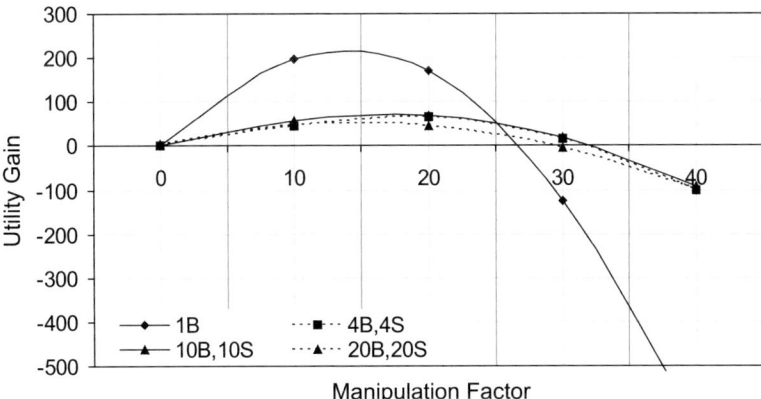

Figure 8.11: Utility gain of manipulating agents using the k-price schema in setting I_1 with approximated allocation decisions

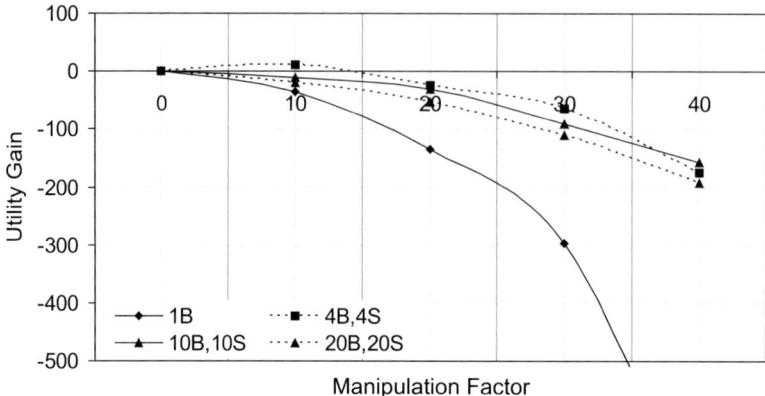

Figure 8.12: Utility gain of manipulating agents using the approximated VCG mechanism in setting I_1 with approximated allocation decisions

To complete the analysis of domain independent bids, Figure 8.12 depicts the results for the approximated VCG mechanism. In contrast to the k-pricing schema, the average utility gains of manipulating agents are negative. In most cases, competition drives the agents to reveal their true preferences to the auctioneer. Agents can only gain a positive utility if 4 buyers and 4 sellers manipulate by a factor of $\lambda = 10\%$. As a consequence, the approximated VCG mechanism has better incentive properties as the k-pricing for the measured samples.

Mean, standard deviation, and CV for the different pricing schemes are given in the Tables B.15 – B.17 in Appendix B.3.

Realistic Bids: The obtained effects with domain independent bids are emphasized by an analysis of the incentive properties with realistic bids. As the expressiveness of the results is comparable to the previous study, the utility gains for all pricing schemes are aggregated in Figure 8.13. The graph illustrates the utilities gained in settings with 1 manipulating buyer ($1B$) and 4 manipulating buyers and sellers ($4B, 4S$). The values reflect the results obtained by the application of the VCG schema (V_1B, $V\_4B, 4S$), the k-pricing schema (K_1B, $K\_4B, 4S$), and the approximated VCG schema (A_1B, $A\_4B, 4S$). The corresponding means, standard deviations, and CVs are given in the Tables B.18 – B.20 (Appendix B.3).

With the application of the VCG schema and the approximated VCG mechanism, agents do worse by manipulating their bids. In all settings, they attain a negative utility on average. With the application of the k-pricing schema, however, one agent can gain a positive utility by manipulating up to $\lambda = 30\%$. However, this case is restricted to settings in which only one agent manipulates and the remaining bidders reveal their preferences honestly. In contrast to the previous study, the use of realistic bids rather decreases the attained utility due to manipulation. If more than one agent manipulates, no agent can gain a positive utility from manipulating.

Although the approximated VCG mechanism outperforms the k-pricing schema in both bidding scenarios, the computational hurdle of the mechanism still remains. With regard to

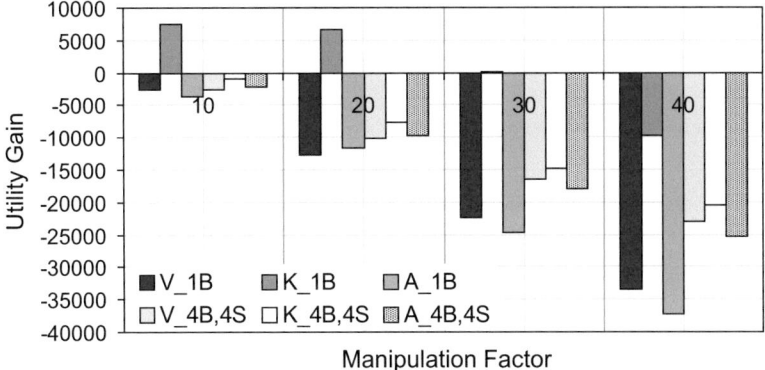

Figure 8.13: Utility gain of manipulating agents with different pricing schemes in setting R_1 with approximated allocation decisions

an increasing number of agents, the computational effort that is required to solve the problem becomes intractable. On the one hand, this fact favors the k-pricing schema due to its computational efficiency. On the other hand, the results obtained by this study demonstrate the tension between computational tractability and economical efficiency (Gomber et al. 2000; Parkes 2001; Kalagnanam and Parkes 2004). With regard to the few cases in which agents can gain a positive utility, the computational efficiency of the k-pricing favors its application for the Grid.

8.3   Summary

The preliminary requirement satisfaction in Section 6.3 revealed open issues that need further evaluation. The previous study examined these issues by analyzing the computational tractability, efficiency, and incentive compatibility of the MACE mechanism.

The runtime analysis showed that the winner determination problem is computationally very demanding. The problem can only be solved optimally in settings with less than 50 agents. With an increasing number of agents, the determination of allocation decisions requires more than 5 minutes. For these settings, the introduction of approximations is indispensable. The simulations emphasized that approximations adequately solve the problem and result in fairly mild efficiency losses. However, for problem instances with more than 450 agents, CPLEX cannot always determine feasible solutions. For these cases, the use of alternative approximations has to be considered.

Transferring the PlanetLab characteristics to the proposed auction schema implies that MACE has to support 340 agents acting simultaneously on the system (cf. Section 4.1.4). With respect to the above presented results, MACE is sufficient to fulfill PlanetLab's resource bids in a meaningful time. Consequently, Requirement R5 (cf. Section 4.2) concerning the computational tractability of the mechanism is fulfilled for the envisioned setting.

The remaining scenarios are concerned with the incentive properties and the resulting efficiency losses of MACE. The results showed that the k-pricing schema does not punish manipulating agents rigorously. Agents can increase their individual utility when they are dishonest and do not reveal their true preferences. However, the utility gains can only be attained by a small manipulation factor and a small number of strategic buyers and sellers. If agents manipulate by a high factor, they considerably raise the risk of not being allocated in the auction. In addition, the efficiency losses caused by a small fraction of agents are fairly small.

The effects obtained with domain independent bids get softened by the use of realistic bidding scenarios. In these settings, the resulting utility gains are restricted to fewer cases. These results further strengthen the application of MACE as a market mechanism for the Grid.

The comparison with the approximated VCG schema showed that the k-pricing schema has similar incentive properties in domain independent settings with an optimal winner determination algorithm. With the application of realistic bids and the use of approximations, the approximated VCG mechanism outperforms the k-price mechanism. However, cases in which agents have a positive utility due to manipulations are restricted to small manipulation factors. With regard to the tension between efficiency and computational tractability, the application of the k-pricing schema for the Grid is superior.

In summary, the study showed that the mechanism is not incentive compatible and – consequently – not efficient. However, the resulting losses are negligible with an increasing number of truthful agents. As such, the auction schema is interpreted as approximative incentive compatible and approximative efficient. Thus, Requirement R1 and Requirement R2 (cf. Section 4.2) are roughly fulfilled. These results evince the practical applicability of MACE for the Grid.

Chapter 9

Summary and Future Work

Treating distributed computation as an economy turns out to be quite fruitful in the analysis, design, and control of such systems. In a sense, economics become a new programming methodology!
(Huberman and Hogg 1995, p. 150)

The increasing standardization of Grid technologies enables the use of computational resources as standardized commodities. Aggregations of computational resources and services are gradually becoming utilities, much like energy. One of the key issues in aggregating these resources is to compute allocation and scheduling decisions. In order to tackle this problem, the main vision of this work is the application of markets for coordinating resource allocations in Grids.

Currently, the canon of available market mechanisms only insufficiently accounts for the peculiarities of the Grid and are thus widely inapplicable. A reason for this problem lies in the different and oftentimes diametric requirements that stem from technical and economical viewpoints. This work attempted to diminish this gap by designing, implementing, and evaluating a market mechanism that is applicable for the Grid.

The previous chapters proposed the derivation of a multi-attribute combinatorial exchange for allocating and scheduling resources in the Grid. In contrast to other approaches, the proposed mechanism simultaneously accounts for a variety of technical and economical requirements. This approach accounts for time and quality attributes of Grid resources, co-allocation restrictions, as well as efficiency, incentive compatibility, and computational tractability of the underlying auction schema. The mechanism provides buyers and sellers with a rich bidding language that allows the formulation of bundles expressing either substitutabilities or complementarities. A simulation study evinced the practical applicability of the proposed auction.

This work is a step towards understanding the effects and strengths of applying markets to the Grid. Contributions include the specification of a realistic Grid environment and an extraction of its underlying requirements, the design and implementation of an auction schema that meets these requirements, and an evaluation of the mechanism by means of a simulation. The results of this work contribute to the further development of market engineering by providing new design principles of combinatorial mechanisms, a simulation tool for their evaluation, and new metrics for evaluating their performance.

9.1 Review of this Work

Chapter 1 briefly outlined the advantages of Grid technologies and motivated the use of markets to allocate Grid resources efficiently. The general objective of this work is the design, implementation, and evaluation of a market mechanism that is applicable for trading Grid resources. In order to fulfill this objective, four research questions were raised and subsequently answered in the course of this work.

The basic concepts of Grid architectures and resource management systems were introduced in Chapter 2. OGSA was highlighted as state of the art architecture for realizing service-oriented Grids in practice. An essential component of this architecture comprises resource management that is responsible for allocating, scheduling, and monitoring Grid resources. A literature review revealed a set of requirements that have to be fulfilled by such resource management systems.

Chapter 3 argued why markets should be applied to the resource allocation problem in Grids and introduced tools and methods that assist in engineering markets. The basic concepts of markets and mechanism design were introduced that built the formal basis for this work. In addition, the market engineering approach was outlined. It offers a structured and systematic procedure to design, implement, and evaluate market mechanisms in practice.

The foundations of Grid technologies and market mechanisms built the basis for the environmental analysis described in Chapter 4. The characteristics of a Grid marketplace were elicited by specifying potential trading objects, user characteristics, and target market segments. On the basis of this analysis, requirements upon an adequate mechanism were deduced by conflating technical and economical objectives of Grids and markets. Related research concerning market implementations for traditional distributed systems and Grids were reviewed with regard to their adherence to the specified requirements. The result of the review emphasized that none of the proposed mechanisms fulfills all requirements.

Chapter 5 addressed the lack of adequate Grid market mechanisms by outlining the design of a multi-attribute combinatorial exchange for allocating and scheduling Grid resources. This included the definition of a bidding language that accounts for multiple attributes and bundle bids, the formulation of a winner determination model that can attain efficient allocations, and the derivation of a pricing schema that provides incentives for agents to bid truthfully.

The implementation of the proposed auction schema was described in Chapter 6. First, state of the art algorithms for solving the winner determination problem of MACE were discussed. After that, the MACE market service was introduced that implements the proposed allocation and pricing schemes. Finally, an analysis of the implemented mechanism revealed open issues that require further evaluation by means of a simulation study.

Chapter 7 was concerned with the design of a Grid market model and its implementation into a software system. The simulation model comprised different bidding scenarios that imitate agents submitting multi-attribute combinatorial bids to an auctioneer. Subsequently, the simulation tool jCase was introduced that implements the proposed model. In addition, the tool can be applied to study the latest available forms of combinatorial auction mechanisms. A set of innovative metrics were introduced that can be applied to measure efficiency and incentive compatibility for auction mechanisms. Further, these metrics are a step towards understanding the effects of suboptimal allocation decisions upon the economical performance of auction mechanisms.

Chapter 8 discussed the results obtained by the simulation study. The runtime analysis showed that the auction schema is computationally very demanding. However, the use of approximated solutions achieved adequate runtime results and fairly mild welfare losses. In addition, the economical requirements upon a Grid mechanism are approximately fulfilled by MACE. Comparing these characteristics with an existing Grid test-bed evinced the practical applicability of the proposed auction.

9.2   Open Questions and Future Directions

In this work, several problems concerning market-based resource allocation in Grids were addressed. However, there are still open issues that can serve as a starting point for future work. First, extensions and limitations of the proposed auction schema are discussed. After that, future work concerning the practical deployment of the mechanism into a real world test-bed is outlined.

9.2.1   Limitations and Potential Extensions of this Approach

The derivation of MACE relies on the market engineering process that divides the underlying problem into different stages. The following paragraphs discuss limitations and potential extensions of the mechanism with respect to the processed stages.

Environmental Analysis of a Grid Market: The specification of the requirements is driven by the identification of general properties and assumptions that are valid for most resource suppliers and consumers. However, there may be application scenarios in which the requirement list is insufficient or some of the items become unimportant. Future work has to consider different application scenarios and – if necessary – refine specific requirements and adapt the mechanism.

In analogy to financial trading systems, the MACE market service will be hosted by a commercial market operator. Consequently, additional factors such as trading fees influence the outcome of the mechanism. Market engineering encompasses these issues by analyzing potential business structures of market operators and their impact on the market performance (Weinhardt et al. 2003; Burghardt 2006). However, such business structures were out of scope for the work at hand. As such, future work has to consider and to analyze possible business models for such operators.

Conceptual Design of MACE: In the design phase, several assumptions upon the technical infrastructure and agents have been made. The most critical one requires agents to formulate their bids in a detailed fashion. This requires the specification of resource demand and resource supply in the future as well as the determination of valuation and reservation prices. Future work has to deal with bidding tools that support agents in specifying their underlying resource characteristics and their preferences. This can be supported by related work on resource prediction models (Smith 2004) and preference elicitation techniques (Conen and Sandholm 2001).

Currently, MACE only supports the specification of cardinal resource attributes. Although this is sufficient for most practical cases, there may be settings in which nominal attributes are also required. In addition, network topology is only considered by the specification of uplink and downlink rates of available network bandwidth. This may be practical in an in-house Grid where network constraints can sometimes be neglected. However, this assumption may fail in networks that do not support advanced bandwidth reservation. Future work has to consider these issues and extend the mechanism to support them.

The bidding language of MACE is based on pairs of attributes and values that syntactically describe resources and their quality attributes. Consequently, demand and supply is matched on the basis of attribute-based matching functions. This may be insufficient if an agent is not only interested in one particular resource configuration but is also willing to accept similar ones. To remedy this drawback, the use of ontology based bidding languages has to be considered in the future (Lamparter and Schnizler 2006).

Algorithmic Considerations: The evaluation showed that the anytime algorithm is only suitable for settings with less than 450 agents. Future research needs to consider alternative heuristics that simplify the winner determination problem. The application of genetic algorithms may be adequate to solve the problem more quickly (Chu and Beasley 1998). Moreover, distributed implementation techniques have to be considered that parallelize the computational effort.

The current implementation neglects the communication complexity when agents submit their bids to the auctioneer. In the future, bidding languages and encoding strategies have to be considered that ensure bid submissions that cause low communication effort. The implementation of an iterative MACE mechanism may be adequate to reduce the average communication complexity (Parkes 2001).

Mechanism Evaluation: Future simulation studies of the mechanism need to consider additional bidding scenarios with varying distribution and initial parameters. A more comprehensive study will improve and strengthen the reliability of the obtained results.

The current evaluation considers the interdependencies between economical efficiency, incentive compatibility, and computational tractability. An interesting future direction lies in an analysis of how these factor influence each other. Among others, this raises the question how accurate a winner determination problem has to be approximated in order to preserve the incentive properties of a mechanism.

9.2.2 Real World Application

A further step towards a functioning Grid market would be to confront the mechanism with real data in a pilot run. Currently, two research projects named CATNETS and SORMA[1] already address this issue by considering the integration of MACE into their middleware infrastructures (Chacin et al. 2006).

In addition, the application in different business scenarios would reveal further insights regarding the applicability and performance of markets in the Grid. On the one hand, this can give insights into the users' acceptance of the mechanism and their individual needs. On the other hand, empirical data can serve as input parameter for further evaluation and refinements of the mechanism.

The application of MACE in real world settings poses several interesting research directions: An important issue concerns the specification of setting-up costs for different services,

---

[1]See http://www.sorma-project.eu/ for details.

network latencies, and penalty costs for jobs that are not performed correctly. In addition, the enforcement of market-based resource agreements as well as a functioning billing and accounting infrastructure have to be considered. Finally, the application of markets in distributed computing infrastructures requires a sound and functionally proven security system.

Appendix

Appendix A

Proof of MACE Properties

Proof. (Theorem 5.4):

MACE Budget-Balance: To proof that MACE is budget-balanced, the prices that buyers have to pay must be equal to the prices that sellers receive for their bundles. On the basis of Definition 5.47 and Definition 5.49, this means:

$$\sum_{n \in \mathcal{N}} \sum_{S_j \in \mathcal{S}} p_{k,n}^N(S_j) = \sum_{m \in \mathcal{M}} \sum_{S_j \in \mathcal{S}} p_{k,m}^M(S_j). \tag{A.1}$$

Let

$$p^N = \sum_{n \in \mathcal{N}} \sum_{S_j \in \mathcal{S}} p_{k,n}^N(S_j)$$

be the prices of all buyers with

$$p^N = \sum_{n \in \mathcal{N}} \sum_{S_j \in \mathcal{S}} \left(x_n(S_j) v_n(S_j) s_n(S_j) - k \sum_{t \in T} \beta_{n,t}(S_j) \right)$$

$$= \sum_{n \in \mathcal{N}} \sum_{S_j \in \mathcal{S}} \sum_{t \in T} \left(z_{n,t}(S_j) v_n(S_j) - k \beta_{n,t}(S_j) \right)$$

$$= \sum_{t \in T} \left(\sum_{n \in \mathcal{N}} \sum_{S_j \in \mathcal{S}} z_{n,t}(S_j) v_n(S_j) - k \sum_{n \in \mathcal{N}} \sum_{S_j \in \mathcal{S}} \beta_{n,t}(S_j) \right)$$

Each buyer n gets allocated at most one bundle S_n^* (XOR-constraint). As a consequence, $\sum_{S_j \in \mathcal{S}} \beta_{n,t}(S_j)$ can be replaced by $\beta_{n,t}(S_n^*)$, due to the fact that $\beta_{n,t}(S_n^*)$ is the only non zero term of the whole summation. Based upon this simplification, the payments can be formulated as

$$p^N = \sum_{t \in T} \left(\sum_{n \in \mathcal{N}} z_{n,t}(S_n^*) v_n(S_n^*) - k \sum_{n \in \mathcal{N}} \beta_{n,t}(S_n^*) \right).$$

For the formalization of sellers' prices, let $\alpha_t(n)$ be defined as

$$\alpha_t(n) = \sum_{m \in \mathcal{M}} \sum_{S_j \in \mathcal{S}} y_{m,n,t}(S_j) r_m(S_j).$$

Based upon this definition, $o_{m,n,t}(S_j)$ can be reformulated as

$$o_{m,n,t}(S_j) = \begin{cases} y_{m,n,t}(S_j) r_m(S_j) / \alpha_t(n) & \text{if } \alpha_t(n) > 0 \\ 0 & \text{otherwise.} \end{cases}$$

As a consequence, it holds that

$$\sum_{m \in M} \sum_{S_j \in S} o_{m,n,t}(S_j) = \begin{cases} \alpha_t(n)/\alpha_t(n) = 1 & \text{if } \alpha_t(n) > 0 \\ 0 & \text{otherwise.} \end{cases}$$

Now, let

$$p^M = \sum_{m \in M} \sum_{S_j \in S} p^M_{k,m}(S_j)$$

be the prices of all sellers with

$$p^M = \sum_{t \in T} \left(\sum_{m \in M} \sum_{S_j \in S} \left[\sum_{n \in N} y_{m,n,t}(S_j) r_m(S_j) + (1-k) \sum_{n \in N} \sum_{S_l \in S} o_{m,n,t}(S_j) \beta_{n,t}(S_l) \right] \right)$$

$$= \sum_{t \in T} \left(\sum_{n \in N} \alpha_t(n) + (1-k) \sum_{m \in M} \sum_{S_j \in S} \sum_{n \in N} \sum_{S_l \in S} o_{m,n,t}(S_j) \beta_{n,t}(S_l) \right)$$

$$= \sum_{t \in T} \left(\sum_{n \in N} \alpha_t(n) + (1-k) \sum_{n \in N} \sum_{S_l \in S} \left[\beta_{n,t}(S_l) \sum_{m \in M} \sum_{S_j \in S} o_{m,n,t}(S_j) \right] \right)$$

The term $\sum_{m \in M} \sum_{S_j \in S} o_{m,n,t}(S_j)$ is only zero if no buyer gets allocated any bundle. If this is the case, the prices of all buyers and sellers are zero, as the decision variables $z_{n,t}(\cdot)$ and $y_{m,n,t}(\cdot)$ are all zero. This results in a budget-balanced exchange.

The following equation only considers cases where at least one buyer gets allocated a bundle, i.e., $\alpha_t(n) > 0$. This allows the reformulation to

$$p^M = \sum_{t \in T} \left(\sum_{n \in N} \alpha_t(n) + (1-k) \sum_{n \in N} \sum_{S_l \in S} \beta_{n,t}(S_l) \right).$$

Replacing $\sum_{S_j \in S} \beta_{n,t}(S_j)$ by $\beta_{n,t}(S^*_n)$ results in

$$p^M = \sum_{t \in T} \left(\sum_{n \in N} \alpha_t(n) + (1-k) \sum_{n \in N} \beta_n(S^*_n) \right)$$

Finally, Equation A.1 can be solved by

$$\sum_{n \in N} \sum_{S_j \in S} p^N_{k,n}(S_j) = \sum_{m \in M} \sum_{S_j \in S} p^M_{k,m}(S_j)$$

$$\sum_{t \in T} \left(\sum_{n \in N} z_{n,t}(S^*_n) v_n(S^*_n) - k \sum_{n \in N} \beta_{n,t}(S^*_n) \right) = \sum_{t \in T} \left(\sum_{n \in N} \alpha_t(n) + (1-k) \sum_{n \in N} \beta_{n,t}(S^*_n) \right)$$

$$\sum_{t \in T} \left(\sum_{n \in N} z_{n,t}(S^*_n) v_n(S^*_n) - \sum_{n \in N} \alpha_t(n) \right) = \sum_{t \in T} \left(\sum_{n \in N} \beta_{n,t}(S^*_n) \right)$$

$$\sum_{t \in T} \left(\sum_{n \in N} z_{n,t}(S^*_n) v_n(S^*_n) - \sum_{n \in N} \alpha_t(n) \right) = \sum_{t \in T} \left(\sum_{n \in N} \left[z_{n,t}(S^*_n) v_n(S^*_n) - \alpha_t(n) \right] \right)$$

$$\sum_{t \in T} \left(\sum_{n \in N} z_{n,t}(S^*_n) v_n(S^*_n) - \sum_{n \in N} \alpha_t(n) \right) = \sum_{t \in T} \left(\sum_{n \in N} z_{n,t}(S^*_n) v_n(S^*_n) - \sum_{n \in N} \alpha_t(n) \right)$$

As a result, MACE is budget-balanced.

MACE Individual Rationality: It is to show that the payment of each buyer n is always less or equal than his valuation. In addition, the payments of each seller m have to be greater or equal than his reservation prices.

For a buyer n, the payment is defined as (cf. Definition 5.47)

$$p_{k,n}^N(S_j) = x_n(S_j)v_n(S_j)s_n(S_j) - k\sum_{t\in\mathcal{T}}\beta_{n,t}(S_j).$$

The payment function of buyer n is individually rational, if

$$k\sum_{t\in\mathcal{T}}\beta_{n,t}(S_j) = k\sum_{t\in\mathcal{T}}\left(z_{n,t}(S_j)v_n(S_j) - \sum_{m\in\mathcal{M}}\sum_{S_l\in\mathcal{S}}y_{m,n,t}(S_l)r_m(S_l)\right) \geq 0$$

As $k \geq 0$, it is sufficient to show that the inequality

$$z_{n,t}(S_j)v_n(S_j) \geq \sum_{m\in\mathcal{M}}\sum_{S_l\in\mathcal{S}}y_{m,n,t}(S_l)r_m(S_l)$$

is not violated for all buyers and sellers. This inequality is inherent by the definition of the objective function of MAP. In case the inequality is violated, the value of the objective function could be increased by not allocating bundle S_j to buyer n.

Likewise, the payment function of seller m is defined as (cf. Definition 5.49)

$$p_{k,m}^M(S_j) = \sum_{n\in\mathcal{N}}\sum_{t\in\mathcal{T}}y_{m,n,t}(S_j)r_m(S_j) + (1-k)\sum_{n\in\mathcal{N}}\sum_{S_l\in\mathcal{S}}\sum_{t\in\mathcal{T}}o_{m,n,t}(S_j)\beta_{n,t}(S_l).$$

To ensure individual rationality, the inequality

$$\sum_{n\in\mathcal{N}}\sum_{S_l\in\mathcal{S}}\sum_{t\in\mathcal{T}}o_{m,n,t}(S_j)\beta_{n,t}(S_l) \geq 0$$

must be true. The term $\beta_{n,t}(S_l)$ is always greater or equal than zero. Otherwise, a higher objective function could be attained by not generating a surplus in this time step (cf. Definition 5.46), i.e., by not allocating the bundle to the buyer. Furthermore, as $y_{m,n,t}(S_j) \geq 0$, the term $o_{m,n,t}(S_j)$ is also greater or equal than zero due to Definition 5.48.

In summary, MACE is individually rational for both, buyers and sellers.   □

Appendix B

Simulation Appendix

B.1 CPLEX Settings

Parameter	Setting
`IloCplex.IntParam.Cliques`	2
`IloCplex.DoubleParam.EpInt`	0
`IloCplex.DoubleParam.EpGap`	0
`IloCplex.IntParam.MIPEmphasis`	1
`IloCplex.IntParam.NodeFileInd`	3
`IloCplex.DoubleParam.TiLim`	300
`IloCplex.DoubleParam.TreLim`	1000
`IloCplex.DoubleParam.WorkMem`	1200

Table B.1: Varied CPLEX settings

B.2   Results: Optimal Winner Determination

B.2.1   Efficiency Loss

Modification	1B		2B,2S		6B,6S		12B,12S	
Factor	μ	σ	μ	σ	μ	σ	μ	σ
5	2.64	16.45	4.22	17.80	7.39	24.67	12.67	24.61
10	3.01	16.79	5.33	18.76	12.83	27.80	21.97	29.35
15	3.35	17.05	7.44	20.95	18.19	29.95	29.78	31.44
20	3.93	17.81	8.64	22.06	22.71	29.33	39.66	33.75
30	5.14	19.05	12.32	24.57	30.68	31.44	55.53	33.48
40	6.10	19.46	14.65	25.84	39.34	33.22	70.45	30.83
50	6.10	19.75	18.23	28.25	47.24	33.16	82.75	25.55
60	6.35	19.90	20.01	28.63	54.55	33.35	90.42	19.20
70	6.75	19.71	23.69	29.37	61.48	33.34	95.27	13.46
80	6.80	19.73	25.72	30.69	65.86	31.88	97.55	10.20
90	6.88	19.78	27.74	31.38	71.33	30.17	99.45	3.89

Table B.2: Mean and standard deviation of the percentage decrease of successful agents in setting I_1 with manipulating agents

B.2.2   Manipulating Agents

B.2.2.1   K-Price Incentive Compatibility

Modification	1B			2B,2S			6B,6S			12B,12S		
Factor	μ	σ	CV	μ	σ	CV	μ	σ	CV	μ	σ	CV
5	163.07	165.26	1.01	28.53	101.65	3.56	12.79	40.09	3.13	-4.72	10.52	-2.23
10	304.11	356.30	1.17	54.49	141.83	2.60	16.75	65.60	3.92	-17.98	27.86	-1.55
15	354.34	651.64	1.84	70.21	198.02	2.82	13.94	88.16	6.33	-37.07	46.59	-1.26
20	394.15	866.14	2.20	76.84	250.30	3.26	10.05	106.91	10.64	-65.64	73.04	-1.11
30	108.03	1496.25	13.85	39.07	347.56	8.90	-15.12	161.18	-10.66	-128.51	122.28	-0.95
40	-337.20	1757.26	-5.21	4.28	416.63	97.34	-68.72	223.90	-3.26	-198.49	171.43	-0.86
50	-782.98	1715.50	-2.19	-106.81	489.54	-4.58	-132.07	261.49	-1.98	-280.96	239.89	-0.85
60	-957.00	1734.06	-1.81	-183.33	573.75	-3.13	-198.24	306.48	-1.55	-330.86	267.63	-0.81
70	-1251.33	1580.29	-1.26	-286.09	576.10	-2.01	-255.08	320.45	-1.26	-362.09	296.93	-0.82
80	-1431.37	1435.13	-1.00	-368.29	606.36	-1.65	-295.69	331.31	-1.12	-376.54	317.72	-0.84
90	-1496.45	1367.35	-0.91	-426.84	637.01	-1.49	-346.02	346.86	-1.00	-385.07	324.90	-0.84

Table B.3: Utility gain of manipulating agents using the k-pricing schema in setting I_1

Modification	1B		2B,2S		6B,6S	
Factor	μ	σ	μ	σ	μ	σ
10	166.14	351.24	41.40	85.51	13.35	61.09
20	160.89	685.72	71.46	142.23	0.33	97.33
30	77.91	996.39	50.09	272.78	-20.72	130.33
40	37.56	1.315.45	26.77	356.05	-44.53	186.56
50	-570.13	1.430.10	-59.81	369.51	-83.29	198.57
60	-966.61	1.263.30	-65.22	415.66	-135.30	226.25

Table B.4: Utility gain of manipulating agents using the k-pricing schema in setting I_2

B.2.2.2   Approximated VCG Incentive Compatibility

Modification	1B		2B,2S		6B,6S	
Factor	μ	σ	μ	σ	μ	σ
10	247.80	299.75	60.65	139.51	19.30	63.26
20	397.93	622.73	85.89	243.45	2.12	124.89
30	377.78	1.011.88	77.42	345.22	-32.12	177.15
40	185.43	1.338.61	47.37	419.44	-86.46	247.08
50	-38.22	1.576.99	-16.98	494.69	-149.16	305.18
60	-404.06	1.722.06	-162.25	566.37	-221.55	321.28

Table B.5: Utility gain of manipulating agents using the k-pricing schema in setting I_3

Modification	1B		2B,2S		6B,6S	
Factor	μ	σ	μ	σ	μ	σ
10	176.55	594.62	61.50	119.84	19.98	63.61
20	196.38	967.55	61.25	237.14	10.07	124.17
30	278.26	1.236.19	80.82	301.73	-20.26	178.25
40	192.58	1.548.19	27.43	398.37	-88.02	240.39
50	-162.84	1.852.99	-15.56	465.04	-157.93	286.43
60	-616.66	1.978.50	-98.05	531.20	-197.39	311.78

Table B.6: Utility gain of manipulating agents using the k-pricing schema in setting I_4

Modification	1B			2B,2S			6B,6S			12B,12S		
Factor	μ	σ	CV	μ	σ	CV	μ	σ	CV	μ	σ	CV
5	3789	8950	2.36	710	6334	8.92	491	3007	6.13	-606	789	-1.30
10	7432	13321	1.79	45	10938	242.25	-265	5573	-21.04	-2734	2416	-0.88
15	8699	20378	2.34	-1459	15258	-10.46	-2234	8116	-3.63	-6034	4374	-0.72
20	8340	26394	3.16	-3820	17948	-4.70	-5307	10866	-2.05	-10727	6824	-0.64
30	5110	37499	7.34	-8717	23232	-2.67	-12275	14927	-1.22	-22706	12111	-0.53
40	-8368	45293	-5.41	-14994	25359	-1.69	-18768	18017	-0.96	-29964	15897	-0.53
50	-25259	43344	-1.72	-21229	26518	-1.25	-24392	19220	-0.79	-30090	15974	-0.53
60	-34996	37251	-1.06	-25075	27299	-1.09	-28544	19652	-0.69	-30090	15974	-0.53
70	-35825	36514	-1.02	-25695	27314	-1.06	-29088	19637	-0.68	-30090	15974	-0.53
80	-35825	36514	-1.02	-25772	27274	-1.06	-29120	19636	-0.67	-30090	15974	-0.53
90	-35825	36514	-1.02	-25761	27320	-1.06	-29154	19657	-0.67	-30090	15974	-0.53

Table B.7: Utility gain of manipulating agents using the k-pricing schema in setting R_1

Modification	1B		2B,2S		6B,6S	
Factor	μ	σ	μ	σ	μ	σ
10	5606.21	9585.14	1390.49	6271.13	256.22	5162.76
20	7740.77	18674.78	-962.85	10474.95	-4045.80	8994.63
30	7443.98	27425.99	-2750.76	14212.49	-9271.00	13804.83
40	8184.50	35272.21	-8783.41	19112.74	-16771.11	17995.05
50	-13853.70	41677.28	-15231.67	18942.00	-22668.13	19402.55
60	-31556.63	34695.92	-21314.57	19056.80	-26914.75	17721.25

Table B.8: Utility gain of manipulating agents using the k-pricing schema in setting R_2

Modification	1B		2B,2S		6B,6S	
Factor	μ	σ	μ	σ	μ	σ
10	8117.21	13518.97	-113.07	10899.92	-960.30	6788.91
20	11088.66	27134.96	-1800.64	17891.14	-4733.49	12159.85
30	1232.84	41729.44	-6006.06	22890.38	-10676.34	16399.31
40	-9254.04	47753.82	-11697.80	25321.33	-17617.81	20288.98
50	-21872.47	47596.41	-18041.74	26180.02	-23253.29	19681.14
60	-32307.83	43529.14	-24505.86	26819.83	-27910.12	19425.77

Table B.9: Utility gain of manipulating agents using the k-pricing schema in setting R_3

Modification	1B		2B,2S		6B,6S	
Factor	μ	σ	μ	σ	μ	σ
10	6181.98	16356.59	-307.60	9439.58	-465.45	5720.34
20	8561.83	27005.44	-2810.05	14083.68	-4790.34	9926.74
30	7591.66	37992.79	-7277.67	20658.21	-10966.21	14580.95
40	-4596.00	47337.30	-12921.74	24155.83	-16862.82	17735.81
50	-24535.79	46427.37	-19632.95	26762.06	-22458.75	19140.19
60	-34616.28	40133.19	-23292.29	26045.47	-26971.86	19365.82

Table B.10: Utility gain of manipulating agents using the k-pricing schema in setting R_4

Modification	1B			2B,2S			6B,6S			12B,12S		
Factor	μ	σ	CV	μ	σ	CV	μ	σ	CV	μ	σ	CV
5	150	175	1.17	26	57	2.17	10	28	2.97	-5	11	-2.23
10	308	391	1.27	49	105	2.13	13	56	4.22	-18	28	-1.55
15	400	608	1.52	58	156	2.68	9	88	10.16	-37	47	-1.26
20	466	787	1.69	61	187	3.05	1	109	84.10	-66	73	-1.11
30	343	1131	3.30	28	258	9.10	-23	163	-7.21	-129	122	-0.95
40	10	1123	109.90	4	348	81.81	-71	243	-3.41	-198	171	-0.86
50	-372	1528	-4.11	-94	401	-4.28	-129	286	-2.23	-281	240	-0.85
60	-481	1602	-3.33	-173	502	-2.91	-194	332	-1.71	-331	268	-0.81
70	-748	1610	-2.15	-271	559	-2.06	-251	343	-1.37	-362	297	-0.82
80	-916	1639	-1.79	-349	612	-1.76	-291	349	-1.20	-377	318	-0.84
90	-979	1603	-1.64	-406	644	-1.58	-340	369	-1.09	-385	325	-0.84

Table B.11: Utility gain of manipulating agents using the approximated VCG schema in setting I_1

Manipulating	Modification factor										
Agents	5	10	15	20	30	40	50	60	70	80	90
1B	0.32	0.48	0.33	0.29	0.13	0.07	0.06	0.04*	0.03*	0.02*	0.02*
2B,2S	0.38	0.30	0.22	0.21	0.34	0.50	0.37	0.41	0.38	0.35	0.35
6B,6B	0.11	0.23	0.22	0.15	0.27	0.44	0.43	0.43	0.43	0.42	0.41

* denotes significant differences between the samples ($p \leq 0.05$).

Table B.12: P-values of a paired t-test with unequal variances to test equality of $UG^O_{n,k}$ and $UG^O_{n,AV}$ in setting I_1

| Modification | 1B | | | 2B,2S | | | 6B,6S | | | 12B,12S | | |
Factor	μ	σ	CV	μ	σ	CV	μ	σ	CV	μ	σ	CV
5	1945	4083	2.10	502	2328	4.63	102	1798	17.55	-608	796	-1.31
10	3458	7697	2.23	-31	6283	-201.25	-949	4202	-4.43	-2734	2417	-0.88
15	3589	11965	3.33	-1309	9186	-7.02	-3002	6697	-2.23	-6024	4380	-0.73
20	2242	16330	7.28	-3551	13217	-3.72	-6135	9773	-1.59	-10713	6836	-0.64
30	-1863	23840	-12.80	-8024	19786	-2.47	-12925	14476	-1.12	-22685	12136	-0.53
40	-14511	43680	-3.01	-13800	24524	-1.78	-18812	18102	-0.96	-29943	15926	-0.53
50	-30342	57575	-1.90	-19448	27878	-1.43	-23889	19809	-0.83	-30069	16003	-0.53
60	-39644	60653	-1.53	-23123	29309	-1.27	-27839	20674	-0.74	-30069	16003	-0.53
70	-40448	60929	-1.51	-23736	29682	-1.25	-28363	20712	-0.73	-30069	16003	-0.53
80	-40448	60929	-1.51	-23835	29722	-1.25	-28398	20692	-0.73	-30069	16003	-0.53
90	-40448	60929	-1.51	-23847	29717	-1.25	-28435	20708	-0.73	-30069	16003	-0.53

Table B.13: Utility gain of manipulating agents using the approximated VCG schema in setting R_1

| Manipulating | Modification factor | | | | | | | | | |
Agents	5	10	15	20	30	40	50	60	70	80	90
$1B$	0.00	0.00	0.00	0.00	0.45	0.00	0.00	0.00	0.00	0.00	0.00
$2B, 2S$	0.00	0.00	0.00	0.12	0.17	0.00	0.00	0.00	0.00	0.00	0.00
$6B, 6S$	0.00	0.00	0.00	0.02	0.48	0.63	0.35	0.26	0.26	0.26	0.26

Table B.14: P-values of a paired U-test to test equality of $UG^O_{n,k}$ and $UG^O_{n,AV}$ in setting R_1

B.3   Results: Approximated Winner Determination

| Modification | 1B | | | 4B,4S | | | 10B,10S | | | 20B,20S | | |
Factor	μ	σ	CV	μ	σ	CV	μ	σ	CV	μ	σ	CV
10	-41.6	365.4	-8.8	-32.2	203.3	-6.3	-24.5	148.5	-6.1	-14.7	177.5	-12.1
20	-170.9	621.2	-3.6	-83.8	242.3	-2.9	-68.1	157.0	-2.3	-73.9	169.7	-2.3
30	-567.4	889.2	-1.6	-181.8	324.4	-1.8	-162.6	227.2	-1.4	-173.0	210.7	-1.2
40	-918.2	1250.5	-1.4	-334.8	463.7	-1.4	-313.4	301.4	-1.0	-314.1	254.9	-0.8

Table B.15: Utility gain of manipulating agents using the VCG schema in setting I_1 with approximated allocation decisions

Modification	1B			4B,4S			10B,10S			20B,20S		
Factor	μ	σ	CV	μ	σ	CV	μ	σ	CV	μ	σ	CV
10	197.9	648.7	3.3	46.0	280.1	6.1	58.2	159.5	2.7	47.1	100.2	2.1
20	171.0	1.245.9	7.3	66.2	440.8	6.7	68.2	235.6	3.5	44.9	155.3	3.5
30	-124.5	1.736.8	-14.0	15.4	631.6	41.0	17.7	361.9	20.5	-3.7	222.7	-60.2
40	-635.4	2.014.3	-3.2	-100.1	764.3	-7.6	-94.0	431.4	-4.6	-99.0	291.5	-2.9

Table B.16: Utility gain of manipulating agents using the k-pricing schema in setting I_1 with approximated allocation decisions

Modification	1B			4B,4S			10B,10S			20B,20S		
Factor	μ	σ	CV	μ	σ	CV	μ	σ	CV	μ	σ	CV
10	-35.1	277.2	-7.9	11.6	171.2	14.7	-10.7	139.2	-13.0	-20.6	141.1	-6.8
20	-134.9	341.8	-2.5	-23.1	200.5	-8.7	-31.4	119.9	-3.8	-52.2	146.7	-2.8
30	-295.4	700.7	-2.4	-63.0	217.7	-3.5	-89.3	182.5	-2.0	-110.7	187.3	-1.7
40	-776.4	1.360.6	-1.8	-175.4	401.8	-2.3	-156.1	256.2	-1.6	-192.1	266.8	-1.4

Table B.17: Utility gain of manipulating agents using the approximated VCG schema in setting I_1 with approximated allocation decisions

Modification	1B			4B,4S			10B,10S			20B,20S		
Factor	μ	σ	CV	μ	σ	CV	μ	σ	CV	μ	σ	CV
10	-2695	16510	-6.1	-2540.5	8558.4	-3.4	-2841	7634	-2.7	-2981	6605	-2.2
20	-12594	29234	-2.3	-10120.2	14149.5	-1.4	-11101	12951	-1.2	-11256	10119	-0.9
30	-22368	36458	-1.6	-16555.1	20340.8	-1.2	-19113	18259	-1.0	-19720	14241	-0.7
40	-33484	42861	-1.3	-23024.0	22489.3	-1.0	-26762	21442	-0.8	-26822	16193	-0.6

Table B.18: Utility gain of manipulating agents using the VCG schema in setting R_1 with approximated allocation decisions

Modification	1B			4B,4S			10B,10S			20B,20S		
Factor	μ	σ	CV	μ	σ	CV	μ	σ	CV	μ	σ	CV
10	7383	16620	2.3	-997	15241	-15.3	-1334	10160	-7.6	-805	7284	-9.0
20	6688	31935	4.8	-7604	23330	-3.1	-9853	17634	-1.8	-9303	12589	-1.4
30	61	43110	710.2	-14747	28951	-2.0	-16977	21450	-1.3	-17130	15753	-0.9
40	-9699	50352	-5.2	-20492	31348	-1.5	-23262	22760	-1.0	-23488	17071	-0.7

Table B.19: Utility gain of manipulating agents using the k-pricing schema in setting R_1 with approximated allocation decisions

Modification	1B			4B,4S			10B,10S			20B,20S		
Factor	μ	σ	CV	μ	σ	CV	μ	σ	CV	μ	σ	CV
10	-3734	17902	-4.8	-2151	8772	-4.1	-3071	8439	-2.7	-3293	7048	-2.1
20	-11655	27494	-2.4	-9821	14126	-1.4	-11496	13459	-1.2	-11701	9645	-0.8
30	-24652	41704	-1.7	-17925	21877	-1.2	-19728	18857	-1.0	-20473	13954	-0.7
40	-37300	51840	-1.4	-25202	26488	-1.1	-27356	21169	-0.8	-27872	15599	-0.6

Table B.20: Utility gain of manipulating agents using the approximated VCG schema in setting I_1 with approximated allocation decisions

Bibliography

Abbas, A. (2004). Grid computing technology – an overview. In A. Abbas (Ed.), *Grid Computing: A Pratical Guide to Technology and Applications*, Volume 1 of *Networking Series*, Chapter 4, pp. 43–74. Charles River Media.

Adar, E. and B. A. Huberman (2000). Free riding on gnutella. *First Monday 5*(10).

Al-Ali, R. J., K. Amin, G. von Laszewski, O. F. Rana, and D. W. Walker (2003). An OGSA-based quality of service framework. In M. Li, X.-H. Sun, Q. Deng, and J. Ni (Eds.), *Grid and Cooperative Computing, Second International Workshop GCC 2003, Shanghai, China, December 7-10, 2003, Revised Papers, Part II*, Volume 3033 of *Lecture Notes in Computer Science*, pp. 529–540. Springer.

Albrecht, J., C. Tuttle, A. C. Snoeren, and A. Vahdat (2006). PlanetLab application management using Plush. *ACM SIGOPS Operating Systems Review 40*(1), 33–40.

Allcock, W. E., J. Bester, J. Bresnahan, A. L. Chervenak, I. T. Foster, C. Kesselman, S. Meder, V. Nefedova, D. Quesnel, and S. Tuecke (2002). Data management and transfer in high-performance computational Grid environments. *Parallel Computing 28*(5), 749–771.

Aloisio, G., M. Cafaro, I. Epicoco, S. Fiore, D. Lezzi, M. Mirto, and S. Mocavero (2005). Resource and service discovery in the iGrid information service. In O. Gervasi, M. L. Gavrilova, V. Kumar, A. Laganà, H. P. Lee, Y. Mun, D. Taniar, and C. J. K. Tan (Eds.), *Computational Science and Its Applications - ICCSA 2005, International Conference, Singapore, May 9-12, 2005, Proceedings, Part III*, Volume 3482 of *Lecture Notes in Computer Science*, pp. 1–9. Springer.

Alonso, G., F. Casati, H. Kuno, and V. Machiraju (2004). *Web Services: Concepts, Architectures, and Applications*. Springer.

Anderson, A. (2005). Predicates for boolean web service policy languages. In L. Kagal, T. Finin, and J. Hendler (Eds.), *Proceedings of the Policy Management for the Web Workshop at the World Wide Web Conference, Chiba, Japan*, pp. 52–56.

Andersson, A., M. Tenhunen, and F. Ygge (2000). Integer programming for combinatorial auction winner determination. In *ICMAS '00: Proceedings of the Fourth International Conference on MultiAgent Systems*, Washington, DC, USA, pp. 39–46. IEEE Computer Society.

Andreozzi, S., S. Burke, L. Field, S. Fisher, B. Konya, M. Mambelli, J. M. Schopf, M. Viljoen, and A. Wilson (2005). Glue schema specificiation version 1.2. Draft specification.

Andrieux, A., K. Czajkowski, A. Dan, K. Keahe, H. Ludwig, T. Nakata, J. Pruyne, J. Rofrano, S. Tuecke, and M. Xu (2005). Web services agreement specification (WS-Agreement). Gwd-r, Global Grid Forum.

Antoniadis, P., C. Courcoubetis, and R. Mason (2004). Comparing economic incentives in peer-to-peer networks. *Computer Networks 46*(1), 133–146.

Ardaiz, O., P. Chacin, I. Chao, F. Freitag, and L. Navarro (2005). An architecture for incorporating decentralized economic models in application layer networks. *International Journal on Multiagent and Grid Systems 1*(4), 287–295.

Arlow, J. and I. Neustadt (2005). *UML 2 and the Unified Process: Practical Object-Oriented Analysis and Design*. The Addison-Wesley Object Technology Series. Addison-Wesley Professional.

Atamtürk, A. and M. W. P. Savelsbergh (2005). Integer-programming software systems. *Annals of Operations Research 140*(1), 67–124.

Ausubel, L., P. Cramton, and P. Milgrom (2006). The clock-proxy auction: A practical combinatorial auction design. In P. Cramton, Y. Shoham, and R. Steinberg (Eds.), *Combinatorial Auctions*, Chapter 4, pp. 115–138. MIT Press.

Ausubel, L. and P. Milgrom (2006). The lovely but lonely Vickrey auction. In P. Cramton, Y. Shoham, and R. Steinberg (Eds.), *Combinatorial Auctions*, Chapter 1, pp. 17–40. MIT Press.

Ausubel, L. M. and P. Milgrom (2002). Ascending auctions with package bidding. *Frontiers of Theoretical Economics 1*(1), 1–43.

AuYoung, A., B. N. Chun, A. C. Snoeren, and A. Vahdat (2004). Resource allocation in federated distributed computing infrastructures. In *Proceedings of the 1st Workshop on Operating System and Architectural Support for the On-demand IT InfraStructure, Boston*.

Bajaj, S., D. Box, D. Chappell, F. Curbera, G. Daniels, P. Hallam-Baker, M. Hondo, C. Kaler, D. Langworthy, A. Nadalin, N. Nagaratnam, H. Prafullchandra, C. von Riegen, D. Roth, J. Schlimmer, C. Sharp, J. Shewchuk, A. Vedamuthu, U. Yalcinalp, and D. Orchard (2006). Web services policy framework. Technical report, BEA Systems Inc., International Business Machines Corporation, Microsoft Corporation, Inc., SAP AG, Sonic Software, and VeriSign Inc.

Bajari, P., R. McMillan, and S. Tadelis (2004). Auctions versus negotiations in procurement: An empirical analysis. Working paper, Duke University and Stanford University.

Ball, M., G. L. Donohue, and K. Hoffman (2006). Auctions for the safe, efficient and equitable allocation of airspace system resources. In P. Cramton, Y. Shoham, and R. Steinberg (Eds.), *Combinatorial Auctions*. MIT Press.

Banks, J. (1998). Principles of simulation. In J. Banks (Ed.), *Handbook of Simulation*, Chapter 2, pp. 3–30. Engineering and Management Press.

Bapna, R., S. Das, R. Garfinkel, and J. Stallaert (2007). A market design for Grid computing. *INFORMS Journal of Computing, forthcoming*.

Bapna, R., P. Goes, and A. Gupta (2005). Pricing and allocation for quality differentiated online services. *Management Science 51*(7), 1141–1150.

Bavier, A., M. Bowman, B. Chun, D. Culler, S. Karlin, S. Muir, L. Peterson, T. Roscoe, T. Spalink, and M. Wawrzoniak (2004). Operating systems support for planetary-scale network services. In *Proceedings of the First Symposium on Networked Systems and Design and Implementation, San Fransisco*.

Becker, J. and M. Clement (2004). The economic rationale of offering media files in peer-to-peer networks. In *37th Hawaii International Conference on System Sciences (HICSS-37 2004), CD-ROM / Abstracts Proceedings*, Volume 7, pp. 70199.2. IEEE Computer Society.

Bell, W. H., D. G. Cameron, L. Capozza, A. P. Millar, K. Stockinger, and F. Zini (2003). Optorsim – a Grid simulator for studying dynamic data replication strategies. *International Journal of High Performance Computing Applications 17*(4), 403–416.

Böhm, V. and K. R. Schenk-Hoppé (1998). Macrodyn – a user's guide. Discussion Paper 400, University of Bielefeld.

Bichler, M. (2001). *The Future of e-Markets*. Cambridge University Press.

Bichler, M. and J. Kalagnanam (2006). Industrial procurement auctions. In P. Cramton, Y. Shoham, and R. Steinberg (Eds.), *Combinatorial Auctions*. MIT Press.

Bichler, M., G. E. Kersten, and S. Strecker (2003). Towards a structured design of electronic negotiations. *Group Decision and Negotiation 12*(4), 311–335.

Bikhchandani, S., S. de Vries, J. Schummer, and R. V. Vohra (2001). Linear programming and Vickrey auctions. In B. Dietrich and R. Vohra (Eds.), *Mathematics of the Internet: E-Auction and Markets*, The IMA Volumes in Mathematics and its Applications, pp. 75–116. Springer.

Bikhchandani, S. and J. M. Ostroy (2000). The package assignment model. *Journal of Economic Theory 107*, 377–406.

Boudreau, M.-C., K. D. Loch, D. Robey, and D. Straud (1998). Going global: Using information technolgy to advance the competitiveness of the virtual transnational organization. *Academy of Management Executive 12*(4), 120–128.

Boutilier, C. and H. H. Hoos (2001). Bidding languages for combinatorial auctions. In B. Nebel (Ed.), *Proceedings of the Seventeenth International Joint Conference on Artificial Intelligence, IJCAI 2001, Seattle, Washington, USA, August 4-10, 2001*, pp. 1211–1217. Morgan Kaufmann.

Brooke, J. M., D. Fellows, and J. MacLaren (2004). Interoperability of resource description across grid domain boundaries. In P. Neittaanmäki, T. Rossi, K. Majava, and O. Pironneau (Eds.), *Proceedings of the European Congress on Computational Methods in Applied Science and Engineering (ECCOMAS 2004), CD*.

Brunett, S., K. Czajkowski, S. Fitzgerald, C. Kesselman, I. Foster, S. Tuecke, A. Johnson, and J. Leigh (1998). Application experiences with the globus toolkit. In *HPDC '98: Proceedings of the The Seventh IEEE International Symposium on High Performance Distributed Computing*, Washington, DC, USA, pp. 81–88. IEEE Computer Society.

Burghardt, M. (2006). Nonlinear pricing of e-market transaction services. In *Proceedings of the Fifth Workshop on e-Business (WeB) 2006, Milwaukee, Winsconsin*.

Buyya, R. (2002). *Economic-based Distributed Resource Management and Scheduling for Grid Computing*. Ph. D. thesis, Monash University, Melbourne, Australia.

Buyya, R., D. Abramson, and J. Giddy (2001). A case for economy Grid architecture for service oriented Grid computing. In *Proceedings of the 15th International Parallel and Distributed Processing Symposium (IPDPS-01), San Francisco*, Washington, DC, USA, pp. 83–98. IEEE Computer Society.

Buyya, R., D. Abramson, J. Giddy, and H. Stockinger (2002). Economic models for resource management and scheduling in Grid computing. *The Journal of Concurrency
and Computation: Practice and Experience 14*(13-15), 1507–1542.

Buyya, R., D. Abramson, and J.Giddy (2000). Nimrod/G: An architecture for a resource
management and scheduling system in a global computational Grid. In *Proceedings
of the 4th Internationall Conference on High Performance Computing in Asia-Pacific
Region (HPC Asia 2000),*.

Buyya, R., D. Abramson, and S. Venugopal (2005). The Grid economy. *Proceedings of
the IEEE 93*(3), 698–714.

Buyya, R. and M. Murshed (2002). GridSim: A toolkit for the modeling and simulation
of distributed resource management and scheduling for Grid computing. *The Journal
of Concurrency and Computation: Practice and Experience (CCPE) 14*(13-15).

Buyya, R., H. Stockinger, J. Ghiddy, and D. Abramson (2001). Economic models for
management of resources in peer-to-peer and Grid computing. In *Proceedings of the
International Conference on Commercial Applications for High Performance, 2001.*

Bykowsky, M. M., R. J. Cull, and J. O. Ledyard (2000). Mutually destructive bidding:
The FCC auction design problem. *Journal of Regulatory Economics 17*(3), 205–28.

Cai, G. and P. R. Wurman (2005). Monte carlo approximation in incomplete-information,
sequential-auction games. *Decision Support Systems 39*(2), 153–168.

Calabrese, G., B. Schnizler, W. Streitberger, and F. Zini (2006). Catnets annual report 2 –
simulation deliverable. Project deliverable, CATNETS Consortium.

Calegari, P., G. Coray, A. Hertz, D. Kobler, and P. Kuonen (1999). A taxonomy of evolutionary algorithms in combinatorial optimization. *Journal of Heuristics 5*(2), 145–158.

Casanova, H. (2001). Simgrid: A toolkit for the simulation of application scheduling.
In *Proceedings of the IEEE International Symposium on Cluster Computing and the
Grid (CCGrid'01)*, pp. 430–437.

Catlett, C. and L. M. Smarr (1992). Metacomputing. *Communications of the ACM 35*(6),
44–52.

Chacin, P., L. Joita, B. Schnizler, and F. Freitag (2006). Flexible architecture for supporting auctions in Grids. In *Proceedings of the 2nd International Workshop On Smart
Grid Technologies 2006 (SGT2006) Workshop.*

Cheliotis, G., C. Kenyon, and R. Buyya (2005). Grid economics: 10 lessons from finance
for commercial sharing of it resources. In R. Subramanian and B. D. Goodman (Eds.),
Peer to Peer Computing: The Evolution of a Disruptive Technology, Chapter 11. Idea
Group Publishing.

Cheon, Y. and G. T. Leavens (2002). A simple and practical approach to unit testing:
The JML and JUnit way. In *Proceedings of the 16th European Conference on Object-
Oriented Programming*, London, UK, pp. 231–255. Springer.

Chu, P. C. and J. E. Beasley (1998). A genetic algorithm for the multidimensional knapsack problem. *Journal of Heuristics 4*(1), 63–86.

Chun, B. N. (2001). *Market-based Cluster Resource Management*. Ph. D. thesis, University of California at Berkley.

Clark, D. and J. Pasquale (1996). Strategic directions in networks and telecommunications. *ACM Computing Surveys 28*(4), 679–690.

Clarke, E. (1971). Multipart pricing of public goods. *Public Choice 2*, 19–33.

Conen, W. and T. Sandholm (2001). Preference elicitation in combinatorial auctions. In *Proceedings of the Third ACM Conference on Electronic Commerce*, New York, NY, USA, pp. 256–259. ACM Press.

Conitzer, V. and T. Sandholm (2003). Computational criticisms of the revelation principle. In *Proceedings of the Workshop on Agent Mediated Electronic Commerce (AMEC V), Melbourne, Australia*.

Cramton, P. (2003). Electricity market design: The good, the bad, and the ugly. In *36th Hawaii International Conference on System Sciences (HICSS-36 2003), CD-ROM / Abstracts Proceedings*, Volume 2, Los Alamitos, CA, USA, pp. 54b. IEEE Computer Society.

Cramton, P., Y. Shoham, and R. Steinberg (Eds.) (2006). *Combinatorial Auctions*. MIT Press.

Curbera, F., M. Duftler, R. Khalaf, W. Nagy, N. Mukhi, and S. Weerawarana (2002). Unraveling the Web Services Web: An introduction to SOAP, WSDL, and UDDI. *IEEE Internet Computing 6*(2), 86–93.

Czajkowski, K., D. Ferguson, I. Foster, J. Frey, S. Graham, T. Maguire, D. Snelling, and S. Tuecke (2004). From Open Grid Services Infrastructure to WS-Resource framework: Refactoring & evolution. White paper, Fujitsu Limited, International Business Machines Corporation and University of Chicago.

Czajkowski, K., D. F. Ferguson, I. Foster, J. Frey, S. Graham, I. Sedukhin, D. Snelling, S. Tuecke, and W. Vambenepe (2004). The WS-Resource framework. White paper, Computer Associates Inc, Fujitsu Limited, Hewlett-Packard Development Company, International Business Machines Corporation, University of Chicago.

Czajkowski, K., S. Fitzgerald, I. Foster, and C. K. Gr (2001). Grid information services for distributed resource sharing. In *Proceedings of the Tenth IEEE International Symposium on High-Performance Distributed Computing (HPDC-10)*.

Czajkowski, K., I. Foster, and C. Kesselman (2004). Resource and service management. In I. Foster and C. Kesselman (Eds.), *The Grid 2 - Blueprint for a New Computing Infrastructure*, Volume 2, Chapter 18, pp. 259–283. Elsevier.

Czajkowski, K., I. T. Foster, N. T. Karonis, C. Kesselman, S. Martin, W. Smith, and S. Tuecke (1998). A resource management architecture for metacomputing systems. In D. G. Feitelson and L. Rudolph (Eds.), *Proceedings of the Workshop on Job Scheduling Strategies for Parallel Processing (IPPS/SPDP'98)*, Volume 1459 of *Lecture Notes in Computer Science*, London, UK, pp. 62–82. Springer.

Dash, R. K., N. R. Jennings, and D. C. Parkes (2003). Computational-mechanism design: A call to arms. *IEEE Intelligent Systems*, 40–47. Special Issue on Agents and Markets.

Davidow, W. H. and M. S. Malone (1992). *The Virtual Corporation: Structuring and Revitalizing the Corporation for the 21st Century*. Harper Business.

De Roure, D., M. Baker, N. R. Jennings, and N. Shadbol (2003). The evolution of the Grid. In F. Berman, G. Fox, and A. J. G. Hey (Eds.), *Grid Computing: Making the Global*

Infrastructure a Reality, Series in Communications Networking and Distributed Systems, Chapter 3, pp. 65–100. Wiley.

de Vries, S. and R. Vohra (2003). Combinatorial auctions: A survey. *INFORMS Journal of Computing 15*(3), 284–309.

DeFanti, T., I. Foster, M. Papka, R. Stevens, and T.Kuhfuss (1996). Overview of the I-WAY: Wide area visual supercomputing. *International Journal of Supercomputer Applications 10*(2), 123–130.

Eerola, P., B. Kónya, O. Smirnova, T. Ekelöf, M. Ellert, J. R. Hansen, J. L. Nielsen, A. Wäänänen, A. Konstantinov, J. Herrala, M. Tuisku, T. Myklebust, F. Ould-Saada, and B. Vinter (2003). The NorduGrid production Grid infrastructure, status and plans. In H. Stockinger (Ed.), *4th International Workshop on Grid Computing (GRID 2003), 17 November 2003, Phoenix, AZ, USA, Proceedings*, pp. 158–165. IEEE Computer Society.

Eymann, T., D. Neumann, M. Reinicke, B. Schnizler, W. Streitberger, and D. Veit (2006). On the design of a two-tiered Grid market structure. In *Proceedings of the MKWI 2006, Business Applications of P2P and Grid Computing, Passau*.

Eymann, T., M. Reinicke, O. R. Werner Streitberger and, L. Joita, D. Neumann, B. Schnizler, D. Veit, O. Ardaiz, P. Chacin, I. Chao, F. Freitag, L. Navarro, M. Catalano, M. Gallegati, G. Giulioni, R. C. Schiaffino, and F. Zini (2005). Catallaxy-based Grid markets. *Multiagent and Grid Systems 1*(4), 297–307.

Fan, M., J. Stallaert, and A. Whinston (1999). The design and development of a financial cybermarket with a bundle trading mechanism. *International Journal of Electronic Commerce 4*(1), 5–22.

Ferguson, D. F., Y. Yemini, and C. Nikolaou (1988). Microeconomic algorithms for load balancing in distributed computer systems. In *Proceedings of the 8th International Conference on Distributed Computing Systems, San Jose, California, June 13-17*, pp. 491–499. IEEE-CS Press.

Foster, I. (2002). What is the Grid? A three point checklist. Discussion paper, Argonne National Laboratory and University of Chicago.

Foster, I. (2005). Globus toolkit version 4: Software for service-oriented systems. In *Proceedings of the IFIP International Conference on Network and Parallel Computing*, LNCS 3779, pp. 2–13. Springer.

Foster, I., J. Gieraltowski, S. Gose, N. Maltsev, E. May, A. Rodriguez, D. Sulakhe, and the other Grid2003 Project Members (2004). The Grid2003 production Grid: Principles and practice. In *Proceedings of the Thirteenth IEEE International Symposium on High-Performance Distributed Computing (HPDC13)*.

Foster, I. and C. Kesselman (1997). Globus: A metacomputing infrastructure toolkit. *The International Journal of Supercomputer Applications and High Performance Computing 11*(2), 115–128.

Foster, I. and C. Kesselman (1998). Computational Grids. In I. Foster and C. Kesselman (Eds.), *The Grid: Blueprint for a New Computing Infrastructure*, Volume 1, Chapter 2, pp. 15–52. Morgan Kaufmann Publishers.

Foster, I. and C. Kesselman (2004a). Concepts and architecture. In I. Foster and C. Kesselman (Eds.), *The Grid 2 - Blueprint for a new Computing Infrastructure*, Volume 2, Chapter 4, pp. 37–64. Morgan Kaufmann.

Foster, I. and C. Kesselman (2004b). *The Grid 2 - Blueprint for a New Computing Infrastructure*, Volume 2. Elsevier.

Foster, I., C. Kesselman, J. Nick, and S. Tuecke (2002a). Grid services for distributed system integration. *IEEE Computer 35*(6), 37–46.

Foster, I., C. Kesselman, J. Nick, and S. Tuecke (2002b). The physiology of the Grid: An Open Grid Services Architecture for distributed systems integration. Technical report, Mathematics and Computer Science Division, Argonne National Laboratory.

Foster, I., C. Kesselman, and S. Tuecke (2001). The anatomy of the Grid: Enabling scalable virtual organizations. *The International Journal of High Performance Computing Applications 15*(3), 200–222.

Foster, I. and C. Kesselmann (2004). The Grid in a nutshell. In J. Nabrzyski, J. M. Schopf, and J. Weglarz (Eds.), *Grid Resource Management – Sate of the Art and Future Trends*, Chapter 1, pp. 3–15. Kluwer Academic Publishers.

Frey, J., T. Tannenbaum, I. Foster, M. Livny, and S. Tuecke (2001). Condor-G: A computation management agent for multiinstitutional Grids. In *International Symposium on High Performance Distributed Computing*, San Francisco, CA, pp. 55–67.

Friedman, D. (1991). The double auction market institution: A survey. In D. Friedman and J. Rust (Eds.), *The Double Auction Market - Institutions, Theories, and Evidence*, pp. 3–26. Cambridge MA, Perseus Publishing.

Fu, Y., J. S. Chase, B. N. Chun, S. Schwab, and A. Vahdat (2003). Sharp: an architecture for secure resource peering. In *Proceedings of the 19th ACM Symposium on Operating Systems Principles, October 19-22, 2003, Bolton Landing, NY USA*, pp. 133–148.

Fujishima, Y., K. Leyton-Brown, and Y. Shoham (1999). Taming the computational complexity of combinatorial auctions: Optimal and approximate approaches. In *Proceedings of the 16th International Joint Conference on Artificial Intelligence*, San Francisco, pp. 548–553. Morgan Kaufmann Publishers Inc.

Gagliano, R. A., M. D. Fraser, and M. E. Schaefer (1995). Auction allocation of computing resources. *Communications of the ACM 38*(6), 88–102.

Gamma, E., R. Helm, and R. Johnson (1995). *Design Patterns: Elements of Reusable Object-Oriented Software*. Addison-Wesley Professional Computing Series. Addison-Wesley.

Garvey, A. and V. Lesser (1994). A survey of research in deliberative real-time artificial intelligence. *Real-Time Systems 6*(3), 317–347.

Gibbard, A. (1973). Manipulation of voting schemes. *Econometrica 41*, 587–602.

Gimpel, H. (2007). *Preferences in Negotiations: The Attachment Effect*, Volume forthcoming. Berlin: Springer.

Global Grid Forum (2005a). Job submission description language (JSDL) specification v1.0. GFD-I.056, OGF Document Series, Global Grid Forum.

Global Grid Forum (2005b). Open Grid Services Architecture: Glossary of terms. GFD-I.044, OGF Document Series, Global Grid Forum.

Global Grid Forum (2005c). Resource management in OGSA. GFD-I.044, OGF Document Series, Global Grid Forum.

Gode, D. K. and S. Sunders (1993). Lower bounds for efficiency or surplus extraction in double auctions. In D. Friedman and J. Rust (Eds.), *The Double Action Market: Institution, Theories , and evidence*, Santa Fe Institute Series in The Science of Complexity, Chapter 15 TODO, pp. 199–219. Addison Wedsley.

Gomber, P., C. Schmidt, and C. Weinhardt (2000). Pricing in multi-agent systems for transportation planning. *Journal of Organizational Computing and Electronic Commerce 10*(4), 271–280.

Gomoluch, J. and M. Schroeder (2003). Market-based resource allocation for Grid computing: A model and simulation. In *International Middleware Conference, Workshop Proceedings, June 16-20, 2003, Rio de Janeiro, Brazil*, pp. 211–218. PUC-Rio.

Gradwell, P. and J. Padget (2005). Markets vs. auctions: Approaches to distributed combinatorial resource scheduling. *Multiagent and Grid Systems 1*(4), 251–262.

Green, J. and J.-J. Laffont (1977). Characterization of satisfactory mechanisms for the revelation of preferences for public goods. *Econometrica 45*(2), 427–438.

Grimshaw, A. S., W. A. Wulf, and T. L. Team (1997). The Legion vision of a worldwide virtual computer. *Communications of the ACM 40*(1), 39–45.

Grosu, D. and A. Das (2006a). Auctioning resources in Grids: Model and protocols. *Concurrency and Computation:Practice and Experience 18*(15), 1909–1927.

Grosu, D. and A. Das (2006b). Combinatorial auction-based resource allocation in Grids. *International Journal of Computational Science and Engineering, forthcoming*.

Groves, T. (1973). Incentives in teams. *Econometrica 41*, 617–631.

Grunenberg, M., D. Veit, and C. Weinhardt (2004). Elektronische Finanzmärkte und Bundle Trading. In *Proceedings der 66. wissenschaftlichen Jahrestagung des Verbandes der Hochschullehrer für Betriebswirtschaft,Graz*, pp. 310–313.

Hardin, G. (1968). The tragedy of the commons. *Science 162*(3859), 1243–1248.

Harsanyi, J. C. and R. Selten (1998). *A General Theory of Equilibrium Selection in Games*. MIT Press.

Håstad, J. (1999). Clique is hard to approximate within $n^{1-epsilon}$. *Acta Mathematica 182*(1), 105–142.

Hayek, F. (1945). The use of knowledge in society. *American Economic Review 35*(4), 519–530.

Hetzel, B. (1993). *The Complete Guide to Software Testing*, Volume 2. John Wiley & Sons Inc.

Holte, R. C. (2001). Combinatorial auctions, knapsack problems, and hill-climbing search. In *Proceedings of the 14th Biennial Conference of the Canadian Society on Computational Studies of Intelligence*, London, UK, pp. 57–66. Springer.

Holtmann, C. (2004). *Organisation von Märkten - Market Engineering für den Wertpapierhandel*. Ph. D. thesis, Economics and Business Engineering, University of Karlsruhe (TH), Germany.

Holtmann, C. and D. Neumann (2003). Market and firm - two sides of a coin. In *Proceedings of the 10th Research Symposium on Emerging Electronic Markets (RSEEM)*, Bremen.

Huberman, B. A. and T. Hogg (1995). Distributed computation as an economic system. *Journal of Economic Perspectives 9*(1), 141–152.

Huhns, M. N. and M. P. Singh (2005). Service-oriented computing: Key concepts and principles. *IEEE Internet Computing 9*(1), 75–81.

Humphrey, M. (2003). From Legion to Legion-G to OGSI.NET: Object-based computing for Grids. In *17th International Parallel and Distributed Processing Symposium (IPDPS 2003), CD-ROM*, pp. 207. IEEE Computer Society.

Hurwicz, L. (1972). On informationally decentralized systems. In C. McGuire and R. Radner (Eds.), *Decision and Organization*. Amsterdam, NL: North-Holland Publishing Company.

Iamnitchi, A. and I. T. Foster (2001). On fully decentralized resource discovery in Grid environments. In C. A. Lee (Ed.), *Grid Computing - GRID 2001, Second International Workshop, Denver, CO, USA*, Volume 2242 of *Lecture Notes in Computer Science*, pp. 51–62. Springer.

ILOG (2005). ILOG CPLEX 9.1 User's Manual. Manual, ILOG, Inc.

Jackson, M. O. (2002). Mechanism theory. In *Encyclopedia of Life Support Systems*, Oxford ,UK. Eolss Publishers.

Jain, R. and P. Varaiya (2004). Combinatorial exchange mechanisms for efficient bandwidth allocation. *Communications in Information and Systems 3*(4), 305–324.

Jehiel, P. and B. Moldovanu (2003). An economic perspective on auctions. *Economic Policy 18*(36), 271–308.

Jennings, N. R., P. Faratin, A. R. Lomuscio, S. Parsons, C. Sierra, and M. Wooldridge (2001). Automated negotiation: Prospects, methods and challenges. *Group Decision and Negotiation 10*(2), 199–215.

Joseph, J., M. Ernest, and C. Fellenstein (2004). Evolution of Grid computing architecture and Grid adoption models. *IBM Systems Journal 43*(4), 624–645.

Joseph, J. and C. Fellenstein (2004). *Grid Computing*. IBM Press.

Kalagnanam, J. and D. C. Parkes (2004). Auctions, bidding and exchange design. In D. Simchi-Levi, S. D. Wu, and Z. M. Shen (Eds.), *Handbook of Quantitative Supply Chain Analysis: Modeling in the E-Business Era*, International Series in Operations Research & Management Science, Chapter 5, pp. 143–212. Kluwer Academic Publishing.

Karp, R. M. (1972). Reducibility among combinatorial problems. In R. E. Miller and J. W. Thatcher (Eds.), *Complexity of Computer Computations*, pp. 85–103. Plenum Press.

Kashani, F. B., C.-C. Chen, and C. Shahabi (2004). WSPDS: Web services peer-to-peer discovery service. In H. R. Arabnia, O. Droegehorn, and S. Chatterjee (Eds.), *Proceedings of the International Conference on Internet Computing, Volume 2 & Proceedings of the International Symposium on Web Services & Applications, Las Vegas, Nevada, USA*, pp. 733–743. CSREA Press.

Kauff, P., R. Schaefer, and O. Scheer (2000). Tele-immersion in shared presence conference systems. In *Proceedings of the International Broadcasting Convention (IBC)*.

Kaye, D. (2003). *Loosely Coupled: The Missing Pieces of Web Services*. RDS Press.

Kee, Y.-S., H. Casanova, and A. Chien (2004). Realistic modeling and synthesis of resources for computational Grids. In *ACM Conference on High Performance Computing and Networking (SC2004)*. ACM Press.

Kersten, G., S. Noronha, and J. Teich (2000). Are all e-commerce negotiations auctions? In *COOP2000: Fourth International Conference on the Design of Cooperative Systems, Sophia-Antipolis, France.*

Kersten, G. E. (2004). E-negotiation systems: Interaction of people and technologies to resolve conflicts. Presented at: UNESCAP Third Annual Forum on Online Dispute Resolution Melbourne, Australia, July 2004.

Kersten, G. E. and S. J. Noronha (1999). WWW-based negotiation support: Design, implementation, and use. *Decision Support Systems 25*(2), 135–154.

Kleinrock, L. (1969). Ucla to be first station in nationwide computer network. Press Release University of California.

Kothari, A., T. Sandholm, and S. Suri (2003). Solving combinatorial exchanges: Optimality via a few partial bids. In *Proceedings of the Fourth ACM Conference on Electronic Commerce*, New York, NY, USA, pp. 236–237. ACM Press.

Krauter, K., R. Buyya, and M. Maheswaran (2002). A taxonomy and survey of Grid resource management systems. *International Journal of Software: Practice and Experience 32*(2), 135–164.

Krishna, V. (2002). *Auction Theory*. San Diego: Academic Press.

Krishna, V. and M. Perry (2000). Efficient mechanism design. Working paper, Pennsylvania State University, The Hebrew University of Jerusalem.

Kroll, P. and B. MacIsaac (2006). *Agility and Discipline Made Easy: Practices from OpenUP and RUP*. The Addison-Wesley Object Technology Series. Addison Wesley Professional.

Kunzelmann, M. (2006). *Zwischen Limit und Market Orders: Innovative Ordertypen im elektronischen Wertpapierhandel*. Number 5 in Studies on eOrganisation and Market Engineering. Universitätsverlag Karlsruhe.

Lai, K. (2005). Markets are dead, long live markets. Technical Report 0502027, HP Labs.

Lamparter, S. and B. Schnizler (2006). Trading services in ontology-driven markets. In *Proceedings of the 2006 ACM Symposium on Applied Computing*, pp. 1679–1683. ACM Press.

Law, A. M. and W. D. Kelton (2000). *Simulation Modeling and Analysis*. McGraw-Hill Higher Education.

Le, L. (2006). *Demand Management at Congested Airports: How Far Are We From Utopia?* Ph. D. thesis, Systems Engineering and Operations Research Department, George Mason University.

Lehmann, D., R. Mueller, and T. Sandholm (2006). The winner determination problem. In P. Cramton, Y. Shoham, and R. Steinberg (Eds.), *Combinatorial Auctions*, Chapter 12, pp. 297–317. MIT Press.

Lehmann, D., L. I. O'Calllaghan, and Y. Shoham (2002). Truth revelation in approximately efficient combinatorial auctions. *Journal of the ACM 49*(5), 577–602.

Leyton-Brown, K., E. Nudelman, and Y. Shoham (2006). Empirical hardness models for combinatorial auctions. In P. Cramton, Y. Shoham, and R. Steinberg (Eds.), *Combinatorial Auctions*, Chapter 19, pp. 479–504. MIT Press.

Leyton-Brown, K., M. Pearson, and Y. Shoham (2000). Towards a universal test suite for combinatorial auctions. In *Proceedings of the Second ACM Conference on Electronic Commerce*, pp. 66–76.

Leyton-Brown, K. and Y. Shoham (2006). A test suite for combinatorial auctions. In P. Cramton, Y. Shoham, and R. Steinberg (Eds.), *Combinatorial Auctions*, Chapter 18, pp. 451–478. MIT Press.

Linderoth, J. T. and T. K. Ralphs (2005). Noncommercial software for mixed-integer linear programming. In J. Karlof (Ed.), *Integer Programming: Theory and Practice*, Operations Research Series, pp. 253–303. CRC Press.

Lohmann, M. (1999). *Dynamische Ressourcenallokation in verteilten Systemen*. Peter Lang Verlag.

Lohmann, M., A. Schmalz, and C. Weinhardt (1997). ADAMCO - an agent architecture with domain independent, adaptive, multiple coordination behavior. In D. Potter, M. Matthews, and M. Ali (Eds.), *Proceedings of the Tenth International Conference on Industrial and Engineering Applications of Artificial Intelligence and Expert Systems (IEA-AIE 1997)*, pp. 151–159. Gordon and Breach Science Publishers.

Lu, D. and P. A. Dinda (2003). Synthesizing realistic computational Grids. In *Proceedings of ACM/IEEE Supercomputing 2003 (SC 2003)*.

Luckner, S., F. Kratzer, and C. Weinhardt (2005). Stoccer - a forecasting market for the FIFA World Cup 2006. In *Proceedings of the 4th Workshop on e-Business (WeB 2005), Las Vegas, USA*.

Ludwig, H., A. Dan, and B. Kearney (2004). Cremona: An architecture and library for creation and monitoring of WS-Agreements. In *Proceedings of the 2nd International Conference on Service Oriented Computing (ICSOC 2004)*, pp. 65–74.

Mahinthakumar, G., F. M. Hoffman, W. W. Hargrove, and N. T. Karonis (1999). Multivariate geographic clustering in a metacomputing environment using Globus. In *Proceedings of the 1999 ACM/IEEE Conference on Supercomputing*, New York, NY, USA, pp. 5. ACM Press.

Mas-Colell, A., M. D. Whinston, and J. R. Green (1995). *Microeconomic Theory*. Oxford University Press.

McAfee, R. and J. McMillan (1987). Auctions and bidding. *Journal of Economic Literatur 25*(2), 699–738.

Meliksetian, D. S., J.-P. Prost, A. S. Bahl, I. Boutboul, D. P. Currier, S. Fibra, J.-Y. Girard, K. M. Kassab, J.-L. Lepesant, C. Malone, and P. Manesco (2004). Design and implementation of an enterprise Grid. *IBM Systems Journal 43*(4), 646–664.

Merriam-Webster (2006). Merrian-webster online. http://www.webster.com/.

Milgrom, P. (1989). Auctions and bidding: A primer. *Journal of Ecnomic Perspectives 108*(2), 245–272.

Milgrom, P. (2004). *Putting Auction Theory to Work*. Cambridge University Press.

Milgrom, P. (2006). Package auctions and package exchanges: the 2004 Fisher-Schultz lecture. *Econometrica, forthcoming*.

Milgrom, P. R. and R. J. Weber (1982). A theory of auctions and competitive bidding. *Econometrica 50*(5), 1089–1122.

Mito, M. and S. Fujita (2004). On heuristics for solving winner determination problem in combinatorial auctions. *Journal of Heuristics 10*(5), 507–523.

Müller, R. (2006). Tractable cases of the winner determination problem. In P. Cramton, Y. Shoham, and R. Steinberg (Eds.), *Combinatorial Auctions*, Chapter 13, pp. 319–326. MIT Press.

Myerson, R. B. (1979). Incentive compatibility and the bargaining problem. *Econometrica 6*, 61–73.

Myerson, R. B. (1981). Optimal auction design. *Mathematics of Operations Research 6*(1), 58–73.

Myerson, R. B. and M. A. Satterthwaite (1983). Efficient mechanisms for bilateral trading. *Journal of Economic Theory 28*, 265–281.

Natrajan, A., M. Humphrey, and A. S. Grimshaw (2001). Capacity and capability computing using Legion. In V. N. Alexandrov, J. Dongarra, B. A. Juliano, R. S. Renner, and C. J. K. Tan (Eds.), *Computational Science - ICCS 2001, International Conference, San Francisco, CA, USA, May 28-30, 2001. Proceedings, Part I*, Volume 2073 of *Lecture Notes in Computer Science*, pp. 273–283. Springer.

Neumann, D. (2004). *Market Engineering – A Structured Design Process for Electronic Markets*. Ph. D. thesis, Economics and Business Engineering, University of Karlsruhe (TH), Germany.

Neumann, D. (2006). Self-organizing ict resource management. In *Proceedings of the Workshop on Grid Economics, eChallenges e2006*.

Neumann, D., S. Lamparter, and B. Schnizler (2006). Automated bidding for trading Grid services. In *Proceedings of the European Conference on Information Systems (ECIS) 2006*.

Neumann, D., B. Schnizler, I. Weber, and C. Weinhardt (2007). Second best combinatorial auctions – the case of the pricing per column mechanism. In *40th Hawaii International Conference on System Sciences (HICSS-40 2007), CD-ROM / Abstracts Proceedings*.

Nicolaisen, J., V. Petrov, and L. Tesfatsion (2001). Market power and efficiency in a computational electricity market with discriminatory double-auction pricing. *IEEE Transactions on Evolutionary Computation 5*(5), 504–523.

Nisan, N. (2000). Bidding and allocation in combinatorial auctions. In *Proceedings of the Second ACM Conference on Electronic Commerce*, New York, USA, pp. 1–12. ACM Press.

Nisan, N. (2006). Bidding languages for combinatorial auctions. In P. Cramton, Y. Shoham, and R. Steinberg (Eds.), *Combinatorial Auctions*, Chapter 9, pp. 215–232. MIT Press.

Nisan, N., S. London, O. Regev, and N. Camiel (1998). Globally distributed computation over the Internet - the POPCORN project. In *Proceedings of the 18th International Conference on Distributed Computing Systems, 26 - 29 May, 1998, Amsterdam, The Netherlands*, pp. 592–601. IEEE Computer Society.

Nisan, N. and A. Ronen (2000). Computationally feasible VCG mechanisms. In *Proceedings of the 2nd ACM conference on Electronic commerce*, New York, NY, USA, pp. 242–252. ACM Press.

Padala, P., C. Harrison, N. Pelfort, E. Jansen, M. Frank, and C. Chokkareddy (2003). OCEAN: The open computation exchange and arbitration network, a market approach to meta computing. In *Proceedings of the Second International Symposium on Parallel and Distributed Computing 2003*, pp. 185–192. IEEE Computer Society.

Pahl, G. and W. Beitz (1984). *Engineering Design*. Bath, UK: The Pitman Press.

Papadimitriou, C. H. and K. Steiglitz (1998). *Combinatorial Optimization – Algorithms and Complexity*, Volume 2. Mineola, New York: Dover Publications, Inc.

Parkes, D. C. (1999). iBundle: An efficient ascending price bundle auction. In *Proceedings of the First ACM Conference on Electronic Commerce*, pp. 148–157. ACM Press.

Parkes, D. C. (2001). *Iterative Combinatorial Auctions: Achieving Economic and Computational Efficiency*. Ph. D. thesis, Department of Computer and Information Science, University of Pennsylvania.

Parkes, D. C. (2006). Iterative combinatorial auctions. In P. Cramton, Y. Shoham, and R. Steinberg (Eds.), *Combinatorial Auctions*, Chapter 2, pp. 41–77. MIT Press.

Parkes, D. C., R. Cavallo, N. Elprin, A. Juda, S. Lahaie, B. Lubin, L. Michael, J. Shneidman, and H. Sultan (2005). ICE: An iterative combinatorial exchange. In *Proceedings of the Sixth ACM Confernece on Electronic Commerce*.

Parkes, D. C., J. Kalagnanam, and M. Eso (2001). Achieving budget-balance with Vickrey-based payment schemes in exchanges. In *Proceedings of the Seventeenth International Joint Conference on Artificial Intelligence*, pp. 1161–1168.

Parkes, D. C. and L. H. Ungar (2000). Iterative combinatorial auctions: Theory and practice. In *Proceedings of the 17th National Conference on Artificial Intelligence*, Austin, Texas, pp. 74 – 81. American Association for Artificial Intelligence: MIT Press.

Pekěc, A. and M. Rothkopf (2006). Noncomputational approaches to mitigating computational problems in combinatorial auctons. In P. Cramton, Y. Shoham, and R. Steinberg (Eds.), *Combinatorial Auctions*, Chapter 14, pp. 337–368. MIT Press.

Pritsker, A. B. (1998). Principles of simulation modeling. In J. Banks (Ed.), *Handbook of Simulation*, Chapter 2, pp. 31–51. Engineering and Management Press.

Raiffa, H. (1982). *The Art and Science of Negotiation*. Harvard University Press.

Raman, R., M. Livny, and M. Solomon (1998). Matchmaking: Distributed resource management for high throughput computing. In *Proceedings of The Seventh International Symposium on High Performance Distributed Computing*, pp. 140–146.

Raman, R., M. Livny, and M. H. Solomon (2003). Policy driven heterogeneous resource co-allocation with Gangmatching. In *12th International Symposium on High-Performance Distributed Computing (HPDC-12 2003), 22-24 June 2003, Seattle, WA, USA*, pp. 80–89. IEEE Computer Society.

Raman, R., M. Solomon, M. Livny, and A. Roy (2004). The ClassAds language. In J. Nabrzyski, J. M. Schopf, and J. Weglarz (Eds.), *Grid Resource Management – State of the Art and Future Trends*, Chapter 17, pp. 255–270. Kluwer Academic Publishers.

Rassenti, S. J., V. L. Smith, and R. L. Bulfin (1982). A combinatorial auction mechanism for airport time slot allocation. *Bell Journal of Economics 13*(2), 402–417.

Regev, O. and N. Nisan (2000). The POPCORN market: Online markets for computational resources. *Decision Support Systems 28*(1-2), 177–189.

Reinicke, M., W. Streitberger, T. Eymann, M. Catalano, and G. Giulioni (2006). Economic evaluation framework of resource allocation methods in service-oriented architectures. In *Proceedings of the 8th Conference on E-Commerce Technology (CEC06), San Francisco, June 26th-29th 2006*.

Reiter, S. (1977). Information and performance in the (new) welfare economics. *American Economic Review 67*(1), 226–235.

Roth, A. E. (1991). Game theory as a part of empirical economics. *The Economic Journal 101*(404), 107–114.

Rothkopf, M., A. Pekěc, and R. Harstad (1998). Computationally manageable combinational auctions. *Management Science 44*, 1131–1147.

Roy, A. and V. Sander (2004). Gara: A uniform quality of service architecture. In J. Nabrzyski, J. M. Schopf, and J. Weglarz (Eds.), *Grid Resource Management – State of the Art and Future Trends*, Chapter 23, pp. 377–394. Kluwer Academic Publishers.

Russell, M., G. Allen, T. Goodale, J. Nabrzyski, and E. Seidel (2004). Application requirements for resource brokering in a Grid environment. In J. Nabrzyski, J. M. Schopf, and J. Weglarz (Eds.), *Grid Resource Management – State of the Art and Future Trends*, Chapter 3, pp. 25–40. Kluwer Academic Publishers.

Saari, D. G. and C. P. Simon (1978). Effective price mechanisms. *Econometrica 46*(5), 1097–1125.

Sandholm, T. (2002). Algorithm for optimal winner determination in combinatorial auctions. *Artificial Intelligence 135*(1–2), 1–54.

Sandholm, T. (2006). Optimal winner determination algorithms. In P. Cramton, Y. Shoham, and R. Steinberg (Eds.), *Combinatorial Auctions*, Chapter 14, pp. 337–368. MIT Press.

Sandholm, T., S. Suri, A. Gilpin, and D. Levine (2002). Winner determination in combinatorial auction generalizations. In *Proceedings of the 1st International Joint Conference on Autonomous Agents and Multiagent Systems*, pp. 69–76. ACM Press.

Sandholm, T., S. Suri, A. Gilpin, and D. Levine (2005). CABOB: A fast optimal algorithm for winner determination in combinatorial auctions. *Management Science 51*(3), 374–390.

Satterthwaite, M. and S. Williams (2002). The optimality of a simple market mechanism. *Econometrica 70*, 1841–1863.

Sattherthwaite, M. A. and S. R. Williams (1993). The Bayesian theory of the k-double auction. In D. Friedman and J.Rust (Eds.), *The Double Auction Market - Institutions, Theories, and Evidence*, Chapter 4, pp. 99–123. Addison-Wesley.

Schmidt, C. (1999). *Marktliche Koordination in der dezentralen Produktionsplanung*. Gabler Verlag.

Schmidt, J. W. (1980). Fundamentals of digital simulation modeling. In *Proceedings of the 12th conference on Winter simulation (WSC '80)*, Piscataway, NJ, USA, pp. 315–323. IEEE Press.

Schnizler, B., S. Luckner, and C. Weinhardt (2006). Automated trading across e-market boundaries. In S. Seifert and C. Weinhardt (Eds.), *Proceedings of the Group Decision and Negotiation (GDN), Karlsruhe*, pp. 199–203.

Schnizler, B., D. Neumann, D. Veit, and C. Weinhardt (2005). A multiattribute combinatorial exchange for trading Grid resources. In Y. Tan (Ed.), *Proceedings of the 12th Research Symposium on Emerging Electronic Markets (RSEEM), Amsterdam, Netherlands*, pp. 220–240.

Schnizler, B., D. Neumann, D. Veit, and C. Weinhardt (2006a). Moving markets to the Grid. In *Proceedings der 68. wissenschaftliche Jahrestagung des Verbandes der Hochschullehrer für Betriebswirtschaft, Dresden*.

Schnizler, B., D. Neumann, D. Veit, and C. Weinhardt (2006b). Trading Grid services – a multi-attribute combinatorial approach. *European Journal of Operational Research, forthcoming*.

Schnizler, B., D. Neumann, and C. Weinhardt (2004). Resource allocation in computational Grids – a market engineering approach. In *Proceedings of the Third Workshop on e-Business (WeB) 2004, Washington*, pp. 19–31.

Schoop, M., F. Köhne, and D. Staskiewicz (2004). An integrated decision and communication perspective on electronic negotiation support systems: Challenges and solutions. *Journal of Decision Systems 13*(4), 375–398.

Schopf, J. (2004). Ten actions when Grid scheduling. In J. Nabrzyski, J. M. Schopf, and J. Weglarz (Eds.), *Grid Resource Management – State of the Art and Future Trends*, Chapter 2, pp. 15–25. Kluwer Academic Publishers.

Schopf, J. M. and L. Yang (2004). Using predicted variance for conservative scheduling on shared resources. In J. Nabrzyski, J. M. Schopf, and J. Weglarz (Eds.), *Grid Resource Management – State of the Art and Future Trends*, Chapter 15, pp. 215–238. Kluwer Academic Publishers.

Schwiegelshohn, U. and R. Yahyapour (2004). Attributes for communication between Grid scheduling instances. In J. Nabrzyski, J. M. Schopf, and J. Weglarz (Eds.), *Grid Resource Management – State of the Art and Future Trends*, Chapter 4, pp. 41–52. Kluwer Academic Publishers.

Schwind, M., O. Gujo, and T. Stockheim (2006). Dynamic resource prices in a combinatorial Grid system. In *IEEE Joint Conference on E-Commerce Technology (CEC'06) and Enterprise Computing, E-Commerce and E-Services (EEE'06); San Francisco*.

Shan, H., L. Olike, W. Smith, and R. Biswas (2004). Scheduling in heterogeneous Grid environments: The effects of data migration. In *International Conference on Advanced Computing and Communication*.

Shan, H., L. Oliker, and R. Biswas (2003). Job superscheduler architecture and performance in computational Grid environments. In *Proceedings of the 2003 ACM/IEEE Conference on Supercomputing*. IEEE Computer Society.

Shneidman, J., C. Ng, D. C. Parkes, A. AuYoung, A. C. Snoeren, A. Vahdat, and B. Chun. (2005). Why markets could (but don't currently) solve resource allocation problems in systems. In *Proceedings of Tenth Workshop on Hot Topics in Operating Systems*.

Sim, K. M. (2006). A survey of bargaining models for Grid resource allocation. *SIGecom Exchange 5*(5), 22–32.

Simon, H. A. (1990). Prediction and prescription in systems modeling. *Operations Research 38*(1), 7–14.

Smale, S. (1976). A convergent process of price adjustment and global newton methods. *Journal of Mathematical Economics 3*, 107–120.

Smith, V. (1989). Theory, experiment and economics. *Journal of Economic Perspective 72*(5), 151–169.

Smith, V. (2003). Markets, institutions and experiments. In L. Nadel (Ed.), *Encyclopedia of Cognitive Science*, pp. 991–998. Nature Publishing Group.

Smith, V. L. (1982). Microeconomic systems as an experimental science. *American Economic Review 72*(5), 923–955.

Smith, W. (2004). Improving resource selection and scheduling using predictions. In J. Nabrzyski, J. M. Schopf, and J. Weglarz (Eds.), *Grid Resource Management – State of the Art and Future Trends*, Chapter 16, pp. 237–254. Kluwer Academic Publishers.

Song, W. and X. Li (2005). A conceptual model for virtual organizations in the Grid. In H. Zhuge and G. Fox (Eds.), *Proceedings of the Fourth International Conference on Grid and Cooperative Computing*, Notes in Computer Science Vol. 3795, pp. 382–393. Springer.

Sotomayor, B. and L. Childers (2006). *Globus Toolkit 4: Programming Java Services*, Volume 1 of *The Elsevier Series in Grid Computing*. Morgan Kaufmann.

Stevens, R., P. Woodward, T. de Fanti, and C. Catlett (1997). From the I-Way to the national technology Grid. *Communications of the ACM 40*(11), 50–60.

Ströbel, M. and C. Weinhardt (2003). The Montreal taxonomy for electronic negotiations. *Journal of Group Decision and Negotiation 12*(2), 143 – 164.

Subramoniam, K., M. Maheswaran, and M. Toulouse (2002). Towards a micro-economic model for resource allocation in Grid computing systems. In *Proceedings of the 2002 IEEE Canadian Conference on Electrical & Computer Engineering*.

Sullivan, W. T., D. Werthimer, S. Bowyer, J. Cobb, D. Gedye, and D. Anderson (1997). A new major SETI project based on project serendip data and 100,000 personal computers. In C. Cosmovici, S. Bowyer, and D. Werthimer (Eds.), *Proceedings of the Fifth International Conference on Bioastronomy*. Editrice Compositori.

Sutherland, I. E. (1968). A futures market in computer time. *Communications of the ACM 11*(6), 449–451.

Tangmunarunkit, H., S. Decker, and C. Kesselman (2003). Ontology-based resource matching in the Grid - the Grid meets the Semantic Web. In D. Fensel, K. P. Sycara, and J. Mylopoulos (Eds.), *The Semantic Web - ISWC 2003, Second International Semantic Web Conference, Sanibel Island, FL, USA, October 20-23, 2003, Proceedings*, Volume 2870, pp. 706–721. Springer.

Taylor, I. J. (2004). *From P2P to Web Services and Grids: Peers in a Client/Server World*. Springer.

Thain, D., T. Tannenbaum, and M. Livny (2005). Distributed computing in practice: the Condor experience. *Concurrency - Practice and Experience 17*(2–4), 323–356.

The Economist (2004a). The future of computing – the next big thing? The Economist Print Edition, January, 15th.

The Economist (2004b). One Grid to rule them all. The Economist Print Edition, October, 7th.

Thiessen, E. M. and A. Soberg (2003). Smartsettle described with the Montreal taxonomy. *Group Decision and Negotiation 12*(2), 165–170.

Thomas, C. J. and B. J. Wilson (2002). A comparison of auctions and multilateral negotiations. *RAND Journal of Economics 33*(1), 140–155.

van Dinther, C. (2006). *Adaptive Bidding in Single Sided Auctions under Uncertainty*. Whitestein Series in Software Agent Technologies and Autonomic Computing. Birkhäuser, Basel, Boston, Berlin.

Varian, H. R. (1992). *Microeconomic Analysis*, Volume 3. W. W. Norton & Company.

Varian, H. R. (1995). Economic mechanism design for computerized agents. In *In Proceedings of the First USENIX Workshop on Electronic Commerce (EC 95), New York*, pp. 13–21.

Veit, D. (2003). *Matchmaking in Electronic Markets – An Agent-Based Approach Towards Matchmaking in Electronic Negotiations*. Number 2882 in Lecture Notes in Artifical Intelligence. Springer.

Veit, D., W. Fichtner, and M. Ragwitz (2004). Agent-based computational economics in power markets – multi-agent based simulation as a tool for decision support. In J. Andrysek, M. Karny, and J. Kracik (Eds.), *Multiple Participant Decision Making*, Volume 9 of *International Series on Advanced Intelligence*. Advanced Knowledge International.

Vickrey, W. (1961). Counter speculation, auctions, and competitive sealed tenders. *Journal of Finance 16*, 8–37.

W3C (2000). Simple object access protocol (SOAP) 1.1. Technical report, World Wide Web Consortium.

W3C (2003). Web services architecture. Third public working draft of the Web Services Architecure specification, World Wide Web Consortium.

Waldspurger, C., T. Hogg, B. Huberman, J. Kephart, and W. Stornetta (1992). Spawn: A distributed computational economy. *IEEE Transactions on Software Engineering 18*(2), 103–117.

Waldspurger, C. A. and W. E. Weihl (1994). Lottery scheduling: Flexible proportional-share resource management. In *Proceedings of the First USENIX Symposium on Operating Systems Design and Implementation (OSDI)*, pp. 1–11.

Weber, I. (2006). *Discounts in Auctions – Theoretical and Experimental Analysis*. Ph. D. thesis, Information Management and Systems (IISM), Universität Karlsruhe (TH), Karlsruhe, Germany.

Weinhardt, C., C. Holtmann, and D. Neumann (2003). Market engineering. *Wirtschaftsinformatik 45*(6), 635–640.

Weinhardt, C., D. Neumann, and C. Holtmann (2006). Computer-aided market engineering. *Communications of the ACM 49*(7), 79–79.

Weinhardt, C., C. van Dinther, M. Grunenberg, K. Kolitz, M. Kunzelmann, J. Mäkiö, I. Weber, and H. Weltzien (2006). *CAME-Toolsuite meet2trade - auf dem Weg zum Computer Aided Market Engineering*, Volume 1 of *Studies on eOrganisation and Market Engineering*. Universitätsverlag Karlsruhe.

Wellman, M. P. (1993). A market-oriented programming environment and its application to distributed multicommodity flow problems. *Journal of Artifical Intelligence Research 1*, 1–23.

Whittaker, J. (2000). What is software testing? Why is it so hard? *IEEE Software 17*(1), 70–79.

Wojciechowski, R. and C. Weinhardt (2002). Web services und peer-to-peer-netzwerke. In D. Schoder, K. Fischbach, and R. Teichmann (Eds.), *Peer-to-Peer (P2P) - Ökonomische, technologische und juristische Perspektiven*, Volume 1, Chapter 7, pp. 99–117. Springer.

Wolsey, L. A. and G. L. Nemhause (1999). *Integer and Combinatorial Optimization*, Volume 1. Wiley-Interscience.

Wolski, R. (1998). Dynamically forecasting network performance using the network weather service. *Cluster Computing 1*(1), 119–132.

Wolski, R., J. Plank, J. Brevik, and T. Bryan (2001). Analyzing market-based resource allocation strategies for the computational Grid. *International Journal of High Performance Computing Applications 15*(3), 258–281.

Wurman, P. R. and M. P. Wellman (2000). A*k*ba: A progressive, anonymous-price combinatorial auction. In *Proceedings of the Second ACM Conference on Electronic Commerce*, pp. 21–29.

Wurman, P. R., M. P. Wellman, and W. E. Walsh (2001). A parametrization of the auction design space. *Games and Economic Behavior 35*(1–2), 304–338.

Xia, M., J. Stallaert, and A. B. Whinston (2005). Solving the combinatorial double auction problem. *European Journal of Operational Research 164*(1), 239–251.

Xing, W., M. D. Dikaiakos, and R. Sakellariou (2005). Design and development of a core Grid ontology. In *Proceedings of the CoreGRID Integration Workshop*, pp. 178–184.